New Dimensions to Energy Policy

New Dimensions to Energy Policy

Edited by
Robert Lawrence
Colorado State University

Lexington Books
D.C. Heath and Company
Lexington, Massachusetts
Toronto

Library of Congress Cataloging in Publication Data
Main entry under title:

New dimensions to energy policy.

  Includes index.
  1. Energy policy—United States—Addresses, essays, lectures. I. Lawrence,
Robert M., 1932–HD9502.U52N46   333.7   78–389
ISBN 0–669–02172–5

Copyright © 1979 by D.C. Heath and Company

Published simultaneously in Canada

Printed in the United States of America

International Standard Book Number: 0–669–02172–5

Library of Congress Catalog Card Number: 78–389

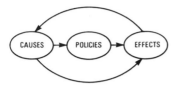

**Policy Studies
Organization Series**

General Approaches to Policy Studies

Specific Policy Problems

Contents

List of Figures

List of Tables

Preface

This book was originally undertaken with two objectives in mind. A third objective was added, together with Part III, as a result of serendipity. The first objective was the standard one in policy studies literature—to illuminate various facets of a particular policy area to increase understanding in a way that leads to better policy. The second objective, also a standard one, was to publish a small sample of work being done in the new area of energy policy. Thus the aim was to encourage communication among those embarking on new research which would not be reported in conventional journals or other regular media. The chapters in Parts I and II were selected to meet these objectives.

As the first two parts of the book were being assembled, a theme emerged quite by accident which suggested that the more traditional social scientists, those not directly interested in particular policy studies such as energy policy, environmental policy, health policy, education policy, and so on, could nevertheless benefit from what Nagel has described as follows: "The policy studies field is a booming growth industry well worth investing one's time and effort in for a variety of pleasing payoffs." The theme referred to is generally familiar to social scientists. It is that in energy policy, as in many situations in which humans are involved, much of the explanation for what happens can be found in the work of Harold Lasswell, whose insights may be summarized by citing the title of one of his best known books—*Politics: Who Gets What, When, How.* For example, the majority of the chapters in Parts I and II focus specifically on "getting" by various groups such as impacted communities, energy boomtowns, competitors for scarce water, electric utilities, the nuclear power industry, Indian tribes, the poor, and certain Western states. The other chapters in Parts I and II examine the getting phenomenon in broader contexts, such as the response of state governments to contending energy demands by various energy groups, the use of technology assessment as a tool in resolving differences over energy alternatives, changing relationships between the public sector and the private sector in energy development and the attendant problem that the latter not exploit the former, and the implications of energy demands set forth by various groups on theories of public administration and policy.

A special variation of the getting theme should be noted, namely the several instances in which the getting under analysis was not the traditional class or group getting, but getting in geographical terms involving various geographical entities. Such getting ranged from local areas downwind from a power station to the energy-rich Western states contesting with the national government. In getting situations the inhabitants of each area pursue conflicting interests taken to be legitimate from their narrow perspective. In such situations one might argue that the larger public interest is ignored. Of course, this Balkanization is not limited to energy matters as the controversy between the Sunbelt and Frostbelt states suggests.

As previously mentioned, the result of the emergence of the getting theme was the addition of Part III and realization by the editor that policy studies offered a special opportunity to those not normally engaged in policy research. The point may be illustrated by a reference to the physical sciences. In the physical sciences at times inquiry into a new area provides the opportunity to further test, refine, or possibly discredit a prevailing proposition, theory, or even law. So it seems with policy studies. Beyond the opportunity to further test the getting explanation of politics are opportunities to test many other propositions regarding the operation of pressure groups, the workings of Congress, the innovation of the states in the federal system, and the operation of public participation in planning. It is the editor's hope that the inclusion of Part III will attract others to use energy policy as a laboratory to sharpen their understanding of various social science concepts. Viewed in this fashion, policy studies need not be a threat to traditional scholars.

A note of thanks is due Professor Stuart Nagel of the University of Illinois, who is secretary/treasurer of the Policy Studies Organization and general editor of the *Policy Studies Journal.* As has often been the case regarding specific public policy areas, it was Professor Nagel who saw the need for examination of the energy policy field by social scientists, likewise, it was he who supported the editor in several ways during the development of the materials presented here, some of which appeared in a briefer form in the autumn 1978 issue of the *Policy Studies Journal.*

The Policy Studies Organization gratefully thanks the Energy Research and Development Administration for its aid to the symposium on which this book is based. Thanks are particularly owed to Harold Young, the education program manager of the ERDA Office of University Programs. However, no one other than the individual authors is responsible for the ideas advocated here.

**Part I
Energy Policy in the
Local, State, and
Regional Contexts**

1

Local Fiscal Effects of Coal Resource Development: A Framework for Analysis and Management

Osbin L. Ervin

Introduction

Limited supplies of natural gas and the unreliability of the supply of imported oil have increased the emphasis on exploitation of domestic coal reserves. Although nuclear, solar, and geothermal energy may hold much promise for the long-term future, it is widely believed that the nation's energy needs over the remainder of this century must be met largely thorugh the use of domestic coal.

President Carter's energy plan calls for the doubling of coal production by 1985, and coal industry executives are devising industry plans to meet that goal. Whether the President's 1985 target is desirable or attainable, it is clear that there will be a considerable increase in coal mining and conversion activity over the next decade, and this prospect poses a major challenge to planners and managers in local coal communities and to community-oriented researchers and policy analysts. The challenge to such administrators and researchers is to provide analysis, plans, and skills for managing coal-related community growth, to the end of translating community economic growth into favorable local government fiscal conditions.

As is well known, local communities across the United States frequently compete with one another for the location of new economic activities. It is generally felt by local officials and citizens that the location of a new industrial activity in the community will result in higher incomes for workers and merchants as well as an improved tax base and better government services for the community as a whole. This assessment of the impact of new industry on the community is largely accurate. However, the research on industrial development suggests that the location of major industrial facilities in small communities is not always accompanied by improved local conditions. There is documentation of cases in which the net fiscal impact on local governments is actually negative, resulting in worse, not better services.[1] Given the current emphasis on the development of domestic coal resources, observations and research of this kind suggest a need for studies in which the local fiscal impacts of new coal mining and conversion facilities are systematically assessed and in which management alternatives are elaborated.

The rural nature of coal resource development makes it especially important

3

to pay attention to local impacts and alternatives for local government action. Domestic coal reserves lie mainly in the mountains of Appalachia, the Illinois Basin, the high plains, and in the Rocky Mountain states. All these areas are essentially rural and have few major population centers. In such rural areas the impacts of new activities on the community are likely to be more severe than in urban areas, and the potential for dislocation problems is increased by a shortage of planning and management capacity in the governments of most rural communities. Further, previous research on growth management has generally focused on urban communities. It is much easier to find management approaches and technologies pertinent to communities such as San Francisco, California, and Montgomery County, Maryland, than to coal communities such as Pinckneyville, Illinois, or Sweetwater County, Wyoming.

Fiscal Problems of Local Government

The development of coal resources in U.S. rural communities poses several especially important fiscal problems for local governments and, from the perspective of the policy analyst, a number of opportunities for applied policy analysis.

First, and perhaps most important, the evidence indicates that the net fiscal impact of new coal facilities is likely to be negative in many cases, at least over the first few years.[2] This is not surprising, for research indicates that this is often the case in community economic development generally. In a study of five small communities in Kentucky, it was found that the net fiscal impact of new manufacturing plants was negative in most cases; a conclusion of the study was that new manufacturing plants had "typically resulted in a negative direct impact on local government finance."[3]

Second, frequently there is a jurisdictional "mismatch" between new revenues and service demands. The new revenues are received in one jurisdiction while the major demand for services is pressed in another. For example, in a study of local impacts of a power plant in Sweetwater County, Wyoming, it was found that the county government was the major beneficiary of new property tax revenues while the major municipality in the county, which could not levy a tax on the plant, was faced with the larger part of the new service demand.[4] This situation has also been documented in the case of industrial development in Kentucky. For example, it was noted that "the impact was by no means uniform among the several units of government studied."[5]

Third, the new revenues from coal developments frequently arrive too late. Negative impacts on the community are felt very early in the development of the project—at the time construction workers or new miners and their families begin to make demands on housing, educational facilities, health and recreation facilities, and municipal services. Major increases in revenue, on the other hand, typically do not arrive until the facilities have been constructed, assessed, and placed on the tax rolls. By this time, the local community may already be in serious fiscal trouble. In a study of an oil shale development in a three-county region in Colorado, it was found that the fiscal impact on local communities would be negative for the first seven years; after that a positive financial return could be expected.[6]

Finally, in most rural communities there is a shortage of planning and management capacity for dealing with local impacts. This should not be interpreted as a criticism of such small communities, for traditionally they have had little need for the sophisticated planning and management skills of their urban counterparts. Management has consisted largely of "balancing the books" of the county or municipality, and the need for planning (at least in the view of local officials) has ended with the development of a "master plan" that would qualify the municipality for federal funds.

A Framework for Analysis

In developing our research on potential community fiscal impacts of coal resource development in Illinois, it seemed important to develop a concise conceptualization of impacts and local policy options. There is a rapidly expanding body of literature in this area. However, much of it is directed toward urban areas and is not directly applicable to processes and problems in small communities. The work of Schuller and Hiltunen at the Oak Ridge National Laboratory,[7] in which an attempt was made to model the budget systems of local governments, is somewhat of an exception in that it is especially oriented toward rural areas, and much of the fiscal impact work of the Urban Institute has wide applicability.[8]

Unless studies of local impacts and policy options are designed within the framework of a conceptual schema, data collection is unlikely to be informed and directed, and individual studies are unlikely to be cumulative. This problem is, of course, very old in social science research. As Meehan has observed, "Without a conceptual framework, a theoretical structure that can assign significance to different perceptions, description is impossible."[9]

In our impact work at the Coal Extraction and Utilization Research Center, Southern Illinois University, we are conceptualizing a local "fiscal system." The system is composed of four interacting subsystems—the economy, land use, service demand, and revenues. The framework is depicted schematically in figure 1-1. The following is a brief description of the interfaces among the four subsystems.

Changes in the economy (for example, growth associated with a coal conversion facility) act as a catalyst to changes in both land use and revenues. The new jobs and associated increase in population are reflected in new or expanded residential, commercial, industrial, and institutional structures. Agricultural and

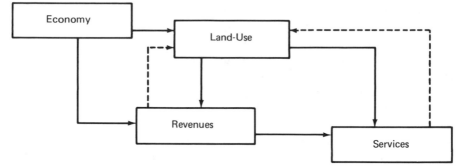

Figure 1-1. The Local Fiscal System.

idle lands are frequently converted to these uses. The relationship between the economy and local revenues is straightforward. Much of the new income in the community is spent for housing and consumer items which increase the yield of the property and sales taxes. Other revenue sources such as the motor fuel tax and income tax are also likely to increase in most states.

The distribution of land uses affects both revenues and services and, in turn, is affected by both. Land use links the economy with the revenue subsystem, and the uses of land determine both the level and the distribution of service demand. In looking at the reciprocal relationships of revenues and services to land use, it is clear that decisions about the distribution and staging of public services (such as the sewerage system) can have a very powerful effect on land use and on private land-use decisions. Similarly, public policies and decisions regarding the revenue subsystem, particularly the property tax, may affect the ways in which land is used. The relationship between revenues and services indicates simply that the provision of public services depends largely on the availability of revenues. These relationships are not, of course, exhaustive. One can think of other direct and indirect linkages between various components of the fiscal system, and the system itself may be very closely related to other sets of relationships in the community.

There are multiple ways in which local decisionmakers can intervene in the system to alter fiscal outcomes. All the relationships shown in figure 1-1 are subject to at least a small degree of local government control. For example, the cost associated with extension of sewer services can be reduced by a zoning ordinance that minimizes the footage which must be laid for a given number of new houses. Regarding the revenues–land use relationship, an increase in the assessed value of idle or low-productivity agricultural land can force the land into commercial or residential use.

As was noted earlier, one can imagine additional linkages in the system and a wide range of ways in which control might be exercised. However, the main point is that one needs to posit the major components and the major ways in which each component (or subsystem) interfaces with others. If one comes to understand the relationship well, then data collection can be made more selective and a wide range of both available and potential management mechanisms become apparent. The calculation of precisely how a public decision might affect the fiscal system is, of course, much more difficult. As Forrester has clearly shown, second- and third-order effects of management decisions may be very difficult to anticipate.[10]

A Preliminary Application of the Framework

In 1975 the Coalcon Company announced plans to build a coal gasification plant near New Athens, Illinois (a village of about two thousand). Although there is now doubt that the plant will actually be constructed at this location, the proposal affords an opportunity for a preliminary use of our conceptual framework in data collection and analysis pertinent to potential fiscal impacts and public policy alternatives. Because of space limitations, only an abbreviated version of this research can be presented.

According to the Coalcon plan, construction and operation of the plant would proceed according to figure 1-2. Thus, construction would start in 1979, followed by the beginning of demonstration operations in 1982 and by full commercial operation in early 1986.

Regarding jobs and economic effects,[11] the plant will employ about one thousand people during construction, followed by reduction to about three hundred during the demonstration phase and by an increase to around six hundred during commercial operation. This is clearly a major economic development for rural New Athens. However, these numbers do not fully reflect the economic impact. As is well known, basic or export employment such as that associated with the Coalcon plant is accompanied by new jobs in service industries. The ratio of service to basic employment is not likely to be as high in New Athens as in some communities. Nonetheless, it is probable that at least fifty to one hundred new jobs will be created in the New Athens area during the demonstration phase and one hundred to two hundred during the commercial phase. Unfortunately, reliable projections of population changes associated with the project are

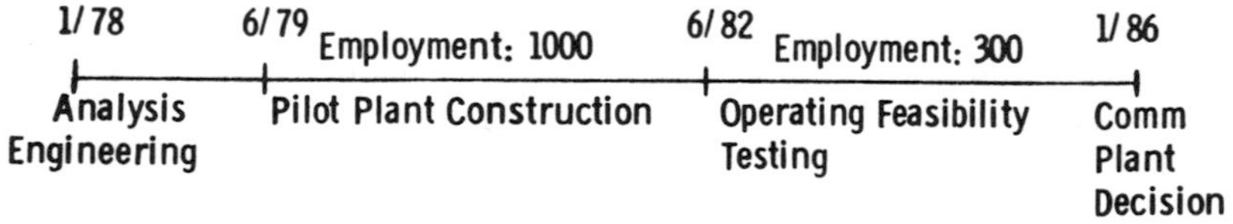

1/78	6/79 Employment: 1000	6/82 Employment: 300	1/86
Analysis Engineering	Pilot Plant Construction	Operating Feasibility Testing	Comm Plant Decision

Figure 1-2. Construction and Operation of the New Athens Coal Conversion Plant.

not available. The best available evidence and opinion indicate that the plant will increase the population of New Athens and its vicinity by about one thousand by the time commercial operations begin. However, the peak of the construction phase may see a fairly large influx of temporary residents.

Our study of land-use conversions likely to be associated with the economic growth relied on an approach generally referred to as the Delphi method. The Delphi method utilizes expert or informed opinion in developing estimates of future changes or conditions. The procedure consists of selecting a panel of "experts" on the matter in question and administering a questionnaire or some other research instrument to each member of the panel.[12]

In applying the Delphi method in New Athens, a reputational approach was used to select a panel of people highly knowledgeable about land-use matters in the area. The group consisted of the newspaper editor, city officials, real estate brokers, a banker, and a merchant. The panelist participated through a three-round process. In each round, the panelist was given a map of the New Athens area and asked to indicate, by means of a grid overlay, the areas within which new residential, commercial, and industrial activities would be most likely to locate over the next ten years. The results were that in general (and in the absence of additional public control) new industrial facilities are likely to locate northeast of the village and near the Coalcon plant. Commercial growth will be largely restricted to the southeastern part of the incorporated area, and residential growth will largely occur immediately south of the village.

Impacts of economic and land-use changes on government services and revenues in the New Athens area illustrate the multijurisdictional nature of impacts. The plant will be located within the boundaries of five local jurisdictions (county, township, school district, fire protection district, and water district) and near the boundary of a sixth (the village of New Athens). Table 1-1 is a list of the impacted governments and associated revenues and services. The fiscal condition of each of the governments will be affected, some negatively and some positively, by the Coalcon plant. Let us very briefly consider the potential for new service demands and additional financial resources.[13]

Construction and operation of the plant will bring a major increase in service demand to the village of New Athens, and existing service delivery systems may have to be expanded considerably in order to meet the new demands. For example, consider police services. The village police department consists of two full-time employees (a chief and a patrolman), a patrol car, and a small office in the Village Hall. The two police officers work eight-hour shifts, and the office is closed from midnight until 8 A.M. There are no detention facilities, and office space is not adequate for filing and investigative activities. Such services do not meet the needs of New Athens today, and they will be woefully inadequate soon after construction of the plant begins. With the beginning of plant construction, work related to traffic control will double and triple quickly, and there is likely to be an increased number of disturbances requiring police action. By 1981 the

Table 1-1
Impacted Governments and Associated Revenues and Services

Government Jurisdictions	County (St. Clair)	Township (New Athens)	Municipality (New Athens)	School District (Unit District 60)	Fire Protection District (New Athens Area)	Water District (Kaskaskia)
Revenues						
Property Tax	X	X	X	X	X	
Sales Tax			X			
State Income Tax			X			
Licenses and State Fees	X		X			
Motor Fuel Tax	X		X			
State Grants	X	X				
Revenue Sharing	X	X	X			
Federal Grants	X			X	X	X
User Fees	X		X			X
Services						
Fire Protection	X					
Police Protection	X		X		X	
Recreation			X			
Health	X		X			
Welfare		X				
Education				X		
Transportation	X	X	X			
Refuse Collection	X		X			
Water						X
Sewerage			X			

Source: Data supplied by the Coal Extraction and Utilization Research Center, Southern Illinois University.

police department will need at least two or three additional officers, two new patrol cars, detention facilities, a considerable expansion of office space, and additional communications and investigative equipment. New and expanded demands also will be made on other municipal services, including street maintenance, garbage collection, and sewerage services.

Services and facilities provided by the school district and the Kaskaskia Water District appear adequate to meet immediate needs. The school system can absorb about two hundred additional students without expansion, and district administrators are already making long-term financial plans for future expansion. The water district was organized in 1973, and a new purification and distribution plant was constructed in 1975. The plant is now operating at only about 33 percent of capacity and appears to be capable of meeting needs over the foreseeable future.

With respect to other local governments in the area, fire protection services will need to be expanded early in the construction phase of the project, and the county and township will face increased demands for road, health, and welfare services.

Local officials expect the demonstration plant to be assessed at about $15 million. This is only a very small percentage of the true market value of the plant. (An assessed/market value ratio of about 13 percent would be the minimum allowed under the Illinois constitution.) Nonetheless, the assessed valuation of all the local governments in the area except the village and the county will increase markedly. For example, the current assessed valuation of the school district is approximately $11 million. Thus, addition of the demonstration plant to the district's tax roll in the early 1980s will bring at least a doubling of assessed valuation. The township, water district, and fire protection district find themselves in a similar condition. The percentage increase in county-assessed valuation will not be very great because the county, which includes East St. Louis, has a very large tax base. The plant will not bring any direct increase in the assessed valuation of New Athens because it lies outside the village boundaries.

The fiscal and management problems discussed earlier are apparent in the New Athens Coalcon project. New service demands are indeed going to be pressed before significant new revenues are available. The demonstration plant, even if completed on schedule, will not be assessed until January 1983; and given the peculiarities of the assessment and billing process, tax bills will not be paid before the middle of 1984. Remember that construction and the accompanying demands for government services will have started a full five years earlier. The need for early "front-end" money is apparent in this case, as in other cases in the past. Also, there is a jurisdictional "mismatch" between governments feeling the most severe impacts and those in which a significant increase in revenues will occur. New service demands associated with the Coalcon project will fall most heavily on the village of New Athens. Yet the village will not be able to levy a property tax on the plant and will have to rely on increases in the sales tax and other sources of revenue.

A wide range of policy and management options are available to local officials in the New Athens area. Two options seem particularly appropriate for the village of New Athens—annexation and home rule. Annexation of the Coalcon plant would add the plant to the village's assessed valuation, and adoption of home rule would give the village the authority and flexibility to tap new sources of revenue.

Regarding the problem of management capacity, the rural local governments in the New Athens area clearly do not have the information and expertise necessary to cope with the problems and opportunities posed by the Coalcon plant. More will be said directly about management capacity, for the development of improved capacity holds promise for local success in dealing with a wide range of coal-related community impacts.

The conceptual framework applied in the New Athens study leads one to ask important research questions about local fiscal impacts and management options, and it directs one to think in systemic terms about these influences and their interrelationships.[14] Further, and just as important, the framework can serve as an organizing rubric for dissemination of policy-related information to local decisionmakers by policy analysts and, in so doing, contribute to an improved local capacity to manage change in coal communities.

Toward Management Capacity Building

Beyond consideration of the various mechanisms of local intervention and control in New Athens and similar coal-impacted communities, there is the more general issue of local government management capacity and of the possibility of capacity building. The need for strengthening the management capacity of local governments is currently receiving a great deal of attention in the public administration community,[15] and it should be especially emphasized in the case of rural coal communities. The capacity of local governments for rational intervention in coal-related events is impeded by inadequate policy-related information and a shortage of planning and management expertise. In the terms of a 1975 report of the U.S. Office of Management and Budget,[16] the need is for improved policy management and resource management, with *policy management* defined as policy analysis and policy making and *resource management* defined as administrative support systems such as financial management and personnel administration.[17]

Reliable and usable information on coal-related impacts is unavailable in most coal communities. Typically, local officials must rely on projections provided by the coal companies and the limited estimates and projections that may be available from the local substate planning agency. In both cases, the information is unlikely to be specific enough for policy and management decision making. The local decisionmaker needs information to calculate the consequences of various combinations of economic, land-use, fiscal, and budgetary options.

University researchers and policy analysts can play an important role in generation and dissemination of this capacity-building information. At Southern Illinois University's Coal Extraction and Utilization Research Center, we are at an early stage in development of a computer-based model that will simulate coal-related fiscal impacts and the consequences of alternative local policies in Illinois communities. One way in which we propose to enhance applicability to local decision making is in modeling each of the funds in the various units of local government. Discussions with local officials have made clear that the structure of specific funds with associated functions and revenue sources is an important constraint in local budgetary decision making. Other efforts to generate locally applicable information and analyses are in progress or have been completed at other academic and research institutions.[18]

There is a need for continued applied policy research to augment the policy-related information base available to local policymakers. In some cases the link between researchers and local government may be direct, and the information provided may be very site-specific. In other cases, the information may need to be more general, and it may need to be channeled through third parties (such as the substate planning agencies) and media (such as the journals of state municipal leagues) to which local officials give attention.

Administrative support systems and, thus the capacity to manage resources, are generally inadequate in coal communities. In the main, these communities do not employ professional planners or financial and personnel administrators. Therefore, planning and management skills familiar to the professional administrator and highly pertinent to growing communities are unavailable to the coal community, and management technique as well as general policy making becomes the responsibility of the part-time elected official.

There are two viable approaches to improvement of resource management capacity in coal-impacted local governments: (1) improvement in the skills and knowledge of the existing planning and management staff, and (2) recruitment of personnel with the requisite management and administrative skills. Universities and governments at the state and federal levels can all play an important role in improving the skills of existing administrative staffs in local governments. Universities and state governments have traditionally offered training workshops and seminars for local administrators. Some of the future workshops in coal-impacted regions might focus specifically on management skills most pertinent to growing coal communities (skills such as capital improvements programming, needs assessment, and personnel testing and recruitment). Federal government help for the administrators of coal communities can be provided through the

Intergovernmental Personnel Act of 1970[19] and the Capacity Sharing Program of the department of Housing and Urban Development.[20] The second approach—recruitment of personnel who possess the requisite training and skills—depends in large part on the fiscal resources available to local governments. As has been suggested earlier, surplus monies may indeed be available over the longrun. But in personnel recruitment as in other local coal-related planning, early front-end funds are needed.

Conclusion

Over the remainder of this century, many small communities in the United States will undergo coal-related economic growth. This growth will have some very positive effects in terms of better jobs and an improved standard of living. One hopes that the improvements in the economy will also be translated into higher-quality public services for the citizens of the various communities. At the least, one would hope that community services and the aesthetic qualities of the region will not deteriorate. If this is to occur, increased attention should be given to applied research on energy-related community impacts, to the management options of local officials, and to possibilities for building local management capacity.

The conceptualizations and research discussed in this chapter are the first step in the development of data-gathering and management approaches thought to be particularly appropriate to the coal communities of Illinois. The next step is the development of a simple computer model that will tie together the major components of the local fiscal system and make the calculations necessary to provide reliable projections of the service demands and revenue needs related to economic and land-use change.

Analysis of local fiscal impacts and management strategies is very important to coal communities and to coal resource development. However, as our knowledge of fiscal impacts improves, attention should increasingly shift to an elaboration of opportunities for local management capacity building. There is opportunity for participation of a wide range of public organizations in the capacity-building process.

Notes

1. Charles E. Garrison, "New Industry in Small Towns: The Impact on Local Government," *National Tax Journal* 24 (December 1971): 493–500.

2. Larry F. Leistritz, Arlen G. Leholm, and Thor A. Hertsgaard, "Public Sector Implications of a Coal Gasification Plant in Western North Dakota,"

Proceedings of the Fort Union Coal Field Symposium, vol. 4 (Billings, Mont.: Eastern Montana College, April 1975), pp. 493–500.

3. Garrison, "New Industry in Small Towns," p. 499.

4. A summary of the research appears in Department of Housing and Urban Development, *Rapid Growth from Energy Projects: Ideas for State and Local Action* (Washington: Department of Housing and Urban Development, 1976).

5. Garrison, "New Industry in Small Towns," p. 495.

6. Department of Housing and Urban Development, *Rapid Growth from Energy Projects, pp. 29–30.*

7. C. Richard Schuller and Ronald A. Hiltunen, *A Generalized Public Budget Analysis,* ORNL/RUS-22 (Oak Ridge, Tenn.: Oak Ridge National Laboratory, 1976).

8. See Thomas Muller, *Fiscal Impacts of Land Development: A Critique of Methods and Review of Issues* (Washington: The Urban Institute, 1975).

9. Eugene J. Meehan, *Explanation in Social Science* (Homewood, Ill.: Dorsey Press, 1968), p. 41.

10. Jay W. Forrester, *Urban Dynamics* (Cambridge, Mass.: M.I.T. Press, 1969).

11. Generally, either impact analysis or economic base analysis (or a combination of the two) is used in forecasting community economic impacts of new industrial activity. For a discussion of these methods and related issues, see Werner Z. Hirsch, *Urban Economic Analysis* (New York: McGraw-Hill, 1973), chaps. 7 and 9; and Charles M. Tiebout, *The Community Economic Base Study* (Washington: Committee for Economic Development, 1962).

12. For an introduction to the method, see Olaf Helmer, *Social Technology* (Basic Books: New York, 1966), and Norman C. Dalkey, *Studies in the Quality of Life* (Lexington, Mass.: D.C. Heath, 1972). And, for a discussion of applications of the method to land-use forecasting, see Osbin L. Ervin, "A Delphi Study of Regional Industrial Land-use," *The Review of Regional Studies* 7 (Spring 1977), and Joseph M. Davis, "Land-use Forecasting: A Delphi Approach," presented at the Regional Science Association Twenty-Second North American Meeting, Cambridge, Mass., November 8, 1975.

13. The monograph by Muller, Fiscal Impacts of Land Development, contains a thorough review and a helpful evaluation of the various approaches to estimation of budgetary/fiscal impacts of community economic growth. Also see Werner Z. Hirsch, "Expenditure Implications of Metropolitan Growth and Consolidation," *Review of Economics and Statistics* 41 (August 1959): 232–241.

14. In addition to the items already cited, the following papers are particularly pertinent to fiscal impacts of energy resource development: Lawrence O. Houstoun, Jr., "Here's What Should Be Done about the Energy Boom Towns," *Planning* 43 (March 1977): 18–20; Girard Krebs, "Technological and Social Impact Assessment of Resource Extraction: The Case of Coal," *Environment and Behavior* 7 (September 1975): 307–329; Lee Nellis, "What Does Energy

Development Mean for Wyoming?" *Human Organization* 33 (Fall 1974): 229–238; C. Smith, T.C. Hogg, and M.S. Reagan, "Economic Development: Panacea or Perplexity for Rural Areas?" *Journal of Rural Sociology* 36 (1971): 173–186; and Gene F. Summers, *Large Industry in a Rural Area* (Madison, Wis.: University of Wisconsin-Madison; Center of Applied Sociology, August 1973).

15. See the report of the Study Committee on Policy Management Assistance, *Strengthening Public Management in the Intergovernmental System* (Washington: Government Printing Office, 1975), and the symposium on "Policy Management Assistance—A Developing Dialogue" in *Public Administration Review* 35 (December 1975).

16. Study Committee on Policy Management Assistance, ibid.

17. Ibid. pp. vii–viii, 4–5.

18. For descriptions and summaries of some of this work, see Department of Housing and Urban Development, *Rapid Growth from Energy Projects;* Leistritz, Leholm, and Hertsgaard, "Public Sector Implications"; Regional Studies Program, *National Coal Utilization Assessment,* vol. 2, ANL-11 (Argonne Ill.: Argonne National Laboratory, 1977), pp. 8.1–9.1; W. Fulkerson et al., *Energy Division Annual Progress Report,* ORNL-5124 (Oak Ridge, Tenn.: Oak Ridge National Laboratory, 1975), pp. 96–147; Resource Planning Associates, Inc., and SCET International, *A Preliminary Approach to Managing Growth in Mercy County, North Dakota* (Washington: Resource Planning Associates, Inc., February 1976); and Irvin L. White "The Energy Issue: An Applied Policy Analysis of Western Energy Resource Development" Paper presented at the Annual Region VII Conference of the American Society for Public Administration, Omaha, Nebraska, October 7–8, 1977.

19. For a discussion of the act, see O. Glenn Stahl, *Public Personnel Administration* (New York: Harper and Row, 1976).

20. The program is described in *Public Administration Times* 1, no. 9 (September 1978): 12.

The Energy Boomtown:
An Analysis of the
Politics of Getting

Norman Wengert

This chapter is based on Lasswell's definition of politics as getting.[1] The following axiom flows from this definition: Using such rationales and rhetoric as seems expedient and effective, American politicians will get as much as they can for their constituents, with only casual attention to the merits of the case and to the extent that they are not likely to be held directly accountable for costs (that is, where they are not directly identified with raising raxes or other adverse local effects).

Two corollaries flow from this axiom:

1. Politicians assess action to benefit constituents in terms of the extent to which it broadens political support and tends to ensure chances for reelection.
2. If friends share uniquely in the benefits (for example, through sales to government or contracts with government), this will not result in political recriminations so long as the district or state also appears to benefit.

Energy Impact Alleviation

This chapter deals specifically with the politics of getting funds and other benefits to mitigate adverse consequences of energy boomtown growth. The merits or needs for actions to mitigate negative impacts are often very important, although identification of negative impacts, particularly those of a secondary character, may prove difficult. In most cases, local perceptions of negative impacts (often confused simply with change) may be the initial stimulus for political involvement and action. In a nation in which ideology plays so small a part as a basis for action programs, squeaking wheels and pinching shoes tend to determine the agenda for political action.

With respect to the alleviation of negative impacts from energy development, *for the politician,* at whatever level he functions, the critical question is, How can I secure funding to deal with impact problems from a level of government where one-on-one relationships between expenditures and taxes are not recognized? None but the very naive believe in the "free lunch." What is important is to have someone else pick up the check! *For the policy analyst,* the issues are normative as well as conceptual, focusing on where the costs of boomtown growth *ought* to fall. And in answering these questions two possible policy positions may be tenable. The one, espoused by many economists, is that those who benefit should pay. The other, less frequently heard today, is that ability to pay should determine on whom the burdens fall. Either position could be consistent with policies to recapture windfalls and unearned increments, balancing excess benefits against severe costs.

To the politician the effective norms are often quite different. First, he is concerned with benefiting all or some of his constituents without arousing hostility. Where some become hostile, his strategy is to deflect hostility. Second, he is constantly concerned with increasing his support. Third, he is concerned with the extent to which his interest in a particular measure or program provides a basis for bargaining with legislative colleagues. Building alliances and alignments and ultimately action majorities is necessary to effectiveness.

The Energy Scene

A variety of national programs and policies have had the effect of encouraging development of Rocky Mountain coal and other energy resources. And when, as expected, Congress enacts a national energy program with incentives and disincentives to encourage domestic energy development, reliance on Rocky Mountain resources will increase substantially.[2] It is in this context that Rocky Mountain environmentalists and political leaders (especially the several governors and members of their personal staffs) have been expressing concern over the damage which will result to Rocky Mountain ecosystems and, in socioeconomic terms, to impacted communities. With respect to the socioeconomic impacts, Rock springs, Wyoming (which became a coal mining boomtown about ten years ago) and Gillette, Wyoming, and Colstrip, Montana (which are more recent sites of coal development) have become symbols of what might be expected locally.

Coal mining is expanding in Eastern states, but for various reasons the political consequences seem different from those in the West. In any case, this chapter deals primarily with developments in the Rocky Mountain West, where coal mine development on the scale now contemplated is something new, where development impact is often starkly evident because it occurs in areas of very low population densities and primitive social infrastructures, where water is scarce, and where substantial acreages of public domain lands may be involved.[3] This is a region, moreover, where in the past decade environmental concerns have been strongly articulated and where the artifacts of ghost towns scattered over the landscape are reminders of past booms and busts primarily from mineral development.

The Political Environment

Depending, of course, on to whom one speaks, the attitudes in the Rocky Mountain West with respect to the mining boom range from outright hostility and opposition to grudging acceptance based on national-interest considerations to muted but enthusiastic support. To towns or counties in which family incomes are often half the national average, to unemployed or underemployed workers, to landowners, speculators, merchants, and others who expect direct benefits from increased economic activity—to all these people the boom is unquestionably welcome. Yet traditional chamber of commerce promotional enthusiasm is muted. In fact, the temper of the times, the thrust of many impact studies, the very real difficulties and frictions in the impacted communities, and statistics on individual social maladjustments have resulted in most attention being directed to negative effects and adverse consequences. Each of these factors requires comment.

The Temper of the Times

Under this heading the environmental concerns expressed so frequently in the past decade and forcefully stated in connection with the recent enactment of state and federal strip mine control legislation should be included. For a vociferous minority, strip mining was evil and should have been stopped. It was considered particularly bad in the arid regions where lack of water complicates reclamation.

Coupled with hostility to strip mining has often been a "no growth" philosophy, reflecting a desire to keep the West as it was circa 1970—a playground for people as well as for deer and antelope—and a hostility to urban growth in the region typified by the bumper sticker "Let's not Californicate Colorado." Undoubtedly such views receive respectful attention just because for at least twenty-five years the Rocky Mountain West had, in fact, been experiencing tremendous changes in its economy as well as in population numbers. Resulting adjustments or failures to adjust intensified problems faced by many communities (even though many individuals may have profited) and highlighted common inadequacies of governmental and social institutions, particularly when measured by critics' expectations of what was happening as well as those of many newcomers who demanded better services and facilities.

The Thrust of Impact Analyses

It has become conventional wisdom in the United States that perceived problems need rarely be just tolerated. They must be studied, researched, investigated

—whether or not the action ultimately taken, in fact, bears much relationship to study findings and recommendations. In the last several decades, moreover, the process of study, research, and investigation has been highly institutionalized, to a large extent as a result of federal largesse and federal law.[4] Federal largesse is exemplified by planning funds (for example, "701" funds and highway funds); federal law is exemplified by the requirements of the National Environmental Policy Act (NEPA), particularly section 102 which mandates preparation of environmental impact statements for major federal actions having an impact on the environment.[5] NEPA is particularly significant to Rocky Mountain energy development because in most of the region federal lands account for one-third to four-fifths of the total land area. In addition, much of the coal and other mineral development may directly involve federal lands. Even where the development itself is on private lands, roads, power lines, or other service facilities are likely to cross federal lands and thus may require preparation of impact statements.

Three factors in the development of impact statements (and other studies) deserve note. First, a strong bias has developed which causes change, whether ecological or socioeconomic, to be equated with negative consequences without much effort being made to assess alternatives or appraise trade-offs. Second, the terms *impact* and *impact assessment* have similarly taken on a strongly negative connotation. Third, the stress on balancing adverse against positive consequences, so well outlined by Judge Skelly Wright in the Calvert Cliffs case[6] interpreting NEPA, has been lost. As a result, many studies are incomplete and often lack both a sense of impact over time and a balanced perspective. More importantly, as discussed in greater detail below, these studies lend themselves readily to the rhetoric of *political getting*.

Difficulties and Frictions

No one could deny that growth has an impact and that rapid growth, where a community may double or triple its population in a decade, creates acute problems. But impacts are by no means all negative. In any case, the purposes of government are to solve problems, as suggested in the Preambles of many American Constitutions!

A brief digression with respect to positive effects probably flowing from growth and development is in order. It is not because Coloradoans are wiser, superior people that unemployment has been hovering around 5 percent and that state revenues for the past decade have shown steady growth, the surplus in fiscal year 1978 being estimated at about $100 million. Various factors account for Colorado's growth since about 1950, although causal relationships are often obscure and conclusions based on simple correlations may be suspect. Population has been increasing at about double the national rate, and personal per capita average income, while increasing, has reached only the national average. Among the factors that seem relevant are, of course, climate and scenery made accessible by interstate highways and jet air travel, Denver being about two hours from two-thirds of the country. The major growth area has been the "Front Range," extending from Pueblo north to Fort Collins, while the area of major change has been the mountain region where ranching, lumbering, and mining have tended to give way to recreation and second homes. At the same time, many other areas of the state remain pockets of depression. Thus it is important to stress that the basic issue in all change is one of equity, identifying *who* benefits and *who* pays the costs, defining both benefits and costs (as does NEPA) in terms broader than simply dollars and direct effects.

Two further factors are relevant. First is the *time* dimension, or that lack of ability to cope may simply be a short-run phenomenon (that is, the need for front-end money). Second is the *institutional* dimension, or that inadequate or unresponsive institutions (including plans, laws, ordinances, jurisdictions, administrative organization, and personnel) may hamper adjustment and intensify adverse consequences. Institutional factors can be changed, but often not without a political struggle. An illustration is Wyoming. Perhaps the most seriously impacted state to date, Wyoming could enact an income tax and could use resulting revenues to alleviate growth problems. But proposals for an income tax and for increased aid to local governments would very likely encounter substantial political opposition. As another illustration, under state water pollution and health laws, even before any energy development had occurred, many small communities in the Rocky Mountain states had inadequate water supply and sewer systems. Perhaps these inadequacies reflected financial inability to comply with state standards. But they more often reflected a crass unwillingness to take on the expenses involved—perhaps because of hope for federal or state aid. In any event, systems already inadequate become grossly deficient in the face of even modest growth.

Social Maladjustments

The statistics on increases in crime, juvenile delinquency, alcoholism, divorce, and so on for Rock Springs, Gillette, and other boomtowns are frightening. They have provided themes for many sermons, as well as subjects for newspaper articles, television features, and academic hand wringing! These data cannot be adequately analyzed here, but one cannot avoid wondering whether those stressing such data on social disorganization in boomtowns have not fallen into the trap of mistaking correlations for causes. Would the alcoholic in Rock Springs have been an alcoholic in Pittsburgh? Would the juvenile delinquent in Gillette have been delinquent in Denver? Would the couple seeking divorce in Colorado perhaps have sought to separate wherever they may have formerly lived? Certainly one can hardly conclude that the Mafia or other organized crime interests, which the CBS News program "Sixty Minutes" suggested may have been operating in Rock Springs, were simply local phenomena triggered by the coal boom. Perhaps the boom created the opportunity for outside criminal interests to move in or the temptation for the local individuals to participate. Analyzed in the above fashion, requests for impact assistance become a commentary upon the human condition but hardly a basis for blaming energy development or justifying special allocations of federal funds.

The Politics of Getting Federal Aid

While it may be assumed that communities in which energy development occurs have a host of new problems, the economic theory or equitable logic which justifies getting federal funds to pay costs of solving these problems is difficult to follow. While the axiom stated at the beginning of this chapter suggests that politicians will seek federal funds, the policy analyst should deal with the reasonableness, the justice, or the equity of the situation. If the objective is to internalize externalities of development, state and local controls and programs should be sufficient. Although the energy self-sufficiency program is a federal action, users of energy resources pay for those resources; and if state or local controls are effective, internalization of development costs should result, including social as well as environmental and operating costs. It may be argued that mining, being exploitative, leaves a residue of problems and costs when mines are depleted. But even these costs can generally be anticipated by state programs, and this usually is a strong rationale for state severance taxes. Whether states, in fact, hold severance tax proceeds in trust for future costs is a different question.

Federal Royalties and Other Payments

Historically, states and local governments have received a portion of federal mineral lease income. The amount going to the states was increased from 37.5 to 50 percent in 1976, and at the same time state legislatures were given greater discretion over allocations. In the same year a law gave counties an in-lieu-of-tax payment for federal lands in the respective jurisdiction. This proposal had been made frequently before 1976, but it had always been rejected. It now is the law of the land![7]

While some may disagree, I firmly believe that neither of these programs, although politically of substantial importance, has much economic justification. They represent a subsidy and as such a transfer from the general funds to specific benefiting localities.[8]

A headline in a recent issue of the Washington *Post* reported that a U.S.

Treasury Department study had found "Many Cities 'Hooked' on Anti-Recession Aid." A similar story might well be written with respect to mineral royalties, in-lieu-of-tax payments, and cost alleviation through federal subsidies. To the political analyst aware of Lasswell's definition of politics as getting, the fact of such distributive programs and of local government addiction to them comes as no surprise. The bargains and trade-offs in Congress involved in authorizing these programs lend credence to the axiom stated at the beginning of the chapter. And local politicians, officials, and various constituent interests support the legislator who does most for his state or district. To the normal political actors in local and state governments who support impact aid must also be added those with a kind of "intellectual" interest in the object—the planning and engineering consultants, the university professors, and others who undertake impact studies to justify local or state needs.

There is probably no introductory course in U.S. politics in which the pork barrel politics of water development (the Corps of Engineers and the Bureau of Reclamation, primarily) is not castigated as representing the worst of the system. Yet what is involved is a standard U.S. political ploy to get benefits for one's constituency while others pay costs or costs are obscured. The search for personal and/or local benefits at the expense of the larger society has always been a major goal of most U.S. politics and politicians. Only by starting from this premise can we make sense out of the intense efforts to secure federal funds to mitigate adverse impacts from energy development, while at the same time ignoring both who pays these subsidies and what other benefits may fall to the impacted region or state.

Despite thousands of words on socioeconomic impacts of energy developments, little or no attention has been directed to the politics of impact abatement in the Lasswellian sense of getting. Identification of who benefits and who pays, in the language of economics, directs attention to the distributive consequences and to externality effects, secondary as well as primary. In political or policy analyses an understanding of who benefits and who pays may be essential both to understanding the network of alliances and alignments supporting action proposals and to recognizing the hidden agendas of powerful, influential groups. Where the "who" is recognized, it may be possible to separate self-seeking goals from public needs and interests. To contribute to this objective has been the purpose of this chapter.

Notes

1. Harold Lasswell, *Politics: Who Gets What, When, How* (New York: Meridian Press, 1958). The original edition was published in 1936.

2. Two points should be noted. First, although the states of California, Oregon, and Washington are anticipating expanded energy consumption, and

hence will be confronted with the need to add to generating capacity, the basic energy resources will generally be brought in from other states. At present there is almost no coal-generated energy in these states, and only a small portion of coal-produced energy is brought in from adjacent states. Second, most development issues are concerned with mining and processing of basic energy raw materials, and far fewer with the use of these materials. A possible exception has been the concern over nuclear energy generating stations which are not dealt with in this chapter.

3. While coal has been mined in Rocky Mountain states since they were first settled, the scale of mining was small. Present-day mining expansion is based on strip mining technology, the environmental consequences of which are more far-reaching and visually apparent than underground mining. According to *Newsweek* (March 20, 1978, p. 35), Western coal in 1977 accounted for about 17 percent of all U.S. production and was estimated to account for 40 percent by 1980. It should also be noted that many counties in which coal mining is likely to occur have population densities of less than 2 per square mile with no communities meeting the census definition minimum of 2,500 to qualify as cities.

4. See Charles Reich, "The New Property," *Yale Law Journal* 73(1964): 733–787, where the idea of government largesse is explored in detail.

5. P.L. 91-190; 42 U.S.C. 4321–4347.

6. *Calvert Cliffs' Coordinating Committee* v. *AEC,* U.S. Court of Appeals, District of Columbia Circuit, 1971, 449 F.2d 1109 ff.

7. During World War II Congress authorized a payment scheme to alleviate the stresses due to military camps and swollen federal payroolls. Over thirty years later these payments, which may have had some justification initially, continue.

8. The following quotation is worth noting: "At the federal level we have no comprehensive understanding of what subsidy programs exist and, correspondingly, what objectives subsidies serve, what good or bad effects subsidies impose upon the treasury and society." And later in the same source the author states: "The arguments used to justify subsidies often have nothing to do with what a subsidy actually can do economically. The arguments for subsidies are also extraordinarily nebulous. Perhaps the most widely used justification is the vague assertion that the activity . . . is in the national interest. . . . An argument of roughly the same analytical merit can be found in statements . . . that there is a great 'need'. . . ." Jerry J. Jasinowski, "The Economics of Federal Subsidy Programs," *Government Spending and Land Values* (Madison, Wis.: University of Wisconsin Press, 1973).

3

Role of the State in Energy Forecasting

Richard J. Timm

Energy forecasting and the results of such forecasts are becoming a major issue in energy policy development. Prior to the oil embargo of 1973, energy forecasting was primarily a responsiblity of the energy suppliers themselves. Since that time, however, numerous agencies, both federal and state, and special interest groups have become involved in energy forecasting. For example, Federal Power Commission witnesses have appeared in Nuclear Regulatory Commission proceedings in support of utilities' energy forecasts.[1] State energy forecasters now appear in both state energy facility siting cases and rate cases and in federal facility siting cases.[2] Even public interest organizations submit testimony regarding energy forecasting in federal and state proceedings. Basic questions now arise as to who should make the energy forecasts and who is ultimately responsible for the results.

Before these questions are discussed, it is important to understand the necessity of an accurate forecast. For the purposes of this discussion, the forecasting has been divided into two time periods: long-range and short-range forecasting. *Long-range forecasting* refers to a period of three to twenty years while short-term forecasting refers to one- to two-year forecasts. Certainly there are other forecasting periods such as day-to-day forecasting to schedule facility dispatching. However, the definitions for short- and long-term forecasting have been adopted simply for clarity of the following discussion.

Necessity of an Accurate Forecast

The general economic climate including employment in a region is related to the energy supply patterns. This is dramatically illustrated in the short term during fuel embargoes and during periods of unusually cold weather if energy shortfalls result. This does not imply that over the long run energy use and the economic activity are *directly* related, but it does imply some relationship between the two activities. Since efficiency of energy use is variable (consider appliance efficiency standards, for example), the relationship between energy use and the economic activity is a *planning variable*. As a result, in planning the economy of a particular region, energy use and supply are crucial factors. Decisions involving

economic development, land use, transportation, environmental control, employment, and housing all require consideration of energy supply and use patterns.

In shaping the long-term economy through legislation (such as tax incentives for certain types of capital investments or energy conservation measures)
or through administrative rules (such as building codes or transportation policies), it is necessary to consider the energy implications. It is a question not of
more (or less) government intervention since government is already there, but
rather of recognizing and understanding the energy implications in both government and private decisions. Thus, there is a necessity for a long-range energy
forecast in making many decisions which affect the overall economic welfare of
a particular region.

More specifically, when a decision is made to construct new energy supply
facilities, a very specific definition of need is required. In dealing with a monopoly such as electric utility regulated by a public utility commission, the decision on need is most important since it directly affects the long-term *cost* of
energy supplies. It is difficult to maintain relatively low-cost utility rates if too
many energy supply facilities have been constructed. In this situation, a long-
term energy forecast is crucial. The construction of too many energy supply
facilities normally leads to excessive energy costs resulting in adverse economic
impacts. The construction of too few facilities, on the other hand, also leads to
higher economic costs and, in severe cases, economic disruptions.

Both long- and short-term forecasts are important in rate design and rate-
of-return decisions. Responses to specific rate designs, that is, energy-use
forecasting, are a basic determinant in selecting one rate design over another.

The short-term forecast is of particular significance in contingency planning. Labor strikes, adverse weather, energy supply embargos, and unforeseen
shortfalls of energy all require reasonably accurate short-term forecasts of
demand under different abatement strategies to enable adequate contingency
planning.

The accuracy of the forecast, whether of long or short range, is a basic element in the soundess of regulatory and planning decisions.

Role of the State versus the Energy Supplier

Both state government and energy suppliers have specific needs for energy forecasting capability. Both should develop forecasting capability for their own
specific needs.

Energy suppliers require long-term energy forecasts for numerous purposes.
The forecast is a basic element in the long-range planning of facility expansion
and operation. For example, long-range planning of the distribution system
requires energy-use forecasts for relatively small areas. Accurate, long-range
forecasts are required to negotiate reasonable fuel contracts for energy supply

facilities. Marketing strategies are developed in part based on future expected consumption patterns given different courses of action. Even the design of consumer rate schedules is now becoming more and more dependent on the long-range energy forecasts.

The short-term energy forecast is also required by the energy supplier for a number of operational functions. Revenue requirements during a future test year are dependent on the short-term forecast for the energy supplier's service area. Scheduling plant maintenance and operation is also dependent on the short-term forecast to enable the most cost-effective maintenance and operation scheduling. To handle various contingency problems such as strikes, fuel embargos, or unusual weather conditions, an adequate short-term forecast also is necessary.

State government has numerous functions which require both a short-range and a long-range energy forecast. The long-range energy forecast is needed to develop and implement a coordinated economic development program. Most state governments, for example, have a department which promotes the development of certain industrial operations. To be effective, such a department must have an adequate knowledge of future energy supply and price. In addition, the impact of energy supply and price on other industries must be examined particularly when the development of energy-intensive industries such as primary metals or paper and allied products is promoted. Thus a forecast is needed first to establish the appropriate economic development policy for the state and then to implement that policy.

Other functions of state government, such as transportation, land use, environmental control, employment, and housing, have similar energy forecasting needs. In fact, a well-developed energy forecasting method can serve as a basis to coordinate the diverse functions of state government.

State government through its regulation of energy monopolies (regulated utilities) also requires a long-range energy forecast to determine the necessity for new energy production facilities. Statutorily the "need" issue is of varying importance in different states; however, the need issue is a key to minimizing rates of regulated energy suppliers. The development of appropriate long-term rate designs also requires a resonably accurate long-range forecast.

The review of the adequacy of a particular state's long-term energy supply depends heavily on the long-range energy forecast. With developing shortfalls of some fuel types, this is of particular significance. A state may want to capitalize on a certain type of energy supply such as geothermal or solar to ensure adequate and stable long-term energy supply. A coordinated program of incentives and regulation must be developed to ensure adequate energy supply.

State government also has need of short-term forecasts. Strikes, embargos, and unusual weather conditions force state government into energy contingency situations which require short-term forecasting capability. Short-term forecasting is also required to determine revenue production from various energy taxes such as the gasoline tax. The determination of the revenue requirements of a regulated energy utility in various rate cases is another function dependent on the short-term energy forecast.

Thus, both state government and the energy suppliers have numerous specific needs for short-term and long-term energy forecasts. Many of the needs in some respects are duplicative. Two significant questions often arise: (1) Who bears the ultimate responsibility for making an accurate forecast and (2) Should a common forecasting method be set forth by the state to provide more consistent energy forecasting?

Who is Responsible Now?

Although the severity of disruptions in energy supply is often overdramatized, an energy shortfall can cause economic disruption and health and safety problems. These can be minimized through effective contingency planning by both the state and energy suppliers. More frequent, but less severe, energy shortfalls require purchases of higher-cost energy, operation of higher-cost facilities at capacity factors higher than economically optimum, and/or reduced system reliability. These actions to overcome the energy shortfalls increase the cost to consumers.

On the other hand, excessive energy supplies usually result in higher cost that can also lead to long-term economic disruptions which, in severe conditions, can even cause health and safety problems. Higher electricity costs resulting from overconstruction (overforecasting) may force lower thermostat settings for customers on fixed or lower incomes and can also increase nonpayments, which ultimately result in service disconnection. These situations can lead to increased illness or even death, particularly with elderly consumers. Who, then, assumes the responsibility for the economic and social costs of both energy shortfalls and oversupply?

Traditionally the energy suppliers have assumed the major responsibility for energy *forecasting*. It is often argued that the energy suppliers should be responsible for preparing the forecast since they have more experience, have greater access to energy-use data, are "closer to the problem," and are legally responsible for supplying adequate service.

Certainly energy suppliers in general have more experience than state energy forecasters. Energy suppliers have long prepared energy forecasts to support increased production facilities and changes in rate levels and/or rate structures. State agencies have generally been satisfied to review the forecast without actually preparing any forecasts themselves.

This additional experience on the part of energy suppliers does not necessarily imply, however, that the *quality* of the forecast is state of the art or even adequate. A study of forecasting methods[3] described a major energy supplier's forecasting manual as "out of date with respect to both data available . . . and techniques in use. . . ." This study continued stating that "[f] or the most part, the energy forecasts [of the public utilities it interviewed] do not depend on statistical estimation techniques. . . . Only one utility has used an ordinary least-squares technique to forecast system energy requirements, but in general there is no broad use of standard statistical techniques." This does not imply that all energy suppliers' forecasts are inadequate. Certain utilities do have generally appropriate forecasting methods.[4] It does illustrate that the added experience does not necessarily yield a forecast of adequate quality.

In certain cases, energy suppliers may have greater access to certain energy-use data than the state has. This is primarily due to the relationship between the energy supplier and the energy user, particularly with large energy users. Certain states (such as Oregon), however, have legislative authority to compel energy users and suppliers to provide certain types of energy-use data.[5] Further and more importantly, the legislation also allows for confidentiality to protect the supplier of the data from any unfair competitive advantages.[6] In states with such legislation, the state actually has greater access to energy data.

More importantly, however, it is not the access to the data that is important but rather the *acquisition* and *use* of the data. For example, a major electric utility could not supply energy price data, service area population and employment, or energy use by customer class as backup data to its basic forecast.[7] This utility simply did not compile these basic data.

It is unreasonable to assume that an energy supplier is closer to the problem and thus able to produce a more correct forecast of future energy use. Future energy use is a function of many variables including economic policies, efficiency standards and guidelines, availability of alternative energy sources, and population growth. Is it reasonable to expect an electric utility forecaster to be more aware of future legislation, availability of alternative energy forms, or population growth than a state forecaster? Certainly not. For example, a forecaster representing a major Midwest electric utility was not even familiar with the federal guidelines set forth for the efficiency of energy used by major industries; yet this same forecaster was sponsoring his own forecast which included a breakdown of future energy use in the industrial sector.[8]

Although energy suppliers have assumed the major responsibility for energy forecasting in the past, have they actually assumed responsibility for the impacts of under- or overforecasting? Ultimately, no. If the actual demand is lower than forecasted, then regulated energy utilities, for example, turn to state regulatory commissions for rate increases to recover the "loss" revenues. If demand has been underforecasted and higher-cost facilities are operated at uneconomically high levels or purchase power is required, these added costs are recovered through rate increases and/or fuel adjustment clauses. With extreme energy shortfalls, government intervention is required to allocate the shortfall, and it bears the brunt of the allocation decisions.

Only if the regulated energy utilities absorb the added cost due to forecasting error can they claim responsibility for such errors. Absorbing the added cost means no pass-through (using fuel adjustment clauses) of added fuel cost and/or high-cost purchases due to forecasting error. The added cost of constructing and maintaining excess capacity built because of overforecasting would also have to be borne by the supplier, not the consumer. Only then would the supplier be responsible for his forecast.

At present, however, the state through the regulatory commissions and ultimately the consumer is assuming the responsibility for forecasting error. Lost revenues because of conservation (which is synonymous with overforecasting) are a stated reason for rate increases. Shortages of supply are allocated according to rules set by regulatory commissions. Fuel adjustment clauses passed through the increased fuel costs resulting from underestimating future demand.

Who Should Be Responsible?

This placement of responsibility of forecasting with the state is appropriate. The interrelationship of energy supply and use with economic activity is too broad to relinquish responsibility of energy forecasting to special interest groups. Future energy use is not a present value but a function of key state decisions on efficiency of energy use, development of particular energy alternatives, economic activity, and population growth. These are primarily concerns of the state, not of energy suppliers.

More specifically, the authorization of energy facilities and the regulation of utility rates are highly dependent on forecasting. Errors in forecasting lead to increased costs and other economic disruptions which are ultimately borne by the general public. Reasonable allocation of energy supplies relies in part on an energy forecast to minimize economic and social hardships.

Not only should the state continue to assume responsibility for forecasting error, but also it should recognize its full responsibility. Adequate state forecasting capability should be developed and maintained. The state forecasting effort should play a prominent role in state and federal proceedings involving energy supply, energy use, and energy rates. The state forecaster should be a full-party intervener in proceedings involving need for new energy facilities and rate design.

Common Forecasting Methods

Because there are incentives, at least for regulated electric utilities, to overforecast and utilities do overforecast,[9] there has been some interest in the state's developing a common forecasting method to provide more consistent forecasting. Such efforts appear to be misdirected for several reasons.

First, different methods of forecasting must be used to answer different questions. For example, the theory of econometric forecasting is appropriate in trying to quantify the effects of various tax incentive programs or to determine the impact on consumption of changing personal income or energy prices. End-use forecasting (which is deterministic) does not provide an adequate theoretical basis to answer such questions but does allow for the quantification of effects of applying efficiency standards or building codes. Econometric modeling is generally inadequate to quantify the energy impacts of such actions.

The time period over which the forecast is made also impacts the level of detail required in the forecasting method. Generally, the longer the time period over which the forecast is made, the greater the need for detail.[10] More factors are subject to change as one projects further into the future; thus more detailed forecasting methods are needed.

Second, state and energy suppliers have different uses for the forecasting results. The state will be more concerned about the overall economic development while energy suppliers will be more concerned about their marketing potentials and strategies. The state will balance the need of one type of energy supply system against another while a particular energy supplier will attempt to justify the need for its type of energy. Energy suppliers will use a short-term forecast to determine the most economic system operation while the state will use the short-term forecast more for contingency planning. Thus, the uses of the forecast are significantly different. Different uses generally require different forecasting methods.

Third, because of the complexities of forecasting and because of the significant and recent changes in forecasting methods, independent energy forecasts provide a check on one another. Understanding the *reason* for differences among forecasts can be as important as the differences themselves. If the differences, for example, are due to input assumptions rather than the methodology, a much more focused discussion on input assumptions can develop. Discussion then focuses not on modeling techniques but instead on more basic questions of future population growth, future application of efficiency standards, expected prices and energy supplies, and future industrial growth. If, however, the major differences are due to forecasting methods, then a more detailed discussion on analytical methods is appropriate. In either case, the scope of the discussion is significantly narrowed.

It is of benefit to both energy suppliers and the state to develop forecasting methods, forecasting assumptions, and actual forecasts independent of one another, but the responsibility of the forecast result rests with the state.

Notes

1. See Nuclear Regulatory Commission (NRC) proceedings on the Pebble

Springs nuclear power plant (docket no. 50-514/515) and the Skaget nuclear power plant (docket no. STN-50-522/523).

2. See State of Oregon Energy Facility Council's record on the application of Portland General Electric Company for a site certificate for the Pebble Springs nuclear power plant; also see State of Oregon testimony in the NRC proceedings on the Skaget nuclear power plant (docket no. 50-514/515).

3. "Review of Energy Forecasting Methodologies and Assumptions," prepared for Bonneville Power Administration, U.S. Department of Interior, by Ernst and Ernst, June 1976.

4. "Principal Observations and Findings," *Oregon's Energy Future—First Annual Report,* prepared by Oregon Department of Energy, January 1, 1977; "Principal Observations and Findings," *Oregon's Energy Future—Second Annual Report,* prepared by Oregon Department of Energy, January 1, 1978.

5. Oregon Revised Statutes 469.070 and 469.080.

6. Oregon Revised Statute 469.090.

7. Interrogatory response of Pacific Power and Light Company to the Oregon Department of Energy's interrogatories in the proceeding before the Oregon Energy Facility Siting Council in the matter of the application of Portland General Electric Company for a site certificate for the Pebble Springs nuclear power plant.

8. See Nuclear Regulatory Commission proceedings on the Midland plant, units 1 and 2 (docket no. 50-329/330), transcript, pp. 1990–1991.

9. "Incentives for Electric Utilities to Overforecast," prepared for Bonneville Power Administration by Ernst and Ernst. U.S. Department of Commerce NTIS no. PB-257 495, July 1976.

10. Anthony Lawrence, "Load Forecasting—Modeling with Judgment," *Electric Power Research Institute Journal,* August 1977.

Western State Energy Policy Development: Inertia Instead of Innovation

Hanna J. Cortner

Introduction

In the past many policy actions with energy significance were made to serve other specific policy objectives. They were not formulated as "energy policy" with a view toward comprehensively managing energy supply and demand.[1] Energy availability and costs were not paramount factors in the decision-making processes of either individuals or governments. Energy, however, is no longer a nonissue. The 1973 Arab oil embargo dramatically signaled the end of the era of cheap, abundant, and reliable energy supply. It prompted political demands and pressures for energy policies designed to overcome past policy omissions and mistakes and to reduce national dependency on energy imports.[2] States as well as the federal government must now respond to these new conditions of energy decision making, formulating and implementing comprehensive and coordinated energy policies focusing on alternatives regarding energy technology, use, and conservation.

Many Western states—which are bound to be the location for increased domestic energy production—have traditionally played a limited role in resource development planning and decision making. In the area of water resources development, for example, the federal government has often worked directly with local and private development interests, forming a federal-local cooperative system of policy making in which states were excluded.[3] Their role eclipsed, the states have had little incentive to develop their own independent planning and information evaluation capabilities.[4] Similarly, in the area of energy, the state role has been a very narrow one, often restricted to the approval or rejection of production sites selected by industry or to the setting of rates charged for service. And it is not surprising that when making those decisions, states have been largely dependent on the utilities to supply and interpret the needed information.[5] Moreover, authority and responsibility for natural resource management at the state level typically have been scattered among a number of weak administrative agencies with rather specialized functions and limited staff and funding support. The states have been unable to do long-range integrated resource planning or to utilize available planning information to develop coherent, unified state policies and positions on important natural resource development issues.

Today, however, Western states are making it known that they are no longer content to play a subordinate role in resource development and planning. They are demanding a greater voice in decisions affecting their interests and are stressing the need to create new organizational and administrative arrangements which will enable them to become more active, effective policy-making participants. These demands for an enlarged policy role in resource development have been characterized by some observers as the "new states' rights."[6]

Yet the states' acknowledgment of the potential importance of the state role and their insistence on assuming a more significant and viable role can easily become empty political rhetoric. Without actual state policy actions to formulate comprehensive state energy policies and to secure the organizational requisites of policy administration, the states will be unable to translate the desire for states' rights into active and effective participation.

This chapter examines the policy actions of five Western states—Arizona, Colorado, Nevada, New Mexico, and Utah—through the spring of 1977.[7] It argues that energy policy development in the five states was characterized by inertia rather than by innovations designed to meet the challenge of an enlarged state policy role.

Comprehensive Energy Policies and the Organizational Requisites for Policy Administration

States have responsibilities to foster research and long-range planning programs that are responsive to individual state conditions and information needs; to analyze and manage the adverse environmental and social impacts of particular production activities on local populations; and to encourage and sponsor educational programs and activities which increase levels of awareness and understanding of the various political, socioeconomic, and environmental consequences of alternative technological and conservation choices. To meet these responsibilities, comprehensive state energy policies must be developed which are balanced, environmentally sensitive, coordinative, flexible, implementable, and politically and economically accountable. To initiate, support, and implement such policies, states must also establish the organizational capacities for capable and aggresive energy policy administration. Centralized and unified energy agencies with broad and inclusive mandates are required. These administrative structures must have the requisite resources for decision making, including staff sufficient in numbers and expertise, an ample budget for administration and research, leadership committed to policy innovation, and a two-way flow of communication with a variety of economic and citizen interests. There must also be a commitment and capacity to do long-range functional energy planning, as well as the mechanisms to facilitate planning coordination vertically among levels of government and horizontally among agencies and programs of government.

When measured by the criteria just described, energy policy development in

Arizona, Colorado, Nevada, New Mexico, and Utah was generally found to be inadequate. These five states had not yet fully resolved how best to organize comprehensively for energy decision making or how best to ensure that the organizations thus established had the basic organizational requisites for energy policy planning, administration, and coordination.

Administrative Framework

Centralized and unified decision-making structures are necessary if states are to have an administrative capacity in energy. Yet by the spring of 1977 only New Mexico and Nevada had acted to create and staff centralized energy agencies. New Mexico created the Energy Resources Board (ERB) in 1975, giving the seven-member board a broad mandate for both energy development and energy conservation functions. In addition to establishing the ERB, the legislature also transferred the responsibility for the state's research and development program to the ERB. This research and development effort was substantial. Between 1974 and 1977, for example, the state committed $6 million to its energy research and development program, far more than any other of the four states.

In Nevada, a specially constituted committee established by the 1975 legislature, the SCR 8 Committee, examined alternatives for the management and planning of the state's natural resources, including state activities in the area of energy. In the energy area, the final report of the SCR 8 Committee recommended the abolition of the Energy Management Division of the State Public Service Commission—a division which had been legislatively mandated in 1975—and the creation of a separate Department of Energy Conservation and Management. The legislature approved these recommendations regarding the new energy department in the spring of 1977.

The other three states studied had not created centralized and comprehensive energy agencies. Instead they had expanded the problem-solving responsibilities of existing agencies, adding such areas as fuel allocation and energy conservation planning to existing duties; or they had added specialized, limited-mandate offices to deal with emergent state activities. Arizona, for example, created the Arizona Solar Energy Research Commission, adding yet another energy agency to the numerous administrative agencies active in energy administration in the state. Colorado established a research group, the Colorado Energy Research Institute. Arizona, Colorado, Nevada, and Utah were also relying heavily on interagency, advisory, and ad hoc mechanisms in order to manage state energy programs and activities, decision-making structures which often operated without any statutory enactments or executive orders to clarify their roles, functions, or authority. The proliferation of limited-mandate energy agencies and special interagency councils had only further fragmented the administrative structure. Moreover, few of these mechanisms had been supplied with sufficient decision-making resources. In most of the states, budget, staff, and expertise were at minimal levels.

Other long-established energy agencies, such as the states' public utility commissions, had failed to alter traditional patterns of energy decision making and adjust to the new energy situation. The emergence of the energy issue presented public utility commissions in the five state with new opportunities and responsibilities for expanding and modifying their traditional role in energy production and demand management. For the most part, however, the commissions still clung to a conventional, limited vision of their role. Lacking commitment to innovation, open channels of communication, and sufficient decision-making resources, they were hard pressed to initiate new programs. Commissioners and their staff expressed resistance to any reorganization of commission missions or decision-making practices that would alter or abolish standard theories and principles of utility regulation—tenets, it can be argued, often applying to regulatory conditions that no longer exist.

Many decisionmakers in the five states examined appeared convinced that reorganization for energy decision making is politically unfeasible and/or undesirable. Some were taking a wait-and-see attitude. Others argued that since energy impinges on so many aspects of our lives and the economy, it is almost impossible to draw together departments and agencies that oversee programs impacting on energy supply and demand. There was much uncertainty about how to use energy as an organizing concept for government.

Legislative Activities

Legislative sanction is often necessary to ensure that strategies for implementation and enforcement extend beyond executive agencies and carry the force of law. Preferably, therefore, efforts to formulate comprehensive state energy policies should involve legislative initiative and deliberation.

By the spring of 1977, however, only Utah had begun efforts to articulate legislatively a comprehensive state energy policy. The previous fall, a blue ribbon committee, which had status as an interim legislative committee, had developed a series of specific policy statements on several energy issues and had prefaced those statements with an overall summary statement. The 1977 legislature passed the energy policy recommendations of the blue ribbon committee. The committee, however, did not discuss in depth the abilities of present administrative arrangements to administer its policy recommendations or tackle the question of administrative reorganization. These items were tabled for future discussion and possible action.

Efforts in the other four states to draft and adopt comprehensive energy policies had not been as extensive. In Colorado, for example, there had been little legislative attention to the need for drafting and adopting a comprehensive energy policy or for reorganizing the state's administrative structure and establishing a comprehensive energy agency. Important legislators indicated resistance to legislative action in these two areas. Legislatures in Nevada, New Mexico, and Arizona had, however, conducted some interim work on selected energy policy issues, including the need for administrative reorganization. The interim work of Nevada's SCR 8 Committee in regard to energy reorganization has been mentioned previously.

The New Mexico legislature established an interim energy committee which operated from the fall of 1975 until the spring of 1977. The legislative committee completed several substantive studies of energy policy issues, including tax relief to offset rising utility costs for low- and fixed-income people; plant siting; energy development; management of the Public Service Commission; and natural gas production, distribution, and pricing. While the committee was not mandated to develop a comprehensive energy policy for the state, it did recommend that the legislature be the primary generator of a unified state energy policy.

In Arizona the most extensive work on energy occurred in the fall of 1975 when a joint legislative interim energy committee met to develop an energy policy framework and a legislative package. The interim process resulted in the introduction of thirty-five bills directly related to energy during the 1976 legislative session, a sixfold increase over previous years. However, only ten energy-related bills were approved by the legislature, none of them really significant. Several reorganization proposals were also discussed, but recognition of the organizational needs associated with energy issues resulted predominantly in extensive introduction and discussion rather than definitive legislative policy action.

Planning and Environmental Assessment Capabilities

Functional planning efforts in energy are beginning to evolve in all states. To date, however, there has been little actual experience which lends insights as to what a comprehensive energy planning process might entail. The newness and complexity of the energy field in governmental planning processes demand innovative implementation techniques and frequent evaluation and monitoring capability. Implementation strategies, for example, require flexibility to respond to changing institutional requirements, political realities, lifestyle modifications, new supply-demand factors, and technical innovations. Much work remained in the five states examined to develop such functional energy planning capabilities.

In addition to the development of functional energy planning capabilities, development of planning coordination capabilities is also needed. Key coordination and communication mechanisms are required to enhance interagency and interprogram relationships. Furthermore, vertical coordination is necessary among levels of government including local, substate, multistate, federal, and Indian entities. Yet of the five states, only Utah had on line a well-developed mechanism for interagency and intergovernmental planning coordination of a broad number of functional planning areas in addition to energy. Utah's system, recognized as the most highly developed in the nation,[8] provided opportunities to link federal and local governments to state activities in energy.

The other states had not yet reached the level of Utah's planning coordination activities, although Arizona, Colorado, and Nevada had established interagency planning coordination mechanisms. While creation of these entities indicates the states' desire to work toward a policy and coordinative approach to planning and decision making, not all these states were using their mechanisms as effectively as they could. In Arizona, for example, meetings of the Planning and Coordination Committee were infrequent. Rather than serving as a forum for information exchange, conflict resolution, and program integration, the committee functioned mainly to facilitate the flow of paperwork associated with federal grants and federal review requirements.

As of 1977 the five states had also not developed, or fully utilized, the environmental assessment and review mechanisms necessary for critical examination of the environmental impacts of energy production. For example, opportunities for increasing state participation in review of the energy projects proposed by federal agencies are provided by the environmental impact statement (EIS) procedures of the National Environmental Policy Act (NEPA). Yet, the states were not using EIS procedures as fully as might be expected, often failing to comment on EISs that discussed important energy projects or neglecting to develop coherent and coordinated state positions on proposed projects. Further, only Utah had, in effect, (by executive order) a general requirement for the preparation of environmental impact statements on state-funded projects. Utah had also established—as part of the state's intergovernmental planning coordination structure—an interagency Environmental Coordination Committee to assist in the formulation and review of both federal and state environmental assessments and impact statements. Utah had thus responded most aggressively to NEPA initiatives, committing itself to playing an active role not only in impact statement review but also in statement preparation. Yet, utilization of environmental assessment and review procedures does not mean that environmental considerations consistently take precedence over developmental considerations when resource development decisions are made. Indeed, there is considerable evidence that Utah's impact assessment and planning coordination processes functioned predominantly to help the state coalesce support for its developmental policies.[9]

Finally, as a study by Wengert and Lawrence reports, [10] only Arizona, Nevada, and New Mexico had adopted specific laws on plant siting by late 1976. Arizona passed siting legislation and created an eighteen-member siting committee in 1971. Nevada and New Mexico, on the other hand, delegated siting regulation to their public utility commissions. Moreover, none of the five states had developed adequate institutional or procedural mechanisms which would allow for the systematic consideration or coordination of the regional factors in siting decisions,[11] an inadequacy that is especially significant since energy production systems in the West exhibit many regional characteristics and dimensions.

Federal Incentives for State Policy Action

There has been a general lack of federal policy direction in energy. The chaotic condition of federal energy policy and organization has often adversely affected policy development in the states. Without knowing the possible future direction of national energy policy, the states have been reluctant to act. But many states have also used the lack of federal initiatives to justify their own inaction. As new institutional arrangements and conditions for energy decision making further develop at the federal level, no doubt there will be greater incentives for the states to act.

Despite past difficulties at the federal level in formulating and adopting a national energy policy, federal grant programs and policy activities have neverless functioned to provide incentives for state energy policy development. For example, the Federal Energy Administration's now defunct state reimbursement program allowed states to be reimbursed for expenditures made in the general areas of energy management, fuel allocation, energy conservation, and energy resources. Without the availability of federal assistance under this program, energy management activities in the five states examined here might well have been cut back.

Federal funding has also exerted considerable influence in the area of energy conservation. Under the Energy Policy and Conservation Act, for example, Congress made available $50 million to the states for preparation, implementation, and modification of state energy conservation plans. And, under the Energy Conservation and Production Act, Congress made available monies for energy audits, public information activities, and weatherization programs for low-income families. A major portion of state conservation activities in the five states was tied to these federal programs. Without the federal financial incentives, conservation planning in the states would not have been receiving as much attention as was the case. Federal money was a strong enticement for the states to move voluntarily toward federal policy objectives.

Conclusions

In the five Western states of Arizona, Colorado, Nevada, New Mexico, and Utah, the institutional arrangements for energy policy planning, administration, and coordination remained fragmented and disorganized. Newly created energy boards and commissions either were ad hoc or lacked adequate legal mandates for comprehensive, long-term energy policy making. Other agencies had failed to adjust their behavior to the new demands and requirements of energy. Almost all agencies had insufficient decision-making resources. Legislative action to formulate comprehensive energy policies and to correct past deficiencies in energy organization had been limited and sporadic. Functional energy planning processes, planning coordination structures, and environmental assessment and review mechanisms all required strengthening. While the states had made extensive and significant studies of their energy situation, overall there had been little actual legislative or administrative policy innovation.

Western states that remain reluctant to face the long-run imperatives of energy policy development will be unprepared to manage future energy problems. Future problem solving will flounder because the states' institutional arrangements do not have the capacity to respond. Further federal incentives, with their inevitable program requirements and attached strings, may be necessary to move states beyond the study and deliberation stage to a point where state policy actions designed to assist the nation reduce energy dependency can be successfully formulated and administered. The "new states' rights" will increasingly become philosophical idealism, not behavioral reality.

Notes

1. U.S. Senate, Committee on Interior and Insular Affairs, *Federal Energy Organization, A Staff Analysis,* 93d Congress, 1st Sess., 1973, 3; and James W. Curlin, "Congressional Initiatives in Energy Policy," in Walter F. Scheffer, ed., *Energy Impacts on Public Policy and Administration* (Norman: University of Oklahoma Press for the University of Oklahoma Advanced Programs, 1974), pp. 117-162.

2. Richard B. Mancke, *The Failure of U.S. Energy Policy* (New York: Columbia University Press, 1974); and Richard B. Mancke, *Squeaking By: U.S. Energy Policy since the Embargo* (New York: Columbia University Press, 1976).

3. Robert D. Thomas, "Federal-Local Cooperation and Its Consequences for State Level Policy Participation: Water Resources in Arizona," *Publius* 1 (Winter 1972): 77-94.

4. Ibid.; and Helen M. Ingram, "The Politics of Water Allocation," in D.F. Peterson and A.B. Crawford, eds., *Values and Choice in the Development of an Arid Land River Basin* (Tucson: University of Arizona Press, forthcoming).

5. Hanna J. Cortner and Helen M. Ingram, *The Arizona Corporation Commission and Electrical Energy Policy* (Tucson: University of Arizona Press, 1976).

6. Timothy A. Hall, Irvin L. White, and Steven C. Ballard, "Western States and National Energy Policy: The New States' Rights," Paper prepared for deliv-

ery at the Annual Meeting of the Western Political Science Association, Los Angeles, Calif., March 16–18, 1978.

7. Most of the data reported on in this chapter were first presented in Hanna J. Cortner, *Energy Policy Planning, Administration and Coordination,* consultant's report to the Four Corners Regional Commission, March 1977.

8. Leonard U. Wilson and L.V. Watkins, draft report, *State Planning: Intergovernmental Policy Coordination* (Lexington, Ky.: Council of State Governments, February 1976), pp. 71.

9. Hanna J. Cortner, "Environmental Impact Assessment and Review in Energy Decision-Making: State Participation in the Lake Powell Region," *Lake Powell Research Project Bulletin No. 43* (Los Angeles: University of California Institute of Geophysics and Planetary Physics, April 1977).

10. Norman Wengert and Robert M. Lawrence, "Regional Factors in Siting and Planning Energy Facilities in the Eleven Western States," Consultants' report to the Western Interstate Nuclear Board, November 1976.

11. Ibid.

Coal Severance Tax Policies in the Rocky Mountain States

Kenyon N. Griffin and
Robert B. Shelton

Introduction

The energy crisis following the Arab oil embargo and subsequent OPEC price increases produced an unexpected boom for energy-exporting states across the United States. While most state governments were confronted with escalating costs attributable to increased energy expenditures, energy-rich states were realizing increased revenue generated by their taxes on energy resources. Each price increase on domestically produced oil and gas has resulted in a comparable increase in tax revenue since energy taxes are commonly tied to selling prices. These price increases, as well as the problems associated with imported oil, have had another important effect: coal has become a more attractive energy resource and will play a major role in any national energy policy. Thus, the nation's energy crisis has created a new policy-making setting for energy-rich states vis-à-vis their tax policies.

The purpose of this chapter is to examine the coal severance tax policies of six coal-exporting states in the Rocky Mountain West—Arizona, Colorado, Montana, New Mexico, Utah, and Wyoming. It is organized into five sections. The first discusses the coal severance tax and economic reasons for using the tax, including the ability to export the tax burden to energy consumers in other states. Second, we examine the conditions necessary for tax exportation to be successful in both an economic and a political context. Third, building on the preceding discussion, we analyze the current situation in these states including coal production, export, reserves, and severance tax policies. Fourth, we undertake a case study of Montana and Wyoming, two large coal-exporting states with high severance taxes, to examine policy decisions on distributing coal-generated revenue as well as public attitudes toward coal severance tax policies. Finally, we conclude with observations about the consequences of the coal severance tax for the states and the nation.

Severance Taxes and Coal Production

The first use of a severance tax in the United States dates back to the nineteenth century when Michigan imposed one on oil production in 1846. The rationale underlying this tax is based on the notion that when a natural resource—oil and gas, coal, minerals, timber, or other resources—is severed from the earth, its value is irretrievably lost. Therefore, the public is justified in recapturing a portion of this lost value through a special tax. The severance tax is presently used by thirty-one states, and it generated over $2 billion in 1976, with oil and gas revenue contributing the largest share of this total.[1]

The severance tax on coal has become increasingly important in the past several years. Recent studies have found that twelve states levy a tax on coal. The coal severance tax was most important in Montana, where it generated over 11 percent of total state tax revenue in 1976. Coal-related revenue was also significant in Kentucky where it produced nearly 7 percent of state tax revenue and in Wyoming where the figure was just under 3 percent.[2]

Among the six coal-exporting states in the Rocky Mountain region which are the focus of this study, Colorado, Montana, New Mexico, and Wyoming currently levy a severance tax on coal production while Arizona and Utah do not. However, recent interest in the development of low-sulfur Western coal has caused legislators in these states to reexamine their state tax policies. Legislative interest in the role of coal-related tax policies is reflected in legislative activity since 1972. During this time, each of the coal-exporting states except Arizona has had legislation introduced or bills passed which relate to the role of coal tax revenue within the total state tax structure.

The debate in these coal-exporting states concerning a coal tax policy includes economic as well as regulatory arguments. Perhaps the most basic is the public interest doctrine—that when the coal is mined, its value is lost for future generations. Related to this contention are two other arguments. In economic terms, it has been argued that the increased demand for coal today has created a situation in which a state is in the desirable position of being able to increase its tax revenue through the taxation of coal. Furthermore, it has also been argued that the state is losing an important part of its tax base as the coal is mined; hence, it is necessary and proper to tax this decreasing resource base now in an attempt to build a reserve fund to be utilized in the future when the coal reserves are depleted.

A second argument which has stimulated legislative debate on the coal severance tax policy involves the "impact" experienced by local communities because of coal-related development projects. "Impacted communities" are characterized by a boomtown scenario. The rapid population growth in small communities stimulated by new economic opportunities has resulted in greatly increased public service needs including services not previously demanded in rural areas. A typical problem for impacted communities has been the need for front-end money—funds available before or in the early stages of growth—to fund the anticipated demands for government services. One response to these expenditure pressures in the public sector has been increased support for taxing the economic activity—coal production—responsible for the growth.

Finally, the argument of tax exportation, whether employed explicitly or implicitly, has also played an important role in the coal severance tax debate in the Western states. *Tax exportation* refers to a tax whose burden or incidence can be "exported" and ultimately paid by out-of-state consumers. A coal severance tax may be exported whenever the product is shipped out of state to be sold at a higher tax-inclusive price. Thus, to the extent that a state is a net coal exporter, the severance tax can generate additional revenue to help meet the financial needs of state government without a comparable increase in the taxes borne by in-state residents. Given the legislators' and the public's interest in the burden of specific taxes as well as the overall tax structure, the tax exportation argument is economically reasonable and politically viable.

These arguments offer strong evidence for the imposition of coal severance taxes. However, severance tax policies in the Rocky Mountain region vary considerably from state to state. We contend that the single most important factor in the legislative decision to levy a coal severance tax, as well as the amount of tax, depends on each state's perception of its ability to export the tax burden. Therefore, before specific state coal tax policies are discussed, it is useful to examine the conditions necessary for a state to export its coal severance tax and the implications of these conditions on legislative policy making.

Conditions for Tax Exportation and Consequences for Legislative Behavior

There are two necessary conditions for tax exportation to be a feasible objective of a state's tax policy: (1) the base which is to be taxed must be exported in sufficient quantities to justify such a goal, and (2) the state which is exporting the base has to have sufficient "market power" to levy the tax (that is, the export demand curve facing the state must be relatively inelastic). Given that a state cannot discriminate between its interstate and intrastate markets in terms of taxation, the most desirable position for a state is to have an interstate market significantly larger than the intrastate market.[3]

A state which is capable of exporting its tax is demonstrated in figure 5-1. The interstate demand is pictured as D_X; the intrastate demand is shown as D_D; and the total demand, which is the sum of the interstate and intrastate demands, is shown as D_T. The supply of a state is depicted as S, with the initial market equilibrium quantities being shown as Q_D, Q_X, and Q_T. For the state to maximize export tax revenues, it must increase the tax rate until the equilibrium price is in the elastic portion of the export demand curve. This will dictate the total (and intrastate) market price and quantities. The effect of increasing the severance tax is shown in figure 5-1 by the shift upward of the supply curve from S to S_1.[4]

It is interesting to note that if the interstate market is dominant, then the

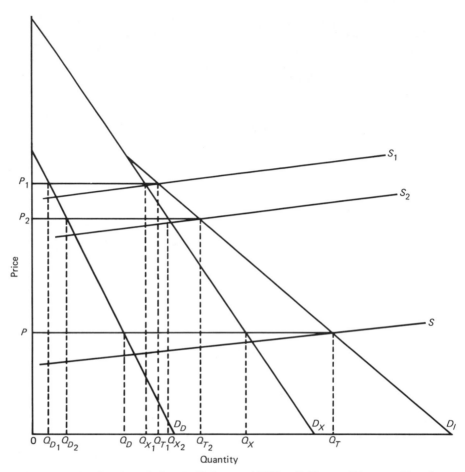

This diagram is taken from Robert B. Shelton, and William E. Morgan, "Resource Taxation, Tax Exportation and Regional Energy Policies," *Natural Resources Journal* 17 (April 1977).

Figure 5-1. A State Which Can Export Its Tax.

tax exportation goal will lead to higher severance taxes than, for example, simply maximizing total tax revenues.[5] The case of maximizing total tax revenue is shown by the shift in the supply curve to S_2 and indicates the lower severance tax policy. Furthermore, the maximization of tax exportation will lead to higher severance taxes as the interstate demand increases. (To see this, one merely has to transpose the interstate and intrastate demand curves in figure 5-1 and then shift the supply curve.)

The ability to export taxes is easily translated into hypotheses concerning legislative behavior by using an economic model. We may assume, using this perspective, that each legislator represents some geographic district within a given state and that the legislator views himself as performing certain actions which produce votes (both positive and negative). We may further assume that the legislator attempts to maximize the likelihood of his reelection by performing actions which will produce the maximum number of positive votes in the next election year.[6] Thus, the legislator is viewed as perceiving the following relationship:

$$V = V(B - t)$$

This equation states that the votes (V) received by the legislator representing the ith district are a function of the benefits accruing to the ith district (B) minus the taxes paid (t) by the residents of that district. Quite simply, then, the legislator is in the position of enhancing the likelihood of his reelection by maximizing the difference between the benefits and the taxes in his district.

One approach to solving this problem is to attempt to have the tax burden shifted to residents of other districts for any given level of statewide benefits. This might be done by trying to push for a tax structure to finance a new state public good which, in fact, minimizes the burden placed on the residents of that particular district. For example, if the legislator represents an agricultural district, he might push for a corporation income tax as opposed to a property tax.

If we carry this analogy to the state level, then we find that the legislature might consider it advantageous to adopt taxes which would be paid by residents of other states. This can be done in an indirect and constitutional manner by adopting a tax structure in which a portion of the taxes is, in fact, paid by residents of other states, that is, by "exporting" part of the tax base. This is essentially the case facing legislators in coal-exporting states.

Coal and Severance Taxes in the Rocky Mountain West

The major assumption of the preceding argument is that a coal severance tax is economically attractive and politically viable if a significant portion of the tax burden can be exported and paid by out-of-state consumers. As noted, one of the necessary conditions for tax exportation to be a feasible state government objective is to have market power as demonstrated by a relatively inelastic demand curve. Estimates of the price elasticity of demand for Western coal indicate that the regional demand curve is, in fact, relatively inelastic.[7] While the demand curve facing any individual state is likely to be more elastic than the regional demand, it is reasonable to assume that the states with the larger interstate "market shares" will have the relatively more inelastic state demand curves. Therefore, these states should possess a greater ability to raise the tax revenue through severance taxation. Coal reserves, we suggest, are a useful long-run proxy for market shares for individual states in the region.

Large reserves of coal exist in Arizona, Colorado, Montana, New Mexico,

Utah, and Wyoming. (See table 5-1). These reserves range from 107,700 million short tons in Montana to 350 million short tons in Arizona; Wyoming has reserves of over 51,000 million short tons followed by Colorado with 14,900 million short tons, New Mexico with 4,400 million short tons, and Utah with 4,000 million short tons. The amount of coal exported by each state corresponds generally with each state's reserves. In 1975 Montana exported 375 trillion Btu's of coal and Wyoming some 304 trillion Btu's; the other states, ranked in order of importance of exported coal, include Arizona, 65 trillion; Utah, 54 trillion; New Mexico, 23 trillion; and Colorado, 8 trillion Btu's.

Three of these states also export electric power produced from coal-fired generating facilities. This is another method through which coal severance taxes can be passed along to out-of-state residents. New Mexico is the largest exporter of electric power in the region with 36 trillion Btu's, while Wyoming exports 22 trillion Btu's and Montana 6 trillion Btu's of electric power generated in coal-fired facilities.

With this background in mind, let us turn to the coal severance taxes employed by these Rocky Mountain states. In 1976 four of the six states levied a severance tax on coal. Three of these states used a tax based on a percentage of the value of the coal, and the other had a flat rate per ton. Montana had the highest rate of 30.5 percent, followed by Wyoming with a 4.8 percent and New Mexico with a 1.25 percent tax rate. Colorado, which used the flat rate, levied a tax of $.007 per ton of coal produced.[8]

The dollar value of the severance tax revenues generated in the four states

Table 5-1
Coal Reserves, Exports, and Severance Taxes for Rocky Mountain State, 1975

State	Coal Reserves,[a] Million Short Tons	Coal Exports (Net),[b] Trillion Btu's	Coal Exported As Electric Power (Net),[b] Trillion Btu's	Coal Severance Tax Rate[c] Rate Per Ton	Coal Severance Tax Rate[c] Percent of Value
Arizona	350	65.3	–	none	
Colorado	14,870	8.0	–	0.7¢	
Montana	107,727	374.5	5.6		30.5
New Mexico	4,394	23.2	35.6		1.25
Utah	4,042	53.7	–	none	
Wyoming	51,228	304.2	21.7		4.8

[a]U.S. Department of Interior, *Coal Reserves of the United States,* Geological Survey Bulletin, January 1, 1974.

[b]U.S. Department of Interior, *Coal Reserves of the United States,* and R.B. Kidman et al., "Energy Flow Patterns for 1975," Informal Report LA-6770, Los Alamos Scientific Laboratory, Los Alamos, N. Mex., June 1977.

[c]Jim Wead et al., *State Coal Severance Taxes and Distribution of Revenue* (Lexington, Ky.: Council of State Governments, September 1976).

varies greatly. In Montana during 1975, the state severance tax on each ton of coal was estimated to be $1.44. This figure was considerably higher than that found in the other states: Wyoming's state severance taxes generated $.24 per ton, New Mexico raised $.08 per ton, and Colorado followed with $.007 per ton.

The contributions of the coal tax revenue to total state tax revenue in the four states represented a significant portion in Montana and Wyoming but not in New Mexico and Colorado. In Montana, 1976 revenue from coal severance taxes accounted for $24.9 million; this was 11.4 percent of total state tax revenue. Comparisons between 1976 and 1972 illustrate that with a lower tax and less coal production, the coal severance tax generated only $483,000 in 1972; this was 0.4 percent of total state tax revenue for Montana.[9]

The findings for Wyoming are similar to those noted for Montana. In 1976 Wyoming received about $5 million from the coal severance tax; this revenue amounted to 2.8 percent of total state tax revenue. Again, the comparison between 1976 and 1972 reveals the growing importance of the coal tax as a revenue source; the tax in 1972 generated only $150,000, which represented 0.1 percent of Wyoming's total state tax revenue.[10]

The figures for New Mexico and Colorado are insignificant when compared to those for Montana and Wyoming. In 1976 New Mexico raised only $735,000 through taxes on coal, and this represented 0.1 percent of total state tax revenue. This revenue figure was up from $216,000 which New Mexico collected in 1972. Based on a 1976 estimate for Colorado, about $50,000 was raised by the tax of $.007 per ton of coal produced.[11]

In table 5-2 we summarize the preceding discussion using a rank-order of the 1976 severance tax burdens, coal reserves, and coal exports for each state. This analysis offers support for the importance of market power or reserves in these states' coal tax policies. Here we see that Montana and Wyoming, which are ranked 1 and 2 in coal reserves and coal exports, are also ranked 1 and 2 in severance tax burdens. Utah and Arizona, states with no severance tax on coal, are ranked last in terms of reserves and are low in terms of coal exportation. New Mexico and Colorado, the middle states in coal reserves, have modest coal severance taxes but rank 4 and 6, respectively, in terms of exports.

The importance of a state's market power is further illustrated in legislative action on coal tax decisions during the 1977 sessions in the six exporting states. Wyoming, with the second largest reserves, increased its coal severance tax by 5.7 percent, bringing its state coal tax burden up to 10.5 percent for 1978. New Mexico, ranked 4 in reserves among the exporting states, increased its coal severance tax to 5.2 percent. Colorado and Utah, which rank 3 and 5, respectively, on reserves, discussed coal severance tax proposals but did not enact legislation. Legislatures in Montana, which has the largest coal reserves and highest tax burden, and Arizona, which has the lowest reserves and no coal severance tax, did not consider coal tax policy changes.

The purpose of the preceding discussion was to outline the coal severance

Table 5-2
Rankings of Coal-Exporting States by Tax Burden, Reserves, and Exports

States	Reserves	Exports[a]	1976 Tax Burden per Ton
Montana	1	1	1 ($1.44)
Wyoming	2	2	2 ($ .24)
New Mexico	4	4	3 ($ .08)
Colorado	3	6	4 ($ .007)
Utah	5	5	None
Arizona	6	3	None

*Rankings based on data in table 5-1.
[a]Includes coal exported in raw form and as electricity generated in coal-fired power plants.

tax policies of the six Rocky Mountain coal-exporting states and to analyze the relationship among coal reserves, coal exportation, and coal tax burdens. The analysis supports the assumption that a coal severance tax policy is economically attractive and politically viable if a significant portion of the tax burden can be exported and paid by out-of-state consumers. We also noted that coal tax monies available to Montana and Wyoming, states with the most significant reserves of coal and the largest severance taxes in the region, are becoming increasingly important as a source of government revenue. Therefore, in the next section we review the allocation of this revenue in these two states.

Distributing Coal Severance Tax Revenue in Montana and Wyoming

The distribution of coal-generated tax monies becomes a more salient policy issue as the amount of revenue in question increases. This generalization is illustrated in the revenue distribution patterns of the four coal-exporting states which use a coal severance tax. In each state—Colorado, Montana, New Mexico, and Wyoming—a portion of tax revenue is designated for the state's general funds. In Colorado, where the severance tax generates an insignificant amount of revenue, the entire sum goes to the general fund. In the other three states, where the revenue is much more substantial, coal tax monies are divided among the general fund, a permanent mineral trust fund, and various earmarked programs to assist local government entities.

An analysis of the distribution of coal-generated revenue in Montana and Wyoming suggests some of the political pressures which faced state legislators when this revenue was allocated. Not only do these states have the largest coal reserves and the highest coal taxes, but they also have the greatest ability to export the tax burden to out-of-state consumers. In 1977 coal revenue amounted to more than \$36 million in Montana and nearly \$19 million in Wyoming—significant revenue for small-population states.[12] The distribution of this revenue in the two states is shown in table 5-3.

The most important point in the distributional patterns concerns the proportion of revenue allocated to the general funds and to earmarked funds. State general funds receive 30 percent of Montana's coal severance tax revenue and 19 percent of Wyoming's revenue, while the remaining monies go to earmarked funds. This allocation reflects the generally favorable revenue situation facing state government in Montana and Wyoming today; at the same time, the allocation of a large proportion of revenue to earmarked funds characterizes special needs of these states as perceived by state legislators.

What are these special needs? First, approximately one-fourth of the coal severance tax revenue goes to the mineral trust fund. These permanent trust funds will set aside revenue now for the time when the coal reserves are depleted and the tax base is substantially reduced. Second, about one-fifth of the revenue in each state is allocated to assist energy-impacted communities. This is a special need for small rural communities which face dramatic population growth as a result of energy development projects. Third, each state has earmarked about 10 percent of the severance tax monies for highways. In Montana the funds are specifically designated for coal-area highways while in Wyoming the revenue goes into the state highway fund.

Table 5-3
Allocation of Coal Severance Tax Revenue in Montana and Wyoming, 1978

	Percent in Montana[a]	Percent in Wyoming[b]
General fund	30.0	19.0
Mineral trust fund	25.0	23.8
Local impact assistance	19.875	19.0
Other earmarked funds		
State highway fund	—	—
Coal area highways	9.75	—
Counties	1.50	—
County land planning	.75	—
School equalization	7.50	—
Water development projects	—	14.3
State capital facilities	—	14.3
Alternative energy research	1.875	—
Renewable resource development	1.875	—
Parks acquisition	1.875	—
Total	100.00%	100.00%

[a]Montana State Department of Revenue, "Allocation of Coal Severance Tax," Helena, 1977.
[b]Percentage distribution based on authors' computation using information provided by the Wyoming Department of Revenue and Taxation, Ad Valorem Division.

In Montana the remaining 15 percent of state coal tax revenue is divided among educational equalization, county governments, parks acquisition, and resource development. Wyoming, on the other hand, has divided the remaining 29 percent of its coal revenue between funding the water development projects and state capital facilities construction projects.

Legislative policy choices on distributing coal revenue, as well as the more basic question of coal tax policy, in these two states have been influenced by interest groups and public opinion. Hence, it is important to understand the preferences of the electorate on these policy issues. We believe that the residents of coal-exporting states such as Montana and Wyoming perceive that the incidence of a coal severance tax is exported to out-of-state consumers. This is reflected in surveys conducted in both states. For instance, in a 1974 survey of Wyoming residents, two-thirds agreed that an increase in the mineral severance tax would be a good idea. In a 1976 statewide survey, two-thirds also agreed that the severance tax should be increased if additional revenue was needed to finance state government expenditures.[13] A 1977 survey of Montana voters confirms the popularity of the coal severance tax in that state. When asked about the Montana coal severance tax, 42 percent judged it to be "about right," 7 percent thought it "too low," and 20 percent suggested it was "too high." The remaining 31 percent were undecided.[14] These results from Wyoming and Montana are consistent with those found in a study of the attitudes of state senators and their constituents toward severance taxes in the Four Corner states (Arizona, Colorado, New Mexico, and Utah) which found overwhelming support for severance taxes.[15]

These favorable public attitudes toward the coal severance tax—at least in Montana and Wyoming if not in other states as well—emphasize that these monies have relieved these residents of an increased tax burden. Without increasing the tax incidence for in-state residents, these states have been able to assist with the financing needs of energy-related problems at the state and local levels, they have increased expenditure possibilities by generating additional revenue for the general funds, and they are putting into trust coal-generated revenue for future generations. The distributions have proved politically feasible in that diverse interests have been satisfied without an increase in the residents' tax burden.

Coal Severance Tax Policies: Some Consequences

The consequences of coal severance tax policies enacted by legislatures in the coal-exporting states in the Rocky Mountain region have significant implications for state and local government finance, but also for any future national energy policy. The United States is fortunate to have an abundance of coal reserves. In fact, coal constitutes 90 percent of conventional U.S. energy reserves, and 40 percent of these are located in the six Western states discussed. Therefore, any future national energy policy will undoubtedly recognize, as did the 1977 Carter proposal, that coal will play an important role in meeting the increased energy needs, at least until the end of this century.[16]

Perhaps the most basic question concerns the effect of coal severance tax policies on the proposals to use coal as an alternative energy resource between now and the year 2000. The present coal tax burden in the Western coal-exporting states, including Montana and Wyoming, will not restrict or limit increased usage of low-sulfur coal. While the present tax policies generate significant revenue for these states, the percentage cost to the ultimate consumer is relatively small.

For instance, low-Btu Montana coal sold for over $23 per ton in the Chicago area during late 1977. This price included $14 per ton for transportation costs and $8.75 per ton for the coal at the mine.[17] The state severance tax of less than $2 per ton was included in the selling price of the coal. The Montana coal severance tax burden was, therefore, less than 9 percent of the delivered price in the Midwest; even when local taxes are included, the tax burden per ton is less than 10 percent of the contract price delivered. In Wyoming, the state and local coal tax burden is even less than that found in Montana. State and local government officials in these two exporting states would agree that their respective coal tax policies are nothing more than a "reasonable cost of doing business" in these states.

Increased dependence on Western coal means more impact for state and local governments. Increased coal production is translated into rapid population growth and increased demands for public services. Few residents or public officials in these coal-exporting states have any expectations that coal tax policies could, however much it might be desired, restrict coal development within their states. The present coal severance taxes are simply an attempt to require that the coal industry pay its own way for public services necessitated by coal-related growth and to put aside revenue for the future when the coal tax base is depleted.

Legislators in these states have been advised by lobbyists for the coal industry that excessive taxation of this industry can produce dire consequences. This argument is not convincing, however. Residents of these Western states view the coal boom with ambivalent feelings. The economic benefits derived from coal development projects are offset by social and environmental problems, problems which focus on the quality of life for these people. The presumed dire consequences, including the argument that state coal tax policies will drive coal companies to other states, are not viewed with the credibility that they would have in economically depressed regions.

Thus the coal industry has turned to the courts to challenge the coal severance tax. A suit, filed in mid-1978, contends that the Montana coal tax is so high that it has created an excessive burden on interstate commerce. The legal basis of this challenge is predicated on the assumption that the incidence of the

Montana coal severance tax is, in fact, being shifted onto out-of-state consumers. If the court's ruling is favorable to the coal companies, the outcome will
be significant for energy tax policy at the state level. Such a decision would provide a precedent which could lead to changes in the severance tax policies of
Western coal-exporting states, as well as in other energy-exporting states such as
Louisiana. Undoubtedly, this issue will be in the courts for the next several years.

Depsite the challenge to Montana's coal tax policy, a more important
threat to prevent legislators from enacting excessive coal taxation policies is the
potential for federal intervention in state tax decisions. This question has not received attention in policy debates or in analyses of tax decisions, but it is reasonable to assume that the federal government would ultimately intervene if a
state's coal tax policy actually hindered the development of coal as an alternative energy resource.

Summary

The purpose of this chapter was to examine the coal severance tax policies of the
six coal-exporting states in the Rocky Mountain West and to analyze these
policies within the context of each state's ability to export the tax burden to
out-of-state consumers. We demonstrated that where states had a large interstate
market as well as large reserves, they were able to utilize a coal severance tax, as
with Montana, Wyoming, and, to a lesser extent, New Mexico. However, where
the intrastate market was important and/or coal reserves were less significant, a
coal severance tax was a less realistic tax objective for state governments. The
discussion also reviewed the distribution of coal tax revenue in Montana and
Wyoming as well as public attitudes toward severance tax policy. The analysis
concluded with observations about the consequences of coal severance taxes in
the Rocky Mountain region, an area which will play a significant role in any
future national energy policy.

Notes

1. U.S. Department of Commerce, *State Government Finances in 1976*
(Washington: U.S. Department of Commerce, Bureau of the Census, 1977),
p. 20.
2. Kenyon H. Griffin and Robert B. Shelton, "Politics and Economics of
State Mineral Taxation: A Look at the Future," *Mineral Taxation Institute
Manual* (Boulder, Colo.: Rocky Mountain Mineral Law Foundation Proceedings,
1977); and Jim Wead, Lois R. Koepf, and Jonathan S. Gaciala, *State Coal Sev-*

erance Taxes and Distribution of Revenue (Lexington, Ky.: Council of State Governments, 1976).

3. For a discussion of tax exportation see the following: Timothy D. Hogan and Robert B. Shelton, "Interstate Tax Exportation and States' Fiscal Structures," *National Tax Journal* 26 (December 1973): 553; Charles E. McLure, "Commodity Tax Incidence," *National Tax Journal* 17 (June 1964): 187; "Interstate Exporting of State and Local Taxes: Estimates for 1962," *National Tax Journal* 20 (March 1967): 49; "Regional Tax Incidence with Estimation of Interstate Incidence of State and Local Taxes," Unpublished doctoral dissertation, Princeton University, 1966; William E. Morgan and Robert B. Shelton, "Natural Resource Taxation, Tax Exportation, and the Stability of Fiscal Federalism," in *Public Goods and Public Policy,* ed. Todd Sandler et al., (New York: Wiley, forthcoming); Todd M. Sandler and Robert B. Shelton, "Fiscal Federalism, Spillovers and the Export of Taxes," *Kyklos* 24 fasc. 4 (1972); "Fiscal Federalism, Spillovers and the Export of Taxes: Reply," *Kyklos* 29 fasc., 2 (1976).

4. See Robert B. Shelton and William E. Morgan, "Resource Taxation, Tax Exportation and Regional Energy Policies," *Natural Resources Journal* 17 (April 1977) for several variations of the diagram set forth in figure 5-1.

5. See Shelton and Morgan, ibid., for a discussion of state government objectives and their economic implications.

6. Jon Cauley and Robert B. Shelton, "National Defense and Legislative Decision-Making," in *Comparative Public Policy: Issues, Theory and Methods,* ed. Craig Liske et al. New York: Halstead Press Division, Wiley, 1975).

7. Shelton and Morgan, "Resource Taxation," p. 280.

8. Wead, Koepf and Gaciala, *State Coal Severance Taxes,* p. 8.

9. Griffin and Shelton, "Politics and Economics of State Mineral Taxation," pp. 8–14.

10. Ibid.

11. Wead, Koepf, and Gaciala, *State Coal Severance Taxes,* p. 18.

12. Revenue figures provided by the State Department of Revenue in Montana and the Ad Valorem Tax Division in Wyoming.

13. Kenyon N. Griffin, "Tax Preferences and Public Services: How They See It in Wyoming," *National Civic Review* 66 (July 1977): 347.

14. Jerry W. Calvert, *Montana Politics Survey 1977* (Bozeman, Mont.: Department of Political Science, Montana State University, 1977), p. 4.

15. Helen Ingram et al., "Policy Representation in the Four Corner States" (Unpublished manuscript, Resources for the Future, 1978), p. 37.

16. Executive Office of the President, *The National Energy Plan* (Washington: Executive Office of the President, Energy Policy and Planning, 1977), p. 68.

17. *Coal Week,* January 23, 1978, p. 5; *Coal Week,* February 6, 1978, p. 6.

An Energy Policy for Indian Lands: Problems of Issue and Perception

David A. Schaller

The national effort to expand development of domestic energy resources has focused wide attention on Indian reservation lands in the Western United States. Some estimates place one-third of all U.S. low-sulfur coal reserves and over half of the nation's uranium ore on Indian lands. With coal and uranium as key fuels in an emerging national energy program, federal, tribal, and state governments, together with the energy industry, are examining a range of policy options addressing the development of these Indian resources.

As with most energy development there are economic, technological, and environmental issues which will influence the policy process on tribal lands. The availability of markets for certain fuels, the demonstrability of extraction and processing techniques, and the applicability of environmental protection measures are issues common to all energy development proposals. However, there are additional issues which are unique to the American Indian. These issues derive in part from the concept of tribal sovereignty and extend to the energy decision-making process. The issues are also influenced by important cultural and political perceptions which participants in the decision-making process bring to the Indian energy policy debate. To understand the potential of a given policy alternative, we must know how relevant issues are defined and under what circumstances individual and particular definitions of issues will prevail.

Many of the significant issues affecting Indian energy policy, and how they are perceived by decisionmakers, raise a number of basic methodological questions for the policy studies to discuss. These include questions on the predictive power of policy-making arenas, the nature of political participation, and the capabilities of an intergovernmental framework in explaining policy outcomes.

Five major issues must be considered in planning energy policy for tribal lands: (1) the availability and cost of development of Indian energy resources, (2) tribal jurisdiction and sovereignty, (3) economic development of the reservations, (4) Indian culture and tradition, and (5) the role of Indian tribes in intergovernmental relations within the federal system.

The Availability and Cost of Indian Energy Resources

Indian energy development is an important factor in the national energy picture largely because of the abundance and accessibility of two valuable resources:

low-sulfur, subbituminous coal and uranium oxide ore. The Indian coal resource is characterized by thick, near-surface coal seams under relatively gentle terrain.

Surface extraction is generally easy and profitable. Sedimentary deposits of uranium ore are also localized across Indian lands, and they are being methodically developed. Low-cost extraction techniques, reduced labor expenses which accompany surface mining, and initially low royalty leases have made Indian energy resources an attractive and inexpensive fuel supply for fossil and nuclear electric generating stations across the West.

Tribal Jurisdiction and Sovereignty

A second major issue which will influence energy policy making on Indian lands is the nature of tribal sovereignty. American Indians have never represented a single legal entity; each reservation remains a product of the treaty, statute, or executive order by which it was created. The federal government, in a trusteeship capacity established and reinforced by Supreme Court decisions, holds exclusive legal title to some 40 million acres of Indian trust land.[1] Through the Bureau of Indian Affairs, the Secretary of the Interior administers the federal trust responsibility on these lands.

Despite surrendering their status as sovereign nations, Indian tribes generally retain authority over their local government affairs. This includes the right to use and manage their trust lands and resources. Individual tribal land-use and resource development proposals are subject to ultimate approval by the Secretary of the Interior. Recently, the Indian Self-Determination Act established as U.S. government policy the maximum participation of Indian tribes in the direction of federal trusteeship services.[2] A clear trend now exists toward greater tribal participation in the administration of U.S. government trust responsibilities.

Less definitive is the legal relationship between Indian tribes and state governments. The Supreme Court has ruled that state control over Indian lands is permitted only if expressly granted by Congress. Water law is one critical and as yet unclear jurisdictional issue in which ultimate water rights and ownership determinations will influence the future of energy development on and off tribal lands. The sovereignty issue—Indian self-determination and treaty rights, states' rights, non-Indian property rights, and the federal trust responsibilities—will be a major consideration in Indian resource policies.

Economic Development of the Reservations

Energy development offers Indian people an opportunity to overcome the impoverished economic conditions they have experienced since their submission to the United States government over a century ago. Tribes have begun to obtain employment opportunities for their people in the mining, processing, and production phases of energy resource development. Labor and industry have also contributed, through purchasing and taxation, to a surge in tribal economies. Although considerable industry profits leave the reservations without ever being "turned over" in local purchases, those which do enter the tribal economy are generally orders of magnitude greater than anything previously experienced by tribal governments. Increases in economic security, reduced unemployment, and more extensive government services are all possible with the revenues generated by energy production.

While the improvement of reservation economies has always been an objective of Indian tribes, there is reluctance on the part of many energy-rich tribes to commit their resources to early development. This is due largely to other policy considerations which strongly temper the lure of economic benefits presented by rapid reservation development.

Indian Culture and Tradition

One of the most powerful issues influencing energy policy decisions on Indian lands has its roots in the clash between centuries-old tribal cultures and the promises of a modern, technological society. The origins of much tribal uncertainty over energy development relate to differing tribal preferences over the level of accommodation to an encroaching non-Indian culture. Older Indians have generally maintained a traditional reverence for the land and the resources which have supported Indian communities over time. The elders view with alarm the specter of social, cultural, and environmental change which generally accompanies energy development. At the same time, younger and more educated Indians are gaining control of tribal governments, and they recognize the short-term economic benefits to be gained from resource development. Cultural integrity and environmental protection on the reservation often become acceptable trade-offs for tribal leaders when measured against the economic promises of energy extraction and production. One of the major tasks facing tribal decision-makers, then, is the accommodation of traditionalist and modernist views in the policy-making process.

Indian Tribes and Intergovernmental Relations within the Federal System

The federal system of government in the United States features a variety of forums in which intergovernmental cooperation can occur on most important public policy issues. These include the formal federal-state clearinghouses, joint federal-state programs, and direct federal grants to the states to implement national programs (highways, education, and so on). Mutual suspicions still occasionally characterize the relations between federal and state governments; however, interaction has been a model of harmony when compared to the struggling and occasionally volatile climate of federal-Indian and state-Indian relations.

While many jurisdictional relationships among Indian tribes and non-Indian governments have been legislatively and judicially defined, many more de facto arrangements have been established which do not now adequately reflect the new trends in Indian self-determination. State and federal agencies once accustomed to a powerful role in Indian policy making must now adjust to a position of reduced influence and control over events on Indian land. There is little to suggest that Indian energy policies can be successfully developed outside the evolving legal framework of tribes and non-Indian governments. A few cases illustrate the significance of this issue.

Mineral Leasing

Under the Omnibus Mineral Leasing Act of 1938, Indian lands may be leased for mineral development pending tribal approval and concurrence by the Secretary of the Interior. In the concurrence process, the Department of the Interior faces a growing need to balance its traditional trusteeship role with the emerging practice of Indian self-determination. There will be increased pressure on Interior to support development proposals initiated by the tribes in lieu of the Bureau of Indian Affairs agreements previously negotiated with industry on behalf of the tribes.[3]

Where the intersecting and "checker boarding" of Indian and state land coincide with energy resource deposits and where no comfortable dialogue has been established between landowners, energy planning could be stalled indefinitely. State governments have traditionally depended on Interior representatives to consider state interests in the course of tribal lease negotiations. A stronger Interior advocacy of Indian interests will force states to accommodate a more dominant tribal role in energy policy making. State-Indian relations could become strongly argumentative in the absence of intergovernmental communication mechanisms similar to those at the interstate and federal-state levels.

Water Rights

Water requirements for energy resource extracting and processing can be significant, particularly in the arid West. Water rights among states have proved difficult to establish, and tribal claims to much of this finite resource complicate an already delicate political issue. The Supreme Court has ruled that reservation tribes have *reserved* rights to water resources sufficient to meet present and future needs.[4] In many instances, reserved Indian water is now committed and occasionally *overcommitted* to non-Indian uses, including energy development. Indian water rights claims have been obscured long enough that most surface-water resources of the West have been allocated without the inclusion of adequate tribal allotments. For energy planning to proceed, tribal and non-Indian water claims will require some conclusive settlement.

Environmental Protection

The requirements of environmental planning and regulation also affect the prospects for energy development on and near Indian lands. Air and water pollution do not conform to political bounds and are now subject to considerable federal regulation.[5]

Federal environmental laws are statutes of general applicability and apply to persons and activities, Indian and non-Indian, without distinction.[6] Many of these statutes do not precisely define the role of Indian tribes in federal environmental programs vis-à-vis state pollution control agencies. The federal statutes also do not confer explicit state or local jurisdiction over regulation of the Indian environment. The Environmental Protection Agency (EPA) must reconcile its established federal-state-local approach toward environmental administration with the growing tribal interest in assuming control of federal programs on Indian lands.[7] State and local government apprehension over the outcome of unilateral tribal regulatory actions (that is, establishment of air quality standards for energy production facilities) will flourish unless the EPA can create effective regulatory and consultative mechanisms which respond to the state's and tribe's fears of each other's environmental planning objectives.[8]

An associated issue which complicates the energy policy picture is the administration of federal environmental programs over non-Indian activities on Indian land. Energy development companies need to know the locus of authority for environmental regulation so facilities may operate within applicable environmental constraints.[9] Financial penalties accrue should industry decisions be delayed unnecessarily or be based on incorrect assumptions of applicable standards and administering authorities. The Supreme Court has ruled that Indian tribes have no authority to enforce tribal law on non-Indian people on the reservation without specific congressional authority.[10] However, such authority is not generally spelled out in existing environmental statutes. As long as this issue remains open, it could seriously affect the timing and attractiveness of tribal energy development options.

Perceptions and Policy

The policy process assumes a more complex nature as each of the above items is considered within separate issue contexts as applied by participants to the energy policy debate. While technical and legal analyses may suggest resolution of some of the major issues, it will be the decisionmakers' perceptions of the energy issues as well as the political arena in which they are focused which largely determine policy outcomes. Four major decision-making groups will lend their perceptions and issue definitions to the resolution of tribal energy development questions.

1. Indian tribes will play a major role in the decision process. Their concerns will be centered on the cultural, economic, and intergovernmental issues related to energy development from the clear perspective of *self-determination*. Territorial claims and traditional Indian culture have been buttressed by recent court decisions affirming general Indian control of Indian lands. The tribes will be weighing energy development proposals against the long-term effect of these proposals (and policies) on the future sovereign power of tribes.

2. A second group represented in the policy process is the coalition of energy producers and consumers interested in obtaining access to the Indian energy resource. Most of the resource availability, economic, and other energy policy issues are viewed by this group in the context of continued low-cost energy production and consumption in support of traditional patterns of national economic growth. The key values which this group brings to the policy process revolve around a faith in the basic market approach to *energy development,* regardless of resource ownership. Cheap, abundant coal is viewed as a national resource which should be developed in a timely fashion. This group is most intent on preserving its economic and political control in making energy policy and, with it, its consequent influence on national social and economic growth. The federal government's national security interest is also served by expanded domestic resource utilization. This interest strengthens support for the overall goals of the energy production advocates.

3. A third participant group is the amalgam of non-Indian interests which compete with tribes and with one another over issues such as water rights, irrigation, grazing, taxation, and general land development practices. Constituencies represented include state and local governments, water conservation districts, livestock producer associations, sport and commercial fishing groups, and ranchers. Each enters the energy policy process when its own particular *self-interests* are threatened by energy development options. At stake for these groups is the ability to maintain control over the universe of political variables influencing their specific interests. Non-Indian constituency groups also argue the need to integrate energy policy on and off the reservations so that decisions can be made more predictable. The concept of predictability can be loosely

translated to mean political control and reinforces the primary perception with which these groups view Indian energy questions.

4. A fourth significant decision group is the federal bureaucracy charged with constitutional *trust responsibility* over Indian lands. At stake for federal agencies, particularly the Bureau of Indian Affairs, is survival as an institutional and political force in tribal decision making. Historically, the executive branch has been slow to innovate in the area of Indian trust administration and has preferred to respond to legislative and judicial policy determinations. Congressional and judicial actions which have expanded the scope of Indian sovereignty now directly challenge the executive agencies' authorities which direct federal services and programs to the tribes. Tribal energy issues could easily be subsumed in a more broadly directed federal agency attempt to maintain influence over all trusteeship issues.

Political Arenas and Policy

Each group involved in the policy process perceives the energy questions in a way which suggests the political arenas preferred for issue debate. Indian court victories on nonenergy issues have encouraged tribes to use the judiciary as an arbiter of many energy-related jurisdiction and development questions. The reluctance of the executive and legislative branches to advance Indian treaty claims further explains the tribal preference for a court interpretation of Indian rights issues.

Tribes have also intensified activity in the public opinion sector in an attempt to build wider support for the trend of legal successes they have experienced. A collective force of Western energy-rich tribes has assembled in a council of Energy Resource Tribes (CERT). CERT hopes to establish itself as a political force which would negotiate with the non-Indian proponents of energy development.[11] While talk of an OPEC-like cartel is premature, CERT leaders have made publicized overtures to the oil-exporting countries for technical and financial assistance. The implications and symbolic importance of such action will not be lightly taken by government and industry policymakers. A Native American Treaty Organization has also been formed to respond to non-Indian efforts at diluting overall tribal legal victories.[12] The Indian energy issue will be brought to the public arena more frequently as tribes build support for their self-determination goals.

A variety of policy arenas are available to the coalition of energy producers and consumers. Both Congress and the federal bureaucracy are generally sympathetic to the economic and national security arguments advanced in support of the prodevelopment alliance. This definition of the energy issue allows prodevelopment interests to generate additional support in the public sector. Here, large segments of the population with poorly defined perceptions of the entire national energy problem are vulnerable to the classical economic justifications offered by developers. The multiple policy arenas available to this coalition of interests signal the widespread success it may have in the tribal energy debate.

Non-Indian constituency groups often prefer the federal legislative branch to address the range of issues tied to energy development. In response to CERT and to tribal court successes, non-Indian groups have begun to encourage legislative action limiting or negating Indian won rights. The most sweeping proposals would abrogate all Indian treaties and so remove any distinction or question of tribal land, water, resource, or other jurisdictional claims.[13] The often weak legal arguments of non-Indian groups may be effectively sidestepped through congressional action (comprehensive or case by case) redefining federal policy toward Indian tribes and trust lands. The dominance of non-Indians in the national legislative forum makes Indian participation in this policy arena difficult if not impossible.

The careful solicitation of public opinion also provides a mechanism for the coalescence of constituency group efforts. As tribal political activity increases, non-Indian groups have begun to mobilize their respective constituencies. Congress could soon be under pressure to respond more directly to the Indian energy development issue. The political strength of Indian tribes will be tested should the congressional arena be chosen by non-Indian interests for resolution of energy questions.

In the executive branch, the White House provides a powerful forum to respond to Indian policy issues. In addition, federal agencies will continue to administer their energy-related programs on most tribal lands. Regulations, guidelines, grants, eligibility criteria, and other instruments of policy administration allow the federal bureaucracy to influence a variety of Indian energy policy questions, including pollution control, water resource management, and mining and reclamation practices. While the Office of the President may establish a policy *tone,* the federal bureaucratic framework provides a more definitive arena for executive branch policy responses.

The concepts of political arenas and issue perceptions help explain why Indian resource development questions will not be resolved on narrow technical, economic, or cultural grounds. Rather, decisions will be based on their perceived benefits and disbenefits within each participant group's overall political strategy. To avoid outright concessions in any forum of the energy debate, most groups will participate, at least nominally, in each of the major political arenas. The mix of arenas chosen and the strength of each group within an arena will be the critical factors in understanding, if not predicting, policy outcomes.

Questions and Methodologies in Policy Resolution

We have identified important substantive issues which define the Indian energy resource question. Together with the issue perceptions and arenas preferred by decisionmakers, these issues raise a number of methodological questions for the policy sciences to consider. The relationship of energy *issues* to the political context in which they are addressed and to eventual *policy outcomes* has been of long-standing analytical concern. Wildavsky's early work noted the value of issue contexts in examining the "why" of policy making.[14] Lowi tied broad issue contexts to political arenas in an attempt to improve the predictive capability of the policy sciences.[15] Neither approach is sufficient to help anticipate possible issue-outcome relationships based solely on the nature of political arenas utilized.[16]

Recently, Edner identified the importance of issue or problem definitions in the study of policy development.[17] Policy outcomes will clearly differ should the Indian energy question be posed and debated as a national economic issue rather than as a tribal sovereignty issue. Policy outcomes will hinge on the ability of decisionmakers to effectively isolate and "sell" the perceptions they assign to particular issues. The policy sciences must develop more refined conceptual tools so that issue perceptions and the *circumstances* under which different perceptions prevail can be better correlated. Until this is accomplished, there remains a policy science discipline largely limited to after-the-fact policy analyses.

Another policy science issue only hinted at in this discussion concerns intergovernmental policy-making frameworks and their utility in a federal-state-Indian context. Trust lands of the United States have rarely been integrated into the body of political science research and subsequent policy science methodologies. Traditional intergovernmental relations frameworks (layer-cake, picket fence, and so on) are generally unable to accommodate the uniqueness of Indian tribal government status.[18] There is also the larger question of a role for political theory in examining many of the issues important to energy policy studies such as political participation and sovereignty.[19] As a relatively small political and cultural minority, the American Indian is seldom presented easy or effective access to the political process where a tribe's legal, economic, or cultural existence may be defended.

Indian energy development questions are now being heightened in public debate. The dominant perceptions of decision groups, together with their preferred arenas for political transactions, will greatly influence a number of important energy policy outcomes. The opportunity for the policy studies discipline to examine questions of perception, participation, and intergovernmental coordination raised here should not be neglected. Development of linkages between issue perception and policy outcomes would greatly improve our understanding of the overall tribal policy process.

Notes

1. *Johnson and Graham's Lessee* v. *McIntosh,* 21 U.S. (8 Wheat.) 240 (1823).

2. The Indian Self-Determination and Education Assistance Act (P.L. 93-638, January 4, 1975).

3. The Department of the Interior has proposed regulations (42 *Federal Register* 18083-99, April 5, 1977) which decrease past emphasis on the leasing option and allow tribes to consider joint ventures, production sharing agreements, service contracts, and other legal arrangements.

4. *Winters* v. *United States,* 207 U.S. 564 (1908).

5. David A. Schaller, "The Applicability of Environmental Statutes to Indian Lands," *The American Indian Journal,* August 1976.

6. *EPC* v. *Tuscarora Indian Nation,* 32 U.S. 99, 116 (1960).

7. J. Kemper Will, "Environmental Protection on Indian Lands and Application of N.E.P.A." (Denver: Environmental Protection Agency, 1976).

8. Council of State Governments, *Indian Rights and Claims: Environmental Management Considerations for the States* (Lexington, Ky., March 1977).

9. Ernst and Ernst, *Comprehensive Analysis of Issues regarding Energy Resource Development on Indian Reservations* (Washington: Federal Energy Administration, October 1977).

10. *Oliphant* v. *Suquamish Indian Tribe, U.S. Law Week,* March 6, 1978 pp. 4210–4216.

11. Jerry Brown, "Resource Rich Indians Form Their Own 'OPEC' to Embarrass Interior," *The Energy Daily,* July 22, 1977, pp. 3–4.

12. "Navajos Trigger Meeting Opposing 'Backlash' Forces," *Yakima Nation Review,* November 14, 1977.

13. On September 12, 1977, John Cunningham (R-Wash.) introduced the Native Americans Equal Opportunity Act. The act provides for the abrogation of all treaties between Indian tribes and the United States government. It also would abolish the Bureau of Indian Affairs.

14. Aaron Wildavsky, "The Analysis of Issue-Contexts in the Study of Decision-Making," *Journal of Politics,* November 1962.

15. Theodore J. Lowi, "American Business, Public Policy, Case Studies and Political Theory," *World Politics,* July 1964, pp. 677–715; and "Four Systems of Policy, Politics and Choice," *Public Administration Review,* July–August 1972, pp. 293–310.

16. Some recent studies have demonstrated the difficulty of using the Lowi framework to predict policy outcomes. See Gabriel Sheffer, "Reversibility of Policies and Patterns of Politics," *Policy Studies Journal* 5, Special Issue 1977, pp. 535–553; Francesco Kjellberg, "Do Policies (Really) Determine Politics? and Eventually How?" *Policy Studies Journal* 5, Special Issue 1977, pp. 554–570; George D. Greenberg, Jeffery A. Miller, Lawrence B. Mohr, and Bruce C. Vladeck, "Developing Public Policy Perspectives from Empirical Research," *American Political Science Review,* December 1977, pp. 1532–1543.

17. Sheldon Edner, "Intergovernmental Policy Development: The Impor-

tance of Problem Definition," in Charles O. Jones and Robert D. Thomas, eds., *Public Policy Making in a Federal System* (Beverly Hills, Calif.: Sage Publications, 1976).

18. Robert D. Thomas, "Intergovernmental Coordination in the Implementation of National Air and Water Pollution Policies," in Charles O. Jones and Robert D. Thomas, eds., *Public Policy Making in a Federal System* (Beverly Hills, Calif.: Sage Publications, 1976).

19. William Ophuls, *Ecology and the Policies of Scarcity* (San Francisco: W.H. Freeman, 1977).

7

Distributive Politics Reconsidered—The Wisdom of the Western Water Ethic in the Contemporary Energy Context

Helen Ingram and *John R. McCain*

Introduction

Distributive politics, where benefits are parceled out to all active participants and no one loses to benefit others,[1] is ordinarily condemned for resulting in overallocated water supplies, inefficient water uses, and no incentive for conservation.[2] While this criticism is valid for past policy choices, we argue here that given the energy industry's redistributive demand for Western water and current federal policy likely to restrict further development of water supplies, a distributive stance on the part of Western states is an intelligent policy strategy. The most damaging effect of distributive politics in past water development policy in the West has been hidden costs. Close consideration of adverse social and environmental consequences was swept aside by Western politicians not wishing to look the proverbial gift horse of huge federal subsidies for large-scale development projects in the mouth. Today, the reluctance of the Western states to abrogate the long-standing distributive rules of equity and mutual accommodation[3] and permit water transfers to energy development from agriculture, and other uses that can not afford to pay as much for water as the energy industry, forces the noneconomic costs of reallocation to be explicitly addressed.

In pursuit of this line of reasoning, first we examine what energy development demand for water could mean for the prevailing patterns of water use in the principal river basin in the arid West, the Colorado River Basin. The existing public and state legislative attitudes about water allocation and traditional relationships among water users are examined next. Finally, we explain how the Colorado River Basin example shows that, contrary to conventional wisdom, a distributive stance on water may actually force closer examination of the social and environmental costs of energy development.

Research for this chapter was supported by a grant from the Office of Water Research and Technology U.S. Department of Interior, Water Resources Research Act of 1964, P.L. 88-279.

Water Supply and Present Use in the Colorado Basin

How much water actually flows in the Colorado is a matter of some public controversy. The negotiators of the Colorado River Compact of 1922, who allocated 7.5 million acre-feet each to the upper and lower basin, assumed an average annual flow of just under 17 million acre-feet. The actual measured virgin flow of the Colorado River, during what hydrologists identify as a dry cycle, from 1931 to 1968, was 13.1 million acre-feet. The bureau of Reclamation's more long-term reconstructed estimate from 1896 is 14.9 million acre-feet. Researchers using dendrochronology techniques have come up with a substantially lower estimate of 13.5 million acre-feet.[4] Whatever the precise amounts available, it is certain that formal allocations to the various states in the basin and to Mexico have exceeded what is physically available. The reasons why the overcommitment is not

Table 7-1
Estimated 1975 Total Depletions by Colorado River Basin States
(1,000 acre-feet; does not include depletions for other minor uses, reservoir evaporations, or conveyance losses)

	Irrigation	Manufacturing and Industry	Minerals	Thermal Electric	Recreation Fish and Wildlife	Total
Arizona	4,242 (91.4)	210 (45)	69 (1.5)	32 (0.7)	89 (1.9)	4,642 (100)
Calif.	24,200 (83.9)	3,903 (13.5)	123 (0.4)	– –	635 (2.2)	28,861 (100)
Colorado	3,630 (90.4)	282 (7.0)	17 (0.4)	30 (0.8)	55 (1.4)	4,014 (100)
Nevada	1,619 (88.5)	137 (7.5)	2 (0.1)	34 (1.9)	37 (2.0)	1,829 (100)
New Mexico	1,789 (87.3)	113 (5.5)	52 (2.5)	39 (2.0)	56 (2.7)	2,049 (100)
Utah	2,608 (79.7)	138 (4.2)	24 (0.7)	13 (0.4)	490 (15.0)	3,273 (100)
Wyoming	2,372 (93.5)	62 (2.5)	88 (3.5)	16 (0.5)	– –	2,538 (100)
Colorado River Basin	40,460 (85.7)	4,845 (10.3)	375 (0.8)	164 (0.3)	1,362 (2.9)	47,206 (100)

Source: Adapted from "Westwide Study Report on Critical Water Problems Facing the Eleven Western States," Department of the Interior, April 1975, table II–31, p. 47.

painfully obvious is that the states, particularly in the upper basin, have not yet developed their total allocations. Further, the reserved rights of Indian tribes have been recognized but not yet quantified and developed. Given the lack of agreement over numbers, estimates of water supply ought not be taken as gospel. However, one estimate published in a popular journal stating that the river is 120 percent committed and 80 percent developed is probably not far wrong.[5] If, as indicated, there is no unallocated and little unused water in the basin, new claimants, such as energy development, will have to be served by reallocation from present uses.

The current pattern of water use varies little among the seven basin states. Table 7-1 shows how the basin states allocate their total water supply. Clearly, agriculture is the largest user of Western water in all states accounting for at least 80 percent of consumptive use.[6] Simply on the basis of amount of water used, agriculture's share is likely to be most threatened by other increasing demands.

Energy and Other Emergent Demands for Western Water

While water is in short supply in the arid Colorado River Basin, the region is rich in energy resources at a time when such resources are scarce. Large formations of coal underlie northwest New Mexico, at Black Mesa on the Navajo and Hopi reservations in northeast Arizona, at the Kaiparowits Plateau in Utah, and throughout western Colorado. Coal development could take a variety of shapes. Strip-mined coal could be burned on or near the mine sites. An electric power complex already exists in the area where the four states' boundaries come to-gether, and utility companies and federal governmental agencies plan to site in the area a number of additional electric power plants. Alternatively, stripped coal can be sent in railway cars or through slurry lines to generating stations out-side the region. Further, there are plans to convert the region's coal into natural gas to replace the nation's dwindling supplies. The highest grade oil shale deposits in the United States are located in northwest Colorado. Government geologists estimate that 2 trillion barrels of oil may be recovered from these deposits and others in nearby Utah and Wyoming. The total amount would be six times greater than all the proved reserves of crude petroleum on earth, enough to sup-ply the oil needs of the United States for several centuries.[7] Uranium also exists in the region in large quantities.

However, every recipe for energy development contains "add water" in its instructions. Again, experts disagree about the exact numbers, but it has been estimated that a 1 million barrel per day oil shale development in western Colorado or eastern Utah would consume approximately 150,000 acre-feet of water per year. A coal gasification plant in Wyoming, New Mexico, or Arizona processing 24 million tons of coal per year to meet the energy needs of a million people would use about 300,000 acre-feet of water per year. A 10,000-megawatt coal-fired thermal electric power plant complex in the Four Corners region would consume about 230,000 acre-feet per year.[8] Were such quantities to be allocated to energy development of these various kinds, energy would consume a much larger share of the available water supply. One utility executive predicted that 28 to 52 percent of the surface water available in the upper Colorado Basin will have to be used for energy development.[9] The Colorado River would soon run short. Weatherford and Jacoby argue that, including both projected and planned energy development, the total projected demand for water may well exceed surface supply in a decade.[10] Further, water consumption for energy will mean greater salinity in the already saline Colorado River and decrease the usefulness of its waters for some purposes.

The demand for water for energy must be understood in the context of the number of other emergent demands for water. Redistributive demands for greater shares of the flow are being asserted by Indian tribes, fish and wildlife, mining, recreational, environmental interests, and the rapidly growing cities in the West. Were the market mechanism allowed to operate freely, energy would be able to outbid agriculture, certainly, as well as most other users except cities and some industries. However, Western states have long been unwilling to simply allow water to flow toward money. Past notions of equity in water have been that everyone gets a share, although some interests have been especially favored. Revenues from municipal water users and profits from hydroelectric development have long been used to subsidize artificially low water prices for irrigated agriculture. Any massive redistribution of water among users must overcome the hurdle of the Western water ethic.

The Distributive Arena of Water Resources

The starting point for unraveling the politics of any substantive issue is the way in which participants see the stakes in the issue—what is at risk and who is likely to benefit or incur costs.[11] Westerners are convinced—some say deluded—that water is different from other commodities.[12] They believe that abundant water is the key to economic prosperity and that it is so important to the quality of life that water supply should be a governmental responsibility.[13] At the same time, water rights, for Westerners, have all the symbolic and emotional value of the Bill of Rights and should be protected from governmental interference. The President of the Colorado Senate articulated this perspective as follows:

> Colorado has the doctrine of prior appropriation. We have a water policy that's been developed over 100 years. . . . We do not want the Federal government to come in. . . . Now, if there's anything that shakes up an irrigator or water user in the West, it's when you start talking about condemning his water right.[14]

The perception of the stakes in the distributive arena is that no participant should be forced to lose in order to benefit others. This is precisely the attitude that Westerners have about more water for energy. Table 7-2 displays the opinions of a sample of voters and the state senators in four out of the seven Colorado River Basin states. While voters and their representatives are quite willing to allocate more or the same amount of water to energy production, they also want more or the same amount of water for all other users. The distributive orientation of the voters is mirrored in the state legislatures. This view is also well reflected in the traditional decision rules of water politics which dictate mutual accommodation among various users.[15]

Mutual accommodation and equity among various water users among different localities and different states have, in the past, been an effective means to put together a package of multipurpose projects in comprehensive river basin bills that can muster broad congressional support. The Colorado River Basin bill that authorized the Central Arizona Project, for instance, contained a string of

Table 7-2

Water Priority of Voters and State Senators

Water use is also an issue of importance in our area. Indeed, the Southwest may eventually have to set priorities among various water users. In your opinion, should each of the following water users get more, *the* same, *or* less *water in the future?*

(Percent Answering More or Same)

	Colorado		Arizona		Utah		New Mexico	
	Voters	Senators	Voters	Senators	Voters	Senators	Voters	Senators
Electric energy production	86	80	88	90	87	95	83	95
Irrigated agriculture	93	88	91	59	93	85	95	95
Water-based recreation	60	72	60	71	62	85	60	77
Industry and manufacturing	77	83	85	86	85	90	80	86
Municipal and residential	86	88	91	95	92	95	88	86
American Indians	66	66	81	88	73	80	76	57
	n = 1,042	n = 25	n = 825	n = 20	n = 626	n = 20	n = 998	n = 22

Source: "Four Corners Policy Study," Institute of Government Research, University of Arizona.

Note: The Four Corners Policy Study administered questionnaires by mail to a sample of registered voters and state senators in 1975 and 1976. Procedures were designed to obtain a high rate of return. The voter response rate was Colorado, 78.1 percent; Utah, 64.4 percent; Arizona, 77.4 percent; and New Mexico, 71.2 percent. The Senators' response rate was Colorado, 83 percent; Utah, 93 percent; Arizona, 70 percent; and New Mexico, 51 percent. Questions ranged over a variety of issues including water, energy, and the environment.

hydrologically and economically unrelated projects in other states put together to gain broad support.[16] Today, Westerners still prefer to deal with water shortage by building a political coalition for federally subsidized water development. Many more voters approve than oppose the construction of interbasin or transmountain diversion projects.[17] The testimony of the President of the Colorado Senate again illustrates this view:

> This is the responsibility of the federal government, not the individual states and I think that when the federal government looks to the West to develop energy resources to supply the nation as a whole, that your trade-off for this area is to help us develop water resources that are not available to us at this time. Then the choices will be a little more easy for us so that we don't have to trade off agriculture for energy development or something of this nature.[18]

An expanding federal water development pie to serve energy without depriving present water users may, however, no longer be politically feasible. The firm stand of the Carter administration against federal investment in construction projects is only the last of a chain of events beginning in the middle 1950s that have brought the Bureau of Reclamation to its knees and new starts of water projects to a virtual standstill.[19] The federal government is now focusing on energy development, embracing subsidies for energy development with enthusiasm reminiscent of the former reclamation zeal to make the deserts bloom by federally funded water development. An entire federal department has been established to promote energy development, millions of dollars are devoted to research and development, and a host of economic incentives are designed to encourage the construction of facilities.

Implications of Distributive Water Ethic
for Energy Development

There is evidence that voters in Western states are favorable to energy development. For instance, 56 percent of Colorado voters and 77 percent of Utah voters favor oil shale development. More than 50 percent of the voters in Colorado, Utah, Arizona, and New Mexico believe that the benefits of nuclear energy outweigh the possible hazards. However, a majority of residents in these states are also unwilling to suffer more air and water pollution to ensure a plentiful supply of energy, nor are they willing to suffer environmental damages for energy produced in their state and used elsewhere.[20] Clearly, residents in the Colorado River Basin would like the benefits of energy without having to pay costs. It may well be that they are even unaware of potential costs.

The policy-making process in energy is poorly designed to illuminate the implications of energy development to changing patterns of water use and water quality. The Department of Energy is separate from water agencies in the Department of Interior and the Environmental Protection Agency. Perhaps planning proceeds partially abetted by unrealistically optimistic estimates from the Bureau of Reclamation about how much water is uncommitted, without explicit consideration of social and environmental costs of altering the pattern of water use. Supplying energy to the nation as a whole is likely to be given a higher priority by the Department of Energy than the adverse impacts of energy development on the sparsely populated but culturally and environmentally delicate region. Unless the Western states combine in defense of their prevailing lifestyles, the adverse regional impacts are not likely to be given much notice.

It is not within the scope of this brief chapter focusing on water to detail all the adverse impacts of energy development on the Colorado Basin. Many analysts believe that implications for land use and air and water quality are likely to be severe, and the boomtowns which accompany energy construction will impose large social costs on their populations.[21] It may be that although full-scale energy development could raise per capita income in Western states, the region will still lag behind the nation as a whole and much of the added income might go to immigrants rather than present residents.[22] Of course, it could be argued that national welfare requires regional sacrifice, present residents in the West have no God-given rights, and more per capita income is an improvement even if the region does not catch up economically. The important point here is that the costs to the region of energy development, including the costs of reallocating water, ought to be recognized in the policy-making process.

Evidence exists that many Western officials are already sensitive to the social implications of reallocating water to energy.[23] Dean Mann illustrates the increasing concern by quoting a report of the Western States Water Council:

> There is more to the issue than this dollar comparison would lead one to believe. The social cost of water used for energy production is the value of all those uses that are sacrificed to make water available for energy. We are coming to realize that almost no diversion of water or new use can be introduced without a sacrifice being made. Even water "in stream" or "in aquifer" has some value to society. Separating out these values or "opportunity costs" is difficult and involved, yet new uses or diversions should be undertaken only when they can be justified.[24]

When the nation is in the grip of a new crisis—in this case energy—the costs of solutions are frequently overlooked. This is especially true when those who bear the cost are unaware. The Colorado River Basin states lack a coherent stand on energy. They have, however, a well-developed stance on water allocation. So long as Westerners continue to perceive water as a priceless birthright and refuse to allow the market mechanism alone to determine water allocation, energy developers will have to justify their use of a larger share of water by more than just the exercise of economic power. If, as Dror has prescribed, "the quality of the best possible policy-making increases as a function of the increases of available policy knowledge,"[25] then there is unrecognized wisdom in the prevailing Western water ethic that forces a public debate over redistribution of water resources based on concerns other than ability to pay.

Notes

1. Lowi states that in many instances of distributive policy the deprived cannot be identified as a class because the most influential among them can be accommodated by further disaggregation of the stakes. See Theodore J. Lowi, "American Business, Public Policy, Case Studies, and Political Theory," *World Politics* 16 (July 1964): 690.

2. See, for instance, Dean E. Mann, "Politics in the United States and the Salinity Problem of the Colorado River," *Natural Resources Journal* 15, no. 1 (January 1975): 113-128; Helen Ingram, "The Politics of Water Allocation," in *Values and Choice in the Development of an Arid Land River Basin: The Colorado River Basin,* eds. D.F. Peterson and A.B. Crawford (Tucson: University of Arizona Press, 1978).

3. Helen Ingram, "The Changing Decision Rules in the Politics of Water Development, *Water Resources Bulletin* 8 (1972): 1177.

4. Gary D. Weatherford and Gordon C. Jacoby, "Impact of Energy Development on the Law of the Colorado River," *Natural Resources Journal* (January 1975): 171-214.

5. George Sibley, "The Desert Empire," *Harpers,* October 1977.

6. Gary Weatherford, "Allocation of the Water Resource: Energy Aspects, Bureau of Reclamation and Its Programs," workshop materials, Conference on Energy and the Public Lands, Park City, Utah, August 23-26, 1976.

7. Neal B. Pierce, *The Mountain States of America* (New York: Norton, 1972), p. 48.

8. Task Force on Water Resources and Uses, Final Report, "Rocky Mountain Environmental Research, Quest for a Future," 1974, p. II-H-5.

9. "Needs for Faster Water Litigation Cited," *Tucson Star,* November 18, 1977.

10. Weatherford and Jacoby, "Impact of Energy Development," p. 187.

11. Lowi, "American Business, Public Policy, Case Studies, and Political Theory."

12. See, for instance, Maurice Kelso, "The Water-Is-Different Syndrome or What Is Wrong with the Water Industry," *Proceedings* of the Third Annual Conference of the American Water Works Association 1977 (1967).

13. Maurice Kelso, William Martin, and Lawrence Mack, *Water Supplies and*

Economic Growth in an Arid Environment: An Arizona Case Study (Tucson: University of Arizona Press, 1973), p. 23.

14. Statement of Senator Fred Anderson, Water Resources Policy Study Public Hearings, Record of Question and Answer Period (Denver, Colo., July 28-29, 1977) Department of Interior Files.

15. Ingram, "The Changing Decision Rules in the Politics of Water Development."

16. Helen Ingram, *Patterns of Politics in Water Resource Development: A Case Study of New Mexico's Role in the Colorado River Basin Bill* (Albuquerque. N. Mex.: Division of Government Research, 1964), p. 14.

17. Southwest Policy Project.

18. Fred Anderson, Water Resource Policy Study, 1977.

19. See Ingram, *Patterns of Politics in Water Resource Development;* (Tucson: University of Arizona Press, 1969); R. Nash, "Wilderness and the American Mind," Ph.D. thesis (Ann Arbor: University Microfilms, 1965), pp. 161-181; Elmo Richardson, *Dams, Parks and Politics* (Lexington: University Press of Kentucky, 1973).

20. Southwest Policy Project.

21. For an assessment of some of the costs see Federation of Rocky Mountain States, Inc., *Energy Development in the Rocky Mountain Region: Goals and Concerns* (Denver, 1975). See also Donald Ropp, "Western Boomtowns: A Comparative Analysis of State Actions" (Denver: Western Governor's Regional Energy Policy Office, June 1976); Leonard D. Bronder, Nancy Carlisle, and Michael Savage, Jr., "Financial Strategies for Alleviation of Socioeconomic Impacts in Seven Western States" (Denver: Western Governor's Regional Energy Policy Office, May 1977).

22. Conclusion reported from Trends and Perspectives Project, Component of Southwest Region under Stress Project, Allen V. Kneese, Director, Annual Meeting, Albuquerque, N. Mex., November 4-5, 1977.

23. Dean E. Mann, *Water Policy and Decision-Making in the Colorado River Basin,* Lake Powell Research Project Bulletin no. 24, July 1976, p. 14.

24. Western States Water Council, *Western States' Water Requirements for Energy Development to 1990,* Salt Lake City, Utah, November 1974, p. 34, quoted in Mann, *Water Policy and Decision-Making.*

25. Yehezkel Dror, *Public Policy-Making Reexamined* (San Francisco: Chandler, 1968), p. 9.

**Part II
Energy Policy in the
National Context**

Organizing for Energy Policy and Administration

Terry D. Edgmon

On August 31, 1977, Congress signed into law the Department of Energy Organization Act. This legislation culminated four years of legislative and executive efforts to consolidate and reorganize federal energy management functions. As such, the new Department of Energy (DOE) not only represents the importance energy has attained as a national problem but also reflects the nature of how we have altered our thinking of what constitutes our energy problems and how we are going to find solutions.

Prior to the "energy crisis" of 1973, energy was not widely utilized as an organizing concept in the formulation and implementation of national policy. To be sure, there existed a nuclear fuels policy, a natural gas policy, and a petroleum imports policy, but few institutions of government were organized to directly address specific aspects of energy policy. Most of the agencies charged with the responsibility of implementing energy policy did so only on a secondary basis. For example, the Atomic Energy Commission, bureaus within the Department of Interior, the Environmental Protection Agency, and the Department of Housing and Urban Development, to name a few, not only operated in separate and distinct policy arenas but also in many instances gave their energy-related activities low priority.[1]

However, since 1973 we have witnessed a rash of legislation and administrative reorganiztion which began with the Alaska Pipeline Authorization (P.L. 93-153) and the Emergency Petroleum Allocation Act in 1973, the creation of the Federal Energy Administration (FEA), the Energy Research and Development Administration (ERDA), the Nuclear Regulatory Commission, and the Energy Resources Council in 1975. In this same year the Energy Policy and Conservation Act was also passed.

Today, with congressional committee reorganization and the Department of Energy, many principal energy management functions of the federal government have been consolidated and centralized on the Presidential cabinet level. A major question exists, however: Will this sweeping reorganization provide for the development and implementation of energy policies which will confront and manage the energy problems of the 1980s and beyond?

The purpose of this chapter is to analyze the concepts that served to organize our thinking and actions in energy policy, patterns of energy politics, and emerging energy "ideologies," so as to assess the potential impact of the latest federal energy reorganization on energy decision making. We will contend that because of the seeming abundance of energy in our recent past, we have ignored its significant ramifications for social and political organization. Institutions created during an era of cheap and abundant energy have not proved to be viable in an era of expensive energy. As the cost of energy climbs, we will require mechanisms to alter its allocation, distribution, and consumption. These alterations, necessary for the maintenance and preservation of social values within a tighter national energy budget, may have a significant impact on the level of control government exerts on our lives, and the consequences and implications of centralizing energy decision making must be carefully scrutinized.

A review of the organizational changes since 1973 indicates that our perceptions of energy and its significance to society are in a rapid state of flux and our past complacency on energy questions has given way to uncertainty as our conventional organizational and policy concepts have failed us.

Traditional Energy Concepts

One of the more troublesome aspects of energy decision making is that there does not seem to be a clear consensus as to what constitutes our set of energy problems. For the consumer, an energy crisis exists when he cannot obtain gasoline for his car or heating oil for his house at any price. He may perceive energy to be a "problem" if his utility rates take on a sharp annual increase. Economists tell us that in the long run we will never truly "run out" of energy resources. Rather, these resources, such as coal, petroleum, and natural gas, at some point will become cost-prohibitive to use, and we will have to search for cheaper substitutes and do without.

Thus, as energy resources, particularly petroleum and natural gas, become scarce, we must increase efficiencies in their allocation, distribution, and consumption; find substitute fuels; or eventually do without. Many studies have indicated that straight-line energy consumption projections for the United States can be maintained only through the deployment of a combination of policies, such as increasing our petroleum imports, rapidly accelerating coal production, and encouraging the proliferation of nuclear reactor technology.[2] Others argue that this may well be a futile gesture since we will eventually "run out" of conventional fossil fuels, so why bother. Attention should be given to the development of renewable energy supplies while time still exists to develop the appropriate technologies.[3] Still others point to the past success of U.S. enterprise and know-how and urge us to keep the faith and place our trust in the U.S. free enterprise system.[4] But the trust has been shaken, and we are realizing that the perceptions of the past may not lead us to safety and comfort in our energy future.

This lack of consensus concerning the nature of our energy problems has led to a peculiar problem. That is, we also suffer from an ambiguity over what national energy goals should be established, what priority each should have, and what types of administrative machinery should be employed to meet them. As a result, our national energy policy goals may be, as Behrens asserts, incompatible or mutually exclusive.[5] The major articulated national goals are to maintain the national economy in the face of large increases in energy prices, reduce our dependence on petroleum imports, maintain our environmental quality standards, and shift energy use from oil and natural gas. Inconsistency is apparent when one begins to realize that petroleum and natural gas are currently the most efficient of our fuels from a utilization point of view and also the most environmentally acceptable. However, our dependence on them in the face of dwindling domestic production increases our dependence on foreign exports. Converting our energy economy to other fuel types has proved to be expensive not only from a capital investment point of view but also from an environmental perspective.

This inconsistency in the establishment of a coherent set of national energy goals has had its impact on the design of administrative mechanisms to solve or find solutions to national energy problems. As a result, executive branch reorganization of energy functions has been almost a preoccupation of the federal government for the last four years. Literally every administrative cliché has been brought to bear with little in the way of satisfactory results. It has appeared that energy has been defined as a problem in public relations, information disorganization, agency fragmentation, technology, monopoly power, economics, or simply institutional.[6]

For example, with the creation of the Federal Energy Office (and later the Federal Energy Administration), the Nixon administration sought to deal with the aftermath of the Mideast petroleum boycott through a combination of strategies, some tried and true, others entirely untried and new. Observers of FEA have indicated that this agency pursued many distinct policy objectives which, if placed in perspective, embodied the great U.S. faith in problem solving through public relations, grant programs, "soft" technological fixes, and regulation.[7] Project Independence was a vast public relations program, geared to mobilize the public for decisive action. Through its energy conservation legislation, grants were made available to states to assist them in developing energy policy management capability and to replicate little FEAs on the state level. A tide of econometric studies on fuel use in economic and industrial sectors flowed forth from the agency, along with countless other publications designed to help the consumer use energy wisely. Instant experts were placed in positions of major responsibility to control the flow of petroleum from market to consumer, often with less than successful results.[8]

Yet confusion on the part of FEA personnel, legislators, and executives over specific objectives to be attained with such policy tools rendered the overall impact of this agency ineffectual, and it has been reorganized into a larger energy administrative structure, the Department of Energy.

The second example of energy policy disorganization was the Atomic Energy Commission (AEC), reborn as the U.S. Energy Research and Development Administration (ERDA) and now lodged within the interstices of the Department of Energy. The AEC stood not only as the symbol of man's technological conquest over nature but also in place of the scientist in public policy making. With the formation of ERDA, this faith was taken from the hands of the scientist and placed on the shoulders of engineers. This was accomplished by breaking off the AEC's nuclear regulatory function, and grafting onto ERDA the top management of the National Aeronautics and Space Administration (NASA), through the appointment of Robert Seamans, former director of NASA. This organizational change reflected a faith in our technological prowess to solve energy problems. However, it later became clear, in Congress and elsewhere, that finding solutions to our energy problems may not be as straightforward as landing a man on the moon, and support for maintaining ERDA in this form waned.[9]

The third great casualty was the Federal Power Commission (FPC). This independent authority embodied our faith in benevolent government, acting to protect the unorganized consumer from the highly organized energy producer and distributor. In respect to its function of regulating the price of natural gas, Breyer and MacAvoy suggest that the FPC pursued two regulation strategies: regulation to control monopoly power of gas producers and later regulation to control the taking of excessive economic rents or windfall profits by producers and pipeline owners.[10] These strategies led to natural gas shortages for which the FPC was criticized in a report by the House Subcommittee on Oversight and Investigations for its failure in natural gas delivery obligations.[11] The major problem, which the FPC could not solve, was how to get a scarce but vital resource out of the ground to consumers at a fair price. Little consensus exists among suppliers and purchasers of what constitutes a fair administered price or how it should be calculated. Consequently, the FPC was also absorbed into the DOE structure.

The fourth organizational assumption to be challenged is the basis of pricing electric power. Existing rate structures and assumptions on which public utilities are organized are coming under scrutiny. New techniques such as marginal cost pricing, inverted rate structures, load management, and lifeline rate setting are being investigated.[12] Fundamentally, however, the utilitarian basis of electric power organization is also being reconsidered.[13] The reconsideration is in respect to the prevailing assumptions that power utilities should meet *all* demands and develop power systems to provide such reserves and that efficiency is attained through scale economics. Given higher energy prices and the increasing demand for capital required to meet anticipated growth, the emphasis is shifting to *demand* management (or how and when the public chooses to use electricity), rather than solely concentrating on supply managements.

If this trend continues, then there will be calls for a greater level of intervention of public institutions as the authority granted to utilities restricts their ability to take direct actions affecting the public welfare. As utilities move in the direction of electricity demand management, other social values, such as income redistribution and lifestyle questions, will increasingly dominate electric power decisions. This will lead to perhaps a reconsideration of both the bases on which we should organize our electric power network and to what ends energy allocations in the form of electricity should be used.[14]

The fifth illustration of shaken faith in traditional concepts lies with nuclear power. The ERDA's *A National Plan for Energy Research, Development, and Demonstration* of 1976 estimated that approximately 40 percent of their budget outlay for the year would be for research, development, and demonstration in the areas of nuclear fission and the nuclear fuel cycle.[15] This represents, once again, our faith in technological solutions and the central place nuclear fission has attained in our energy future. Yet uncertainties associated with its safety, possible environmental effects, and reactor deployment have been critical issues not yet resolved. Further, the widespread deployment of nuclear power has implications for the future organization of our energy systems. This is in respect to its inflexibility of use. Nuclear reactor technology is geared to the generation of electricity. Reliance on nuclear power to fill the gaps created by a reduction in our reliance on petroleum imports and natural gas while meeting increased electric power demands may lead to a highly centralized energy system based on electrification. Thus, the policy question of how large a share of the total energy picture electric power should play in the future is implicit in nuclear research and development decisions made today. Given research, development, and technological lead times stretching into the decades, such research and development decisions may not provide us with the appropriate technologies thirty years hence if they are not based on premises which take into consideration the electrical distribution systems of which nuclear power will only be a part.[16]

The sixth organizational assumption challenged during the energy crisis of 1973 was within the area of petroleum policy. The aftermath of the oil embargo witnessed an aroused Congress bent on seeking respite from constituent wounds by entertaining policy proposals for the creation of a national petroleum corporation and the break-up of multinational petroleum corporations. Domestic petroleum policies, once designed to aid and protect producers from the vagaries of cheap foreign oil, became obsolete as OPEC pushed up the price of petroleum produced by its members. Regulatory policies, once designed to benefit producers, have been altered into more punitive forms.[17]

In summary, we have witnessed major organizational transformations since

1973. These alterations were based on the realization that past organizing concepts were developed in an era of abundant and cheap energy. Today, with the acknowledgment that energy prices will never return to the levels of the 1960s, new policies and organizational structures are being developed. In respect to the above examples, these policies and structures will emerge from the Department of Energy, which can be seen as a centralization of energy policy formation and implementation mechanisms. This structure will provide for the implementation of organizing concepts for energy, which will allow for a greater degree of integration and control of energy-related administrative activities. Whether this enhanced integration will be effective depends to a large extent on the relative integration of political forces which seek to influence federal energy policies. In the next section we review the major components of energy politics.

Energy Politics

The above institutional shortcomings, which by no means include all witnessed in our scramble to reorganize in the face of threats to our energy future, demonstrate an inadequacy in defining our energy problems in ways that allow for the taking of concentrated social and political action to resolve them. As in all areas of policy administration, our energy disorganization stems from the nature and context of energy politics. Davis has pointed out that traditional energy politics constituted separate and distinct policy systems, organized around principal fuel systems.[18] Each fuel type or energy system (natural gas, petroleum, electric power generation, coal, and nuclear power) has operated on the basis of different historical and political events, political actors, legislation, agencies, and government rules.

   While the consolidation of energy administrative functions under the banner of the Department of Energy may offer the potential for a comprehensive approach to energy policy implementation, the centrifugal forces of energy politics may forestall such efforts. These centrifugal forces are associated with the following dimensions of energy politics: (1) the organization of interests among those who supply energy and those who consume it, (2) the differentiation of impacts of energy policies within the United States along income and geographical lines, (3) the rapidly changing substantive content of energy issues and problems, and (4) the inadequacy of traditional conflict management techniques used to resolve conflicts of interest. Each of these characteristics is reviewed below.

   In our competitive pluralistic system, energy producers and suppliers, by virtue of their organization, have been able to impact the development of our energy policies in ways the consumer never could. While it is an oversimplification to suggest that energy politics is dichotomized among those who produce it and those who consume energy, we can observe that inequities exist in the distribution of power between the energy producer and the energy consumer.[19] In most fuel policy areas, power is concentrated on the supply side and fragmented on the demand side. Production or technology groups range from utilities to petroleum corporations to nuclear engineers. Such groups are sensitive to minute alterations in energy policy. While the impact of such changes may produce slight or marginal immediate impacts, they may have long-range implications for the welfare of the consumer. Consumer interests, however, can be differentiated along income and social class lines. For example, since rising energy costs affect people of different incomes differently, consumer issue cleavages are laid bare in debates concerning the implementation of lifeline utility rate structures for natural gas which, in effect, are energy subsidies for the poor.

Light and others have written about emerging sectional cleavages created by energy politics. Coalitions among states have emerged as indicated by divisions in Congress between producer and consumer rates.[20] Regional organizations, such as the Western Governors' Energy Policy Office and the Southwest Regional Energy Council, are organizational manifestations of the sectional interests of producer states. Thus with energy problem impacts falling differently among income groups, producer regions, and consumer regions, conditions for rancorous conflicts among interests exist that make the development of consensus on a systematic course of national policy difficult to achieve. This, in turn, makes coordinated policy implementation through a centralized administrative structure a difficult undertaking.

A second observation of energy politics also bodes ill for conducting the energy policy administration through a centralized administrative system. This is in respect to the changing substantive nature of energy issues. That is, not only are energy problems multifaceted, but they are also dynamic over time. Because technological lead times associated with energy research and development decisions alter public attention to natural gas shortages, electric brownouts, and localized protests over nuclear reactor siting policies, our ability to achieve an equilibrium of political forces may not be able to keep pace with the technological, financial, and resource "moving equilibrium" of the technical aspects of energy decision making. For example, it takes approximately ten years to build a nuclear power plant from scratch. It has taken approximately thirty years to establish the extensive petroleum and natural gas intrastructure within the United States. It will take approximately just as long to switch to alternative technologies and fuel types.[21]

Increasingly, our petroleum and natural gas economy has become dependent on our foreign supplies as our domestic reserves dwindle. The current level of petroleum imports is approximately 50 percent. At some point in the near future, continuing to increase foreign fuel imports will not be a viable option for balance-of-trade factors, if not for reasons of national security.[22] In order to meet our national security and international trade goals, decisive decisions concerning the conservation of petroleum and natural gas should be made soon. But will our policy resolution machinery, the Congress, the executive branch, the courts, and the states be able to respond fast enough to resolve energy-induced problems? Or, will we need to seek structural modifications in conflict-of-interest resolving procedures in order to speed up the policy decision and implementation process? Solving these problems requires the development of consensus of a radically different nature from what is now required to pass energy legislation. Such decision making may require the centralization of authority going beyond the legislation authorizing the creation of the Department of Energy.

Another characteristic of the U.S. political style which may be threatened is related to the issue raised above. That is, the manner by which we have historically attempted to solve political problems appears not to be able to solve our energy problems. Political conflicts and problems have historically been managed through a compromise, logrolling process. Grants are administered to allow dissatisfied, but politically influential, groups to "buy into" the political arena. The responsibilities for the regulation of resources and trade have been assigned to independent regulatory bodies which, some claim, fall under the influence of those regulated.[23] This process of conflict management, well documented in the literature, is likened to a non-zero sum game in which there exist no losers in the political struggle, only winners. However, given a declining resource base, we may not possess sufficient resources in the near future to continue this practice, and political conflicts may begin to resemble zero-sum games in which compromise is impossible to achieve, given the structure of the game.

Such problems, if real, require the mobilization of the public on some other basis than slogans or energy conservation leaflets and TV spots. Such problems can be solved only within the context of an ideological base, which legitimizes actions taken by decisionmakers on behalf of the public and society. Carter's stern warning that solving our energy problems will require efforts on the magnitude of the "moral equivalent to war" may appear to be cosmetic. But given what we may have to do over the next ten years in terms of making social adjustments necessary to accommodate dwindling petroleum and natural gas supplies, such invocations may become more and more common to Presidents.

Energy Ideologies

Yet the centralization of federal energy administrative functions and the reliance on central governmental direction and control are only one manifestation of energy organization. There exist several other possible ways by which we may organize ourselves to manage our energy problems. These directions are articulated in the emerging energy ideologies currently espoused by various energy interests. Three major ideological positions may be identified: (1) The market proponents argue that energy is a matter of pricing, supply, and demand and that with the proper adjustments to the marketplace individuals and firms will increase energy efficiencies and producers will supply more energy as prices rise.[24] (2) The central government planning approach is articulated in *A Time to Choose,* and it constitutes the Carter administration's strategy. (3) The decentralist approach stresses policies to decentralize our energy systems and government control.[25] Each of these ideological positions, while used to justify interest positions on discrete policy issues, represents different notions of both social organization related to society's ability to adapt to changes in its resource environment and the locus of decision making within society. In theory, the market approach maximizes individual preferences; but such choice maximization and resource utilization efficiencies are a function of the organization of energy suppliers and the public's perception of the nature of the good being exchanged. If competitive markets existed in all fuel areas and few opportunity costs were associated with switching from one fuel to another, then such a basis for energy organization might be viable. However, producers and distributors of energy represent highly concentrated and centralized organizations for which market principles may not strictly apply. Also, fuels and electricity may not be considered to be private goods, subject to disposition and consumption through the exercise of private preferences. Society perceives values other than Btu's and kilowatts associated with energy decision making. This fact is evident in the numerous social and environmental issues raised in relation to the making of energy policy decisions.

Central energy planning on the part of the federal government may be seen as a viable response to the concentration of energy decision making among suppliers. Since there has been a gradual centralization of our national energy system through vertical and horizontal corporate integration, such integration on the part of the federal government may be necessary to apply controls for the balancing of supply and demand with domestic and foreign policy concerns. However, central planning has never had much success in our history, and given the pluralistic nature of energy politics, whether comprehensive legislation can emerge out of the congressional process remains to be seen.

The third major ideological position is articulated by those who believe that the concentration of energy decision making in either the private or the public sector is not a viable course of action, given the fundamental nature of our energy situation. This line of thinking, embodied in the writings of Schumacher and Lovins, attacks the notion of energy problem solving through the application of high technology and centralized organization. Reliance on centralized energy systems that rest on a dwindling resource base and complex technologies may not, in the long run, allow for the flexibility society requires to respond to new resource situations. What is recommended is a realization of the finite nature of our resource base and the pursuit of alternative energy sources and systems on vastly smaller scales than is being conducted today. Through the development of simple energy technologies, communities and subnational regions may be able to achieve relative energy independence, which frees the federal government from having to plan and act for such communities. Thus, consumer flexibility and decision autonomy are maintained and not sacrificed for central government control. Also, such decentralized systems would avoid another problem of centralized control—the compounding of errors in information and failures of decisions to solve problems. However, such a "path," while in the spirit of U.S. individualism and self-reliance, carries with it a price. This price is related to the alteration of existing lifestyles and technologies. As energy conservation planners have discovered, getting people in the United States to alter their lifestyles for the sake of diminishing their consumption of energy requires techniques other than the conventional ones available to them.

Summary

Thus it appears that energy organization in the short run will follow the centralization path as represented by the Department of Energy. However, given the fragmented and pluralistic nature of energy politics, the management of this department may prove to be as difficult as that of the Department of Health, Education, and Welfare. Any increase in the federal government's capability to manage our energy problems may require structural changes of a fundamental nature, which will affect the relationship of the citizen to his government. As these decision points are reached, the public may be forced to choose between maintaining existing lifestyle patterns and losing a degree of freedom or maintaining existing freedoms of choice but altering lifestyles based on a given pattern of energy use. Such decisions are usually not clearly articulated at specific times but rather are implicit in the countless choices made by the public, in terms of how it chooses to consume energy, and by policy makers who attempt to maximize the interests they represent in the policy arena. However, it is incumbent upon us to recognize the trends established by decisions made in the past and to consider the implications of choices made now for the future organization of society and government. If anything, energy is fundamental to society. Energy decisions, like those related to the economy, will always embody political, social, and economic considerations. Given our reliance on a dwindling resource base, how we choose to organize now will affect our ability to make choices in the future.

Notes

1. *Federal Energy Regulation: An Organization Study,* prepared by the Federal Energy Regulation Study Team (Washington: GPO, April 1974).
2. Edward L. Allen and Chester L. Cooper et al., *U.S. Energy and Economic Growth, 1975-2010* (Oak Ridge, Tenn.: Institute for Energy Analysis, September 1976); Walter G. Dupree, Jr., and John S. Corsentino, *United States*

Energy through the Year 2000, rev. ed. (Washington: GPO, 1975); ERDA 76-1, *A National Plan for Energy Research, Development and Demonstration,* vol. 2 (Washington: GPO, 1976); John Hagel, III, *Alternative Energy Strategies: Constraints and Opportunities* (New York: Praeger, 1976); and Roger F. Neill, *Managing the Energy Transition* (Cambridge, Mass.: Ballinger, 1977).

3. Wilson Clark, *Energy for Survival* (Garden City, N.Y.: Anchor Books, 1975); Amory B. Lovins, "Energy Strategy: A Road Not Taken," *Foreign Affairs,* October 1976, pp. 65-96; and E.F. Schumacher, *Small Is Beautiful: Economics as if People Mattered* (New York: Harper & Row, 1973).

4. Edward J. Mitchell, *U.S. Energy Policy: A Primer* (Washington: American Enterprise Institute, 1974).

5. Carl E. Behrens, *Energy Famine in Late 20th Century America* (Washington: Library of Congress, Congressional Research Service, 1977).

6. John F. O'Leary, "A Resource vs. Institutional Crisis?" in *Energy: Public Policy–1972* (New York: The Conference Board, Inc., 1972), pp. 238-240.

7. William A. Johnson, "Why U.S. Energy Policy Has Failed," in *Energy Supply and Government Policy,* eds. Robert J. Kalter and William A. Vogely (Ithaca, N.Y.: Cornell University Press, 1976), pp. 280-305; Alfred R. Light, "The Rise of the Energy Policy Arena," Paper presented at the American Society for Public Administration Annual Meeting in Chicago, April 2, 1975; and Richard B. Mancke, *The Performance of the Federal Energy Office* (Washington: American Enterprise Institute, 1975).

8. Johnson, ibid., pp. 196-305; Light, ibid., p. 8.

9. Office of Technology Assessment, U.S. Congress, *An Analysis of the ERDA Plan and Program* (Washington: GPO, October 1975).

10. Stephen G. Breyer and Paul W. MacAvoy, *Energy Regulation by the Federal Power Commission* (Washington: Brookings Institution, 1974).

11. *Federal Regulation and Regulatory Reform,* Report by the Subcommittee on Oversight and Investigations of the Committee on Interstate and Foreign Commerce, House of Representatives, 94th Cong. 2d. Sess., October 1976.

12. John S. Ferguson, "Building Blocks of Rates–Revisited," *Public Utility Fortnightly,* November 20, 1975, pp. 38-43; Herbert B. Cohn, "Current Proposals in Rate Design," *Public Utility Fortnightly,* December 18, 1975, p. 21.

13. Kenneth Sayre, *Values in the Electric Power Industry* (Notre Dame, Ind.: University of Notre Dame Press, 1977).

14. Lovins, "Energy Strategy," pp. 65-96.

15. ERDA 76-1, *A National Plan for Energy.*

16. Lovins, "Energy Strategy," pp. 69-71.

17. Walter J. Mead, "Petroleum: An Unregulated Industry?" in Kalter and Vogely, *Energy Supply and Government Policy* (Ithaca, N.Y.: Cornell University Press, 1976), pp. 130-160.

18. David Davis, *Energy Politics* (New York: St. Martin's Press, 1974).

19. Robert Engler, *The Politics of Oil* (Chicago: University of Chicago Press, 1961) and *The Brotherhood of Oil* (Chicago: University of Chicago Press, 1977).

20. Hanna J. Cortner, "Energy Policy Planning, Administration and Coordination in the Four Corners States," Consultant's Report, Submitted to the Four Corners Regional Commission, Farmington, N. Mex., March 1977, pp. 131–133; and Alfred Light, "From the Declaration of Independence to Valley Forge: Intergovernmental Relations and the Energy Crisis of 1973-76", Paper presented at the National Meeting of the American Society for Public Administration, Atlanta, Ga., April 1, 1977.

21. Chauncey Starr, "Energy and Power," in *Scientific American, Energy and Power* (San Francisco: W.H. Freeman, 1973), pp. 3-18.

22. Central Intelligence Agency, *The International Energy Situation: Outlook to 1985,* April 1977.

23. Louis M. Kohlmeier, Jr., *The Regulators* (New York: Harper & Row, 1969); Paul W. MacAvoy, ed., *The Crisis of the Regulatory Commissions* (New York: Norton, 1970); and Roger Noll, *Reforming Regulation* (Washington: Brookings Institution, 1971).

24. Edward J. Mitchell, *U.S. Energy Policy.*

25. Lovins, "Energy Strategy"; and Schumacher, *Small Is Beautiful.*

Technology Assessment as an Energy Policy Tool

Irvin L. White, Steven C. Ballard, and *Timothy A. Hall*

Introduction

Technology assessment was first introduced as a kind of applied policy analysis in 1966.[1] What it promised so tantalized policymakers that the administration commissioned studies by the National Academies of Engineering and Science to evaluate the concept and the Office of Science and Technology contracted with the MITRE Corporation for a study of how to do technology assessments;[2] Congress established an Office of Technology Assessment;[3] and the National Science Foundation funded a number of first-generation technology assessment studies, including several focused either directly or indirectly on some aspect of energy policy.[4] Both the Department of Energy and the Environmental Protection Agency now have major technology assessment (TA) programs intended to inform their own and the nation's energy policies and programs.[5] In this brief chapter, technology assessment as a kind of applied policy analysis is described and its contribution to better informed energy policy making is discussed.

Technology Assessment as a Kind of Applied Policy Analysis

Technology assessments are interdisciplinary applied policy studies[6] undertaken (1) to inform public and private policymakers and interested citizens about the likely consequences of a decision to develop and deploy a technology and (2) to identify, evaluate, and compare alternative policies and implementation for dealing with the problems and issues likely to arise when a technology is deployed. To achieve the first objective, three questions must be answered: Are the conse-

The technology assessment approach described in this chapter is a product of the University of Oklahoma's Science and Public Policy (S&PP) program. The policy analysis framework discussed here is an outgrowth of a three-year Technology Assessment of Western Energy Resource Development being sponsored by the Environmental Protection Agency, Office of Energy, Minerals, and Industry, under contract number 68-01-1916. In addition to the authors of this paper, members of the S&PP interdisciplinary team conducting the Western Energy Study are Michael A. Chartock, R. Leon Leonard, Frank J. Calzonetti, Mark S. Eckert, Martha W. Gilliland, Edward J. Malecki, Gary D. Miller, and Edward B. Rappaport.

quences that have been anticipated likely to occur? Are there also likely to be consequences that have not been anticipated? And if either or both kinds of consequences occur, how serious will they be? To achieve the second objective of technology assessment, the answers to these three questions must be related to the social and political context within which the technology will be developed and deployed. The questions to be answered in this case are, What alternative policies and implementation strategies can reasonably be used to maximize benefits and minimize costs and risks when the technology is developed and deployed, and how will these alternatives distribute costs, risks, and benefits throughout society?

Technology assessment (TA), as does applied policy analysis generally, involves two kinds of analyses: technical and policy.[7] Technical analyses evaluate and compare technologies on the basis of objective and, to the extent possible, unbiased scientific and technical criteria.[8] Policy analyses interpret the results of the technical analyses in the context of the social and political system(s) within which the technology is developed and deployed.

Technical Analysis

As figure 9-1 shows, impacts occur when the inputs and outputs of a technology interact with the conditions existing where the technology is sited and operated. Therefore, the evaluation and comparison of technologies for developing energy resources begin with a description and comparison of inputs, outputs, and existing conditions. Energy technologies can be evaluated and compared in terms of inputs (such as capital, labor, and land requirements) and outputs (such as the quantities of electricity and air pollutants produced). The conditions existing at an energy development location can be evaluated and compared on the basis of such factors as the availability of public services, sectors of eco-

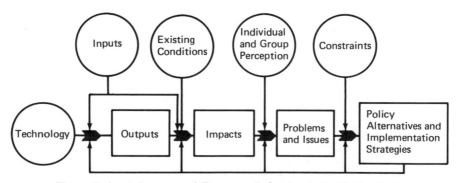

Figure 9-1. A Conceptual Framework for Assessing Technologies.

nomic activity, air dispersion potential, water availability and quality, and attitudes toward energy development.

Engineering studies can provide detailed data on an energy technology's inputs and outputs and the effects of configuration changes (such as installing environmental controls and minimizing water consumption). Impact analyses can estimate changes in such things as air quality (air dispersion modeling), water quality (water quality modeling), and local and national economies (economic base and input-output models). The results of these and similar technical analyses make it possible to compare the impacts of energy development alternatives on the basis of such factors as changes in ambient air concentrations of sulfur dioxide, per unit energy costs, and demand for public services such as water and sewage treatment. Impacts can also be compared in terms of how likely they are to occur and how serious they will be.[9]

In short, the descriptions of energy development technologies and locations and the results of the analyses of the impacts likely to occur when technologies and location are interacted can be used to inform policymakers about the costs, risks, and benefits of various technology and siting options. However, the results of technical analyses will always be incomplete, largely because of the limited explanatory power of existing theories and either the inadequacy or unavailability of data and analytical tools. Even if it were possible to overcome these limitations, the results of the technical analyses would not be an adequate basis for policy making. Policymakers need to know more than the costs, risks, and benefits of technological and siting alternatives evaluated and compared on the basis of objective criteria. They need to know how costs, risks, and benefits will be distributed, which interests and values will be promoted at the expense of which others, how to promote the interests and values they wish to promote, and how to avoid unwanted costs and risks.[10] The policy analyses performed as a part of a TA are intended to produce results responsive to these needs.

Policy Analysis

Policy analyses in a TA are conducted in three steps: the identification and definition of problems and issues;[11] the description of the social and political context within which the technology will be deployed; and the identification, evaluation, and comparison of alternative policies and implementation strategies.

Identification and Definitions

Problems and issues are identified from the following sources: those already anticipated and being dealt with by the political system; those identified by the interdisciplinary research team based on a review of the results of its technical analyses; and those identified by the interdisciplinary research team during the policy analyses themselves.

Description

The second step requires the identification and description of the relevant policy system(s). This "issue systems" approach is based on the observation that political systems vary according to the substance of the issue being processed.[12] The interests and values at stake, relevant institutional arrangements, applicable laws and regulations, governmental and nongovernmental participants, and intensity of involvement of various participants can vary on the basis of substance. For example, the substance of health care problems leads to a different issue system definition than would oil and gas problems.

For issues that the political system has dealt with in the past, the identification of the issue system begins with an examination of key questions in the historical development of the issue: When did the issue arise? Which participants in the system perceived that it was an issue and what interest and values did they represent? When and how did government respond? What policies were enacted and who has administered them? And how have these policies and their administration affected the issue? This step also includes a more detailed identification and description of the existing system for dealing with the issue: What are the relevant current public and private, formal and informal institutional arrangements? What interests and values are at stake, who represents them, and what strategies and tactics are they employing? And are there situational or social and physical environmental conditions and circumstances that either affect or could potentially affect whether and how the issue is processed?[13]

Identification, Definition, Evaluation, and Comparison of Alternative Policies and Implementation Strategies

In the policy analysis step of a TA, policy alternatives and implementation strategies are identified, defined, evaluated, and compared. Alternatives and implementation strategies for dealing with issues already being processed by the system will have been identified in the second step. However, the interdisciplinary research team also formulates alternatives itself, both for issues already being processed and for issues likely to arise as a consequence of unanticipated impacts identified when results of the technical analyses are reviewed. Drawing from both sources, the team reduces the number of alternatives and strategies to be evaluated and compared in detail to a manageable number. This is accomplished by applying a number of filters to isolate those alternatives and strategies that appear to be most significant and feasible.[14] Since alternatives distribute costs, risks, and benefits differently, filtering alternatives requires at least a preliminary assessment of distributive effects. For example, (1) which individuals, groups, or organizations would benefit more than or at the expense of others; (2) which costs, risks, or benefits would be transferred from some individuals. groups, or organizations to others; and (3) would existing regulations have to be modified and/or eliminated, would new regulations have to be added to existing programs, or would new regulatory programs have to be established?

Implementation strategies can also affect the distribution of costs, risks, and benefits. However, the first evaluation and comparison of implementation strategies are in terms of the relative ease or difficulty of implementing an alternative.[15] But the analysis of implementation strategies also includes identifying means for gaining acceptance of an alternative and achieving its objectives.

Another key consideration in the evaluation and comparison of alternatives is utilization. An essential component of applied TA is the participation of the potential users in the production of the interdisciplinary team's research products. This includes participation by representatives of the broad range of interests and values at stake. This includes involving users in identifying and filtering alternatives and implementation strategies.[16] Regarding energy policy, potential users may include many federal and state agencies, local governments, Indians, regional organizations, industries, and a variety of public interest groups.

Despite many policymakers' desire to have a "bottom line," no single measure or evaluation criterion can provide an adequate summary of the costs, risks, and benefits of alternative policies and implementation strategies. Multiple measures are required; the combination of measures and criteria to be used is determined both by what is being evaluated and by the interest and values at stake. Although economic measures and criteria are used most frequently, they are not always applicable and do not always provide an adequate basis for evaluation. For example, dollars are not an adequate measure of aesthetics, nor do they always provide the best indication of how equitably an alternative may distribute costs, risks, and benefits. And while it is possible to determine the dollar cost of environmental controls, the associated social costs often cannot be determined quantitatively. By themselves, economic measures and criteria can be used to evaluate only one component of overall costs, risks, and benefits.

Interaction of Technical and Policy Analysis

Although the above abbreviated description of technical and policy analyses may make it appear that the two are performed in sequence, they actually overlap and are mutually informing. For example, initial decisions concerning which technical analyses to undertake are informed by a preliminary policy analysis which identifies what problems and issues policymakers are likely to have to deal with; and the later, more detailed policy analyses will almost certainly raise questions that will necessitate additional technical analyses. Over the duration of a TA, emphasis shifts from technical to policy analyses. But technical analyses uninformed by the results of policy analysis are likely to be wasteful and inadequate to inform the final policy analyses; and policy analyses uninformed by the results of technical analysis do not provide a basis for well-informed policy making.

Properly performed, the TA process is iterative: the initial technical analyses are informed by preliminary policy analyses; the results of the technical analyses help to define the scope and focus of policy analyses; the policy analyses identify a need for additional technical analyses; and so on. There is constant interaction between the two kinds of analysis.

The Contribution of Technology Assessment to Energy Policy Making

The results of the technical and policy analyses described above will seldom (if ever) eliminate all the uncertainties associated with the development and deployment of energy technologies. However, these kinds of analyses can offer public and private policymakers a knowledge base for making better informed energy policies than would otherwise be possible. In part, this is because the policymaker will be better informed concerning the consequences of technological development. For example, the development of energy technologies in the West will result in impacts in several categories, including water availability and quality, air quality, social/economic/political, ecological, health, transportation, noise, and aesthetic impacts.[17]

Some of these impacts, such as the social and economic problems faced by local communities near energy facilities, can be anticipated independently of a TA. However, the results of a TA can better inform policymakers about how serious impacts, problems, and issues are likely to be, what groups will be most affected, and how long problems will last. Also TAs can identify impacts not generally anticipated in the policy system. For example, as shown in White,[18] urban population increases resulting from Western energy resource development will often produce more serious air quality problems than will the energy facilities themselves.

A TA can also contribute to better informed policy making by relating consequences to existing response mechanisms. Responses to some consequences may actually be impeded by existing mechanisms. For example, in the case of rapid population growth in small Western towns, air quality problems are largely attributable to mobile sources. This highlights a weakness in the current system of pollution control: state and local governments have very little control over mobile sources, yet these governments are responsible for meeting ambient air standards that can be violated largely as a consequence of increased automobile pollution produced by energy workers and their families. When response mechanisms are not so well developed, policymakers may have more flexibility and a greater opportunity to be innovative and creative.

The TA approach for applied energy policy analysis described above marries the incrementalists' emphasis on process and the systems analysis/operations research emphasis on outcomes.[19] This moves, or makes it possible to move, energy policy making beyond a pluralist/incrementalist accommodation of a broad range of interests and values. Given knowledge about likely outcomes, policymakers and stakeholders can assess alternatives and press for policies that also take outcomes into account.

Notes

1. Congress was becoming increasingly aware of the need to anticipate the broad range of consequences that would result from a decision to acquire and utilize knowledge. Historically, most decisions of this kind had been made on the basis of limited knowledge, which usually focused primarily on first-order costs. See U.S. Congress, House, Committee on Science and Astronautics, Subcommittee on Science, Research and Development, *Inquiries, Legislation, Policy Studies Re: Science and Technology; Review and Forecast,* 2d. Progress Report, Committee Print (Washington: Government Printing Office, 1966).

2. Committee on Public Engineering Policy, *A Study of Technology Assessment* (Washington: National Academy of Engineering, 1969); *Technology: Processes of Assessment and Choice* (Washington: National Academy of Sciences, 1969); and *A Technology Assessment Methodology,* 6 vols. (Washington: MITRE Corporation, 1971).

3. Technology Assessment Act of 1972, P.L. 92-484, 86 Stat. 797.

4. Don E. Kash and Irvin L. White et al., *Energy under the Oceans: A Technology Assessment of Outer Continental Shelf Oil and Gas Operations* (Norman: University of Oklahoma Press, 1973); *Technologies and Methods of Conserving Energy* (Vienna, Va.: Braddock, Dunn and McDonald, 1977); and *A Technology Assessment of the Transition to Advanced Automotive Propulsion Systems,* 3 vols. (Columbia, Md.: Hittman Associates, 1972).

5. Indeed, the growing government awareness of and interest in TA is reflected in the number of studies which have been undertaken or are being funded by federal agencies. See Vary T. Coates, *Technology and Public Policy: The Process of Technology Assessment in the Federal Government,* 2 vols. (Washington: George Washington University, Program in Science and Technology, 1972). Some of these assessments deal directly with energy issues and policy. For example, the Council on Environmental Quality funded an early study of North Sea oil and gas operations (Kash and White et al., *Energy under the Oceans*). In addition, the Office of Technology Assessment has pro-

duced a major TA report on solar energy (forthcoming) and one on offshore energy systems (1976) and is currently engaged in assessments of coal and slurry pipelines (1977). As noted, the Environmental Protection Agency is sponsoring assessments of energy resource development. See Irvin L. White et al. *Energy from the West: A Progress Report of a Technology Assessment of Western Energy Resource Development,* 3 vols. (Washington: Environmental Protection Agency, 1977); and *First Year Report* (draft), *An Integrated Technology Assessment of Electric Utility Energy Systems,* vol. 1: *The Assessment* (Berkeley, Calif.: Teknekron, Inc., n.d.). The TA work of the Energy Research and Development Administration is to be continued within the new Department of Energy. Of course, the performance and/or funding of TA is not limited to the federal government (that is, states, industry, and universities have performed and underwritten TAs); nor is the application of TA as a policy tool limited to the study of societal impacts of energy development. Assessments have been completed on other topics, including medical logistics, airport siting, recreational opportunities, aircraft noise and air pollution, and timber harvesting. For a survey of these and other TA applications, see *A Survey of Technology Assessment Today* (Washington: Peat, Marwick, Mitchell & Co., 1972); *A Comparative State-of-the-Art Review of Selected U.S. Technology Assessment Studies* (Washington: MITRE Corporation, 1973); Willis W. Harmon and Joe E. Armstrong, *Study Strategies for Technology Assessment,* Draft of final report, National Science Foundation Contract 75-22788 (Stanford: Stanford University, Department of Engineering Economic Systems, 1977); and Martin V. Jones and Richard M. Jones, *Twenty-five National Science Foundation Technology Assessment Studies: An Analytical Bibliography* (Rockville, Md.: Impact Assessment Institute, 1977).

6. Inherently TA is an interdisciplinary activity and belongs to the policy sciences class of applied policy studies. No single discipline such as political science, public administration, or economics provides an adequate knowledge or methodological basis for performing a meaningful TA. On the inherently interdisciplinary character of TA, see Irvin L. White, "Interdisciplinarity," in *Perspectives on Technology Assessment,* eds. Sherry R. Arnstein and Alexander N. Christakis (Jerusalem: Science and Technology Publishers, 1975), pp. 87–96.

7. These two labels are not altogether satisfactory since both kinds of analysis are a part of policy analysis. The analyses labeled *policy* in this section are those which emphasize the political aspects of the overall applied policy analysis.

8. Although the technical analyses required in an energy resource development study are focused amost exclusively on engineering studies and impacts, technical analysis need not be so limited. Technical analysis can include the use of both quantitative and qualitative tools. These tools are generally useful in policy analysis only to the extent that policy objectives can be precisely defined,

relevant variables identified, quantified, or described, and alternatives comprehensively identified, evaluated, and compared.

9. For a more detailed description of this TA conceptual framework and the kinds of technical analyses that are appropriate in a TA of energy resource development, see Irvin L. White et al., *First Year Work Plan for a Technology Assessment of Western Energy Resource Development* (Washington: Environmental Protection Agency, 1976).

10. For example, see E.J. Meltsner, "Political Feasibility and Policy Analysis," *Public Administration Review,* November /December 1972, pp. 859-867; and Carol H. Weiss, "Where Politics and Evaluation Research Meet," *Evaluation* 1973, pp. 37-45.

11. The terms *problem* and *issue* are not synonymous. The key distinction is that issue denotes conflict whereas problem does not.

12. An issue system may focus on a single issue such as what the ambient concentration standard for sulfur dioxide should be or a category of problems and issues such as air quality. See Irvin L. White, "Policy Analysis and International Law: Interdisciplinary Research in Law of the Sea," Paper presented at the annual meeting of the International Studies Association, New York, N.Y., March 14-17, 1973.

13. Not all the items listed here apply to all problems and issues. Which ones do apply is determined by the stage of development of the problem or issue. Some will be "well developed," in which case most of these items will apply. Others will be emerging or not yet anticipated independently of the technology assessment, and few if any of the listed items will apply.

14. The identification and comparative assessment of alternatives are a critical component of applied policy analyses, as distinguished from policy analysis which attempts to understand causes and consequences of particular policies. Elaboration of the analysis of alternatives in applied policy analysis is discussed in Yehezkel Dror, *Design for the Policy Sciences* (New York: American Elsevier, 1971); and Jacob B. Ukeles, "Policy Analysis: Myth or Reality?" *Public Administration Review,* May/June 1977, pp. 223-228.

15. Policy analysts have increasingly turned their attention to problems concerning the application or implementation of public policies. See Jeffrey L. Pressman and Aaron B. Wildavsky, *Implementation* (Berkeley: University of California Press, 1973); and Walter Williams and Richard F. Elmore, (eds.), *Social Program Implementation* (New York: Academic Press, 1976). On the specific point that implementation is a feasibility constraint in translating policy into performance, see Donald S. VanMeter and Carl E. Van Horn, "Policy Implementation Process: A Conceptual Framework," *Administration and Society,* February 1975, pp. 445-488. On approaches to implementation, see Peter House and David Jones, Jr., *Getting It Off the Shelf: A Method for Implementing Federal Research* (Boulder, Colo.: Westview Press, 1977).

16. Irvin L. White et al. *Work Plan for Completing a Technology Assessment of Western Energy Resource Development* (Washington: Environmental Protection Agency, forthcoming).

17. Elaboration of these consequences and the policy problems and issues arising as a result can be found in White et al., *Energy from the West.*

18. White, ibid.

19. Allen Schick, "Systems Politics and Systems Budgeting," *Public Administration Review,* March/April 1969, pp. 137-151.

10 Toward an Alternative Energy Future

Gregory A. Daneke

Introduction

As Lovins suggests, the United States, and the world for that matter, stands at the energy crossroads. A decision must be made relatively soon about whether to pursue the "hard path" (centralized, high technology, capital-intensive, heavily nuclear) or the "soft path" (decentralized, diversified, low technology, primarily solar).[1] The decision, unfortunately, is not as simple or clear as Lovins' dichotomy and subsequent analysis imply. A vast structure of artificial incentive has paved and lighted the hard path, while an intricate web of constraints has obscured the soft path. In other words, previous political and economic machinations make the formulation of alternative energy futures tenuous at best. Reinstating some sort of market in which energy options could compete on an economic basis is nearly impossible. Even if it were within the realm of political probability to place the various energy alternatives on equal footing, the Gordian knot of subsidies, tax breaks, and research funding is so difficult to unravel that, one would be at a loss as to where to begin. Nevertheless, an alternative energy future (basically solar) is not without hope. The hard alternative is faltering under the weight of an ailing nuclear industry, and soft systems (basically solar) are taking off despite institutional discouragements. The tiny David may eventually topple the mammoth Goliath, given the following scenario:

1. Advantages provided to the nuclear industry are either reduced or maintained at existing levels.
2. A reasonable level of conservation reduces the growth in energy demand to 3 or 4 percent.
3. Legal and institutional constraints on solar development are relaxed.

In order to build a case for just such a set of policy alternatives, this chapter explores briefly the relative economics of nuclear and solar energy and outlines the various types of incentives and disincentives associated with these energy resources. Oil and coal are conspicuously excluded from this analysis because,

---

*The author would like to acknowledge the helpful comments of Jack Salmon, Professor of Political Science, Virginia Polytechnic Institute.

generally speaking, both the hard and soft paths rely on certain levels of usage for these conventional fossil fuels (along with other resources such as geothermal and hydroelectric). Moreover, the most direct way to visualize the continuum of alternative energy futures is through the bipolarity of nuclear and solar.

The Changing Economies of Nuclear Development

To begin, whether or not one perceives the nuclear industry as safe, a vast array of fairly substantial uncertainty costs attend continued nuclear development. As resource economist Kneese suggests, an adequate cost-benefit analysis of nuclear development is rendered impossible by the fact that these uncertainties are difficult to calculate and involve moral dilemmas involving burdens on future generations.[2] However, gradually more information is being compiled regarding existing and potential risks, and irrespective of exact measurement these risks cannot easily be ignored. Generically these risks include:

1. Nuclear accidents brought on by operational defects, human error, and/or sabotage[3]
2. Existing health hazards from normal operations[4]
3. Disposal of high-level nuclear wastes and the eventual decommissioning of the installations themselves[5]

These uncertainties or potential costs take on added significance if one forecasts the economic impacts of a debilitating accident or health threat at a time when the United States is largely dependent on nuclear power (the Ford administration wanted 80 percent dependency by the year 2000). There are, of course, the added risks of proliferation of nuclear weapons as a result of continued international nuclear development (the enriched fuels used in reactors, the artificial element plutonium produced by neutron bombardment in a reactor, or the wastes from a nuclear plant can be used to produce nuclear weapons).

Nevertheless, even if we assume for the moment that these eventualities are highly improbable and that nuclear energy is relatively, if not absolutely, safe (the assumption being made by the nuclear industry), it still remains a highly tenuous economic proposition at best. Like many industries, the nuclear industry has suffered rapidly rising capital costs which entail labor, materials (excluding fuels), construction, and the interest on building loans. In the early 1960s these costs were relatively low, for the nation generally was in a boom period. The capital costs computed in dollars per kilowatt were about $135 in 1960—comparatively cheaper than the cost of coal-fired plants.[6] While the industry predicted slight cost increases to $200 per kilowatt, the actual increase was to $500 per kilowatt during the next ten years. At present, the cost of building a nuclear plant is increasing about 15 percent per year. Therefore, a plant ordered now for completion in 1988 will cost over $1,200 per kilowatt. Roe and Young explained that cost overruns resulted from the following factors:

1. The allowance for inflation has been too low.
2. The stretching out of construction schedules led to higher costs for interest during construction.
3. Most of the schedule stretchout before 1971 occurred after construction had begun.
4. Field labor or construction costs were adversely affected by extended construction time as well as increases in the scope of the work.
5. Additional safety measures, unanticipated regulatory proceedings, additional environmental tests, and increases in equipment prices all contributed to cost increases.[8]

These authors fail to mention that the nuclear industry has also been hampered by its own ineptitude. A study by the Federal Power Commission pointed to over forty-five instances in which managerial problems accounted for construction delays.[9]

Rising fuel costs also plague the nuclear industry. The industry began with the assumption that uranium was an abundant, and thus cheap, fuel source. Uranium is actually quite scarce, constituting about 2 parts per million of the earth's crust. If one could mine all this uranium, only a small fraction would be the much sought after U-235. While the United States has a relatively large supply of uranium, its price, like that of everything else, is soaring. Uranium prices were fairly stable until 1973, at about $6 to $8 per pound, but by 1978 they were up to $45 per pound. Sources predict that by 1985 the price could be over $300 per pound.[10]

In addition to costing more, nuclear plants have delivered less than initial estimates. Atomic Energy Commission (AEC) cost-benefit assessments relied on an 80 percent efficiency figure (that is, that plants would operate at 80 per cent of their maximum capacity). In reality, plants have achieved little more than 50 percent efficiency; and as Comey points out, nuclear plants become less efficient with age. After seven years of operation, the combined impact of corrosion, aging components, fuel leaks, and the pile-up of radioactive "crud" reduces efficiency to about 40 percent.[11] Moreover, the larger plants (1,000+ megawatts) presently being built operate at considerably less overall efficiency (45 to 50 percent) than the older installations.[12]

Apocalytic Politics

The apparent resiliency of the nuclear alternative does not stem from its once-promised economic competitiveness. The myth of energy "too cheap to meter" has faded. Nuclear energy remains viable as a result of geometric growth forecasts and policies and an elaborate set of political advantages. Unlike most regulatory experiences which gradually evolve into clientele relationships, since its inception the nuclear industry has been a subtly veiled government enterprise. Beginning in 1954, commercial nuclear power was initiated through the AEC's various promotional activities. The AEC's mission of "promoting the peaceful use of the atom" was basically a manifestation of the United States' guilt complex at being the first to develop and use the bomb. Early attempts by the AEC to give away technological know-how produced few private investments. Thus, in 1955, under pressure from Congress, the AEC launched its "power reactoi demonstration program," which provided construction subsidies and five years of free fuel. Despite these inducements, many corporations were reluctant to enter the nuclear business because of the insurance problem. The AEC's *Brookhaven Report* (1957) (calculated on much smaller reactors than presently in service, located at least 30 miles from a major city) estimated maximum possible property damage in a nuclear accident at $7 billion. In response, the Joint Committee on Atomic Energy (JCAE) introduced the Price-Anderson legislation (P.L. 88-703) which limited the aggregate liability for a single nuclear accident to $500 million. Also, the industry established a self-imposed $60 million insurance pool. Total liability has subsequently been fixed at $0.5 billion.

Price-Anderson gives a necessary but not quite sufficient condition to sustain the industry. Even after Admiral Rickover's creation of the "nuclear navy" provided the major vendors with design and manufacturing experience, more government funding was required to stimulate the needed technological development.[13] Thus, over the years most of the research and development relevant to commercial nuclear power has been federally funded. The Energy Research and Development Administration (ERDA) figures point up the fact that $7 billion had been spent on directly applied research as of 1976.[14] These figures do not include basic physical research nor related military research. They also neglect government-provided enrichment and waste disposal programs.

In addition to generous research funding, the nuclear industry, like most other major industries, has received a good deal of direct and indirect government support. The less apparent forms of federal aid are injected at several strategic junctures in the nuclear fuel cycle. To begin, uranium mining receives a mineral depletion allowance of 22 percent (coal's allowance is less than 10 percent, and oil's was dropped). According to the Ford Foundation project, this allowance saved the uranium industry $15 million in 1974.

Once the uranium is taken out of the ground, the government takes over the enrichment process which makes it suitable for use in the standard light-water reactor (LWR). All enrichment plants prior to 1955 were considered a defense expense. In recent years, ERDA has taken over the enrichment program and passed on a portion of the cost to the nuclear industry and ultimately to consumers. But a portion, about half, has remained tax-supported. Moreover, ERDA has provided the enrichment service at "bargain basement" prices. On occasion ERDA has agreed to allow the industry to forego penalties on canceled enrichment contracts during production cutbacks. These programs, appropriately entitled "open season," saved the industry several hundred million dollars.[15]

The nuclear industry has also enjoyed the benefits of a complex set of taxing policies. The present policy of "accelerated depreciation" will afford the industry an $18 billion tax break by 1985. Furthermore, the process of "normalized accounting" used by the nuclear industry means that the tax is passed along to the customers which would have been paid had the industry not used accelerated depreciation. The industry receives an additional $18.5 billion in tax breaks as a result of the federal "investment tax credit."[16]

Beyond these various supports, the nuclear industry probably gains additional advantages from its close relationship with governmental activity. This relationship has afforded a good deal of lateral mobility for industry employees. Even after the breaking up of the schizophrenic functions of the AEC [regulatory to the Nuclear Regulatory Commission (NRC) and promotional to ERDA], the problem of mixed loyalties seems to have continued.[17] A study by Common Cause highlighted the following potential problems:

1. Of the top 139 employees of ERDA, 52.5 percent (or 73) used to work for private enterprises in the energy field, and 75 percent of these 73 employees came from ERDA contractors.
2. Of the top 429 employees of the NRC, 72 percent (or 307) have been employed by private energy enterprises, and 90 percent (279) of these 307 employees came from enterprises holding NRC licenses or contracts. Common Cause research also showed that 192 of these 279 employees came from firms that, in addition to having dealings with NRC, also had contracts with ERDA.
3. Of NRC's 162 consultants 65 percent are presently working for both the NRC and private enterprises that are recipients of NRC licenses or contracts.[18]

These incestuous relationships are, of course, a regular part of business ethics in the United States and elsewhere. Yet the nuclear business has always had a certain preferred status. Whether or not this preferred status continues may well dictate the nation's energy future.

Solar Energy: The Forgotten Alternative

Solar energy is not a new idea. Nearly every ancient civilization used solar energy widely. Legend suggests that the Greek mathematician Archimedes used solar energy to set fire to the Roman fleet in 212 B.C. In the 18th century the French chemist Lavoisier developed a "solar concentrator" which produced temperatures of 3,000+ degrees. Until the 20th century passive solar design was a fine art in nearly every civilization. Remnants on the North American continent include the Pueblo Indian dwellings and the New England "salt box." Solar production plants were being built in the United States at the turn of the century; one such plant was built near Phoenix, Arizona, in 1904. Residential solar thermal units found widespread use in Florida and California in the 1930s. And, of course, wind systems (another form of solar energy) were a common feature in the rural United States until recently. With the coming of the nuclear age in the 1950s, solar energy was virtually abandoned, with the exception of photovoltaics (silicon cells) for the space program.

The primary arguments against solar usage are economic; however, such arguments are made within the context of the highly manipulated energy marketplace. Even given the biased structure of incentives, solar energy for heating and cooling is becoming highly cost-effective, and solar electric generation (from wind, solar thermal, and photovoltaics) is not very far behind.[19] Nevertheless, until very recently government and industry sources were placing solar development as far away as the year 2000, and solar potential is still grossly underestimated. For example, President Carter's energy plan suggested 2.5 million solar heaters by 1985; Energy Secretary Schlesinger subsequently cut this estimate to 1.3 million. However, Wilson Clark, Energy Advisor to the state of California, contends that California alone will surpass federal estimates.[20] The Solar Energy Industry Association (representing major manufacturers) suggests a conservative estimate of 11 million units by 1985.[21] With mass production and active government support, these figures, of course, might easily be surpassed.

However, very early on, governmental support for solar energy was withheld, even after considerable interest in solar energy was generated during the early 1950s. The well-known Paley Commission report (presented during the Truman administration) predicted that solar energy would play a major role in the nation's energy development by 1975.[22] In 1959 an economic assessment conducted by the University of Maryland concluded that solar energy would be far more cost-effective than nuclear energy.[23] The Maryland study was met with open hostility by the then burgeoning Atomic Energy Commission. Consultants who had worked on and approved the results of the study were so intimidated that few would allow their names to be placed on the final report.[24] Blatant discrimination against solar energy alternatives continued through the 1960s. In 1972 the federal government was spending only $2 million on all solar-related research. By 1977 spending rose to $290 million, still relatively small when compared to the billions spent on nuclear research. Moreover, much of this funding goes to fairly exotic, and perhaps unrealistic, systems such as space platforms. As Nadler suggests, federal research tends to focus on macro-level applications rather than on the pragmatic problems of community-level planning.[25]

Solar energy presently finds its most practical use in direct solar and solar thermal heating for residential and small to medium-size commercial structures. Yet, solar thermal electric generation and photovoltaic conversion are certainly viable alternatives for the future. A recent study supported by the United Nations concluded that energy from photovoltaic cells could be produced more cheaply than nuclear energy after an initial investment of $1 billion (the cost of one nuclear plant).[26] The U.S. Office of Technology Assessment (OTA) contends that total solar systems (including solar electricity) may be cost-competitive by 1985.[27]

The OTA study also illuminated a number of policy impediments which currently constrain the solar industry. These include:

1. A federal research focus on centralized solar energy rather than the more practical decentralized alternatives
2. A false price structure with regard to competitive fuel sources
3. Insufficient tax incentives to encourage individual solar investments
4. Legal and regulatory conditions which discourage individual solar investments[28]

An inquiry conducted by the Florida Solar-Energy Center into state institutional arrangements magnifies OTA's findings. Essentially the Florida study points out that in those states which have tax incentives, the rate is so miniscule that it merely serves to reduce the penalty rather than encourgae solar investments. Moreover, most tax breaks are granted to individual homeowners only, and not to developers and contractors who intend resale. Thus, existing tax incentives are unlikely to stimulate large-scale solar investments. The report also noted other problems:

1. A general lack of public information regarding solar energy
2. A lack of quality and performance standards for solar units
3. Discriminatory electrical rates for solar homeowners[29]

Generally speaking, the United States has a set of institutional arrangements designed to buttress existing energy systems. The return of an ancient energy alternative raises many new legal and political questions. The Environmental Law Institute addressed some of these questions associated with solar development and constructed the following list of unresolved issues:[30]

1. *Solar access,* or "sun rights" (for example, codes which would prevent the building of units that would shade existing collectors)
2. *Existing building codes* (for example, limits on types of structures, citing requirements, and hot-water levels)

3. *Loan and financing* problems with regard to solar construction and improvements
4. *ERDA patent policies* which prohibit solar innovations under research contract
5. *Antitrust* issues involving existing utilities and their involvement in solar energy
6. *Labor union* resistance to solar standards (for example, plumbers)
7. *Insurance, liability,* and *warranties* involving solar units

Until these issues are resolved, the solar industry will move forward cautiously and under a cloud of uncertainty. Ultimately, however, the pure force of economic logic is likely to prevail even in an environment of hostile institutional arrangements. Yet, whether this evolution will occur soon enough to save the United States from the economic and social disorder which will accompany the impending energy crunch is highly problematic.

Conclusions: Changing the Energy Policy Picture

Following the above discussion, the question of how, if at all, solar energy can assert istself as a policy priority looms large. In the aftermath of the various nuclear initiatives, it would seem that the new unholy alliance between the existing energy industries and labor has the upper hand. Yet, an optimistic appraisal would follow the admonition of Abe Lincoln: "You can fool some of the people some of the time, but you can't fool all of the people all of the time." Thus, a very rudimentary strategy is to provide more and more information regarding the major myths of the centralized energy economy, that is, that growth in energy consumption and continued nuclear development are vital to economic well-being. In actuality, conservation (not sacrifice but merely elimination of waste) and solar energy develpment would provide more jobs and more general economic well-being.[31] European countries duplicate and/or excel the U.S. standard of living while using less than half, and in some cases one-third, the energy. Under a reasonable growth scenario (such as the Ford Foundation model of 2 or 3 percent) nuclear development would be unnecessary, and the general state of the economy would be boosted. Using a lower growth equation, an Oak Ridge study concluded that the economic impacts of a nuclear moratorium would be minimal.[32] Moreover, coupled with conservation, solar energy could reduce strains on remaining fossil fuels. This economic rationality may make inroads on prevailing labor/business coalitions. Initially, new labor movements might be created within the solar sector drawing support from plumbers, steamfitters, and solar architects and builders. As conservation strategies such as industrial cogeneration (where industries generate their own electricity and utilize the waste heat) take hold, broader coalitions of decentralized interest may be possible.

For the time being, Gerald Ford's plan for a multibillion-dollar "plutonium breeder fuel cycle bailout"[33] of the nuclear industry has been placed on the back burner by the Carter administration. But, Congress as well as elements of the Carter camp still strongly promotes the industry, and this back burner may be heating up.[34] Therefore, the short-range strategy of solar advocates should be to maintain the current atmosphere of benign neglect, instead of seeking immediate regulatory support for decentralized systems. Solar advocates should avoid being co-opted by a small piece of the regulatory pie, while nuclear development continues to get the whipped cream. In essence, by preventing the nuclear industry from gaining further advantages, the cause of solar energy is strengthened. In this regard, solar interests should continue to rally the support of a variety of liberal thinkers who see in the highly risky nuclear alternative the potential for police-state security measures because, it is claimed, of the necessity to control the larger amounts of fissionable material in an expanding nuclear economy. In the meantime, solar research should explore a number of social and design science questions regarding the interface between community development and alternative energy systems.

In the final analysis, ecologists have argued for some time that people will eventually and inexorably adapt to a new set of decentralized and diversified energy systems.[35] Whether this transition takes place before or after the destruction of existing economic and environmental conditions is the critical question.

Notes

1. Amory Lovins, "Energy Strategy: The Road Not Taken?" *Foreign Affairs,* October 1976, pp. 65–96.

2. Allen V. Kneese, "Benefit-Cost Analysis and Unscheduled Events in the Nuclear Fuel Cycle," Mimeo, Washington, D.C.: Resources for the Future, 1973.

3. Operational and fuel cycle safety has been an issue of considerable debate in the scientific community, particularly since William Ergen demonstrated that emergency core cooling systems would not work. See Ergen et al., *Emergency Core Cooling* (Oak Ridge, Tenn.: Oak Ridge Laboratory, 1967); also note Daniel Ford, " A Re-evaluation of Reactor Safety," in Barry Commoner et al., *Energy and Human Welfare,* vol. 1, (New York: Macmillan, 1975). The industry, however, relies on the safety assessment provided in the much touted Rasmussen Report. Yet, Rasmussen fails to consider human error and/or the possibility of sabotage. Norman Rasmussen et al., *Reactor Safety Study: An Assessment of Accident Risks in U.S. Commercial Nuclear Power Plants* (Washington: Nuclear Regulatory Commission, 1974). Draft WASH-1400.

4. Note the assessment of health hazards by medical researchers Gofman and Tamplin in *Poisoned Power* (Emmaus, Pa.: Rodale Press, 1971); also note Donald P. Geesman, "Plutonium and Public Health," in Commoner et al., *Energy and Human Welfare,* vol. 1 (New York: Macmillan, 1975), pp. 167–178; and Thomas Mancuso, "Preliminary Report: Hanford Radiation Study," Testimony before the House Committee on Health and the Environment, January 24, 1978.

5. William W. Hambleton, "Storage of High Level Radioactive Wastes," in Commoner et al., *Energy and Human Welfare,* pp. 158–166. For a more optimistic and yet uncertainty-ridden appraisal, see Arthur S. Kubo and David J. Rose, "Disposal of Nuclear Wastes," *Science,* December 21, 1973, pp. 1205–11; also note Gene I. Rochlin, "Nuclear Waste Disposal: Two Social Criteria," *Science,* January 7, 1976, pp. 24–29.

6. George L. Weil, *Nuclear Energy* (Washington: George Weil, 1972); also note Federal Power Commission, *National Power Survey* (Washington: FPC, 1974), pp. 79–80.

7. Ron Lanore, *Nuclear Plants: The More They Build, The More You Pay* (Washington: The Center for Responsive Law, 1976), p. 60.

8. Cited in Edward Berlin et al., *Perspectives on Power* (Cambridge, Mass.: Ballinger, 1974), p. 5.

9. Michael Rieber and Ronald Halcrow, *Nuclear Power to 1985: Possible vs. Optimistic Scenarios* (Urbana, Ill.: Center for Advanced Computation, 1974), p. 3.

10. Lanore, *Nuclear Plants,* p. 44.

11. David Comey, "Nuclear Power Plant Reliability," *Not Man Apart,* April 1975, pp. 12–13.

12. Wilson Clark, *Energy for Survival* (New York: Anchor, 1975), p. 289.

13. John Hogerton, "The Arrival of Nuclear Power," *Scientific American,* February 1968, pp. 21–31.

14. Jim Harding, "President Ford's Energy Menu," *Not Man Apart,* March 1976, p. 8.

15. Robert McCoy, *Commercial Nuclear Power and Uranium,* November 1975, p. 16.

16. Philip Caeser et al., *Investment Planning in the Energy Sector* (Berkeley, Calif.: The Lawrence Laboratory, 1976).

17. John Abbotts, *The NRC's Promotional Activities* (Washington: Public Interest Research Group, 1976).

18. Andrew Kneier et al., *Serving Two Masters: A Study of Conflicts of Interest in the Executive Branch* (Washington: Common Cause, 1976), p. ii.

19. Office of Technology Assessment, *Application of Solar Technology to Today's Energy Needs* (Washington: OTA, 1977).

20. Cited in Dennis Hayes, "We Can Use Solar Energy Now," *The Washington Post,* February 26, 1978, p. D1.

21. Ibid.

22. The Paley Commission, "The Promise of Technology," 5, *Resources for Freedom* (Washington, D.C.: Government Printing Office, 1952).

23. Bureau of Business and Economic Research, "Solar and Atomic Energy —A Survey" (College Park, Md.: University of Maryland, 1959).

24. Cited in Clark, *Energy for Survival* p. 381.

25. Arnold Nadler, "Planning Aspects of Direct Solar Energy Generation," *Journal of the American Institute of Planners,* October 1977, p. 339.

26. Robert H. Murray and Paul A. LaVolette, "Assessing the Solar Transition," in *Goals in a Global Community,* ed. Irving Laslow (Elmsford, N.Y.: Pergamon Press, 1977).

27. OTA, *Application of Solar Technology,* p. I-2.

28. Ibid.

29. Florida Solar Energy Center, *Solar Energy Commercialization at the State Level* (Cape Canaveral: Florida State Energy Commission, 1977).

30. Environmental Law Institute, *Legal Barriers to Solar Heating and Cooling of Buildings* (Washington: Environmental Law Institute, 1976).

31. Dennis Hayes, "Post-Petroleum Prosperity," and Joel Darmstadter, "Energy Conservation and Economic Well-Being," Papers presented at the Symposium on Economic Growth and Energy Conservation, Conference of the American Association for the Advancement of Science, Washington, 1978.

32. Oak Ridge Associated Universities, *Economic and Environmental Impacts of a U.S. Nuclear Moratorium, 1985-2010* (Oak Ridge, Tenn.: OAV, Institute of Energy Analysis, 1976).

33. John Abbotts, "The Fuel Cycle Bail-Out: ERDA's Plutonium Pork Barrel" (Washington: Public Interest Research Group, 1976). For a discussion of breeder economics, see Brian G. Chow, *The Liquid Metal Fast Breeder Reactor: An Economic Analysis* (Washington: American Enterprise Institute, 1975), p. 18; and Brian G. Chow, "The Economic Issues of the Fast Breeder Reactor Program," *Science,* February 11, 1977, pp. 551-556. Also note General Accounting Office, *The LMFR Program—Past, Present and Future* (Washington: Government Printing Office, 1975).

34. The Carter administration has already been turned around on issues of nuclear exports. See "The Turnabout on Nuclear Policy," *Wall Street Journal,* October 19, 1977.

35. Howard and Elizabeth Odum, *Energy Basis for Man and Nature* (New York: McGraw-Hill, 1976).

11

Energy Policy and Changing Public-Private Relations

Mary R. Hamilton

Introduction

The Importance of Energy in Public Policy Today

Energy is now a highly visible, high-priority area of public policy. As such, it is considered too important to be left entirely to the private sector. As a result, current energy policy prescribes a substantially increased role for government in all aspects of energy policy formulation and implementation.

Before 1973 energy was primarily a private sector concern. The majority of energy projects—whether the exploration and production of energy resources (for example, oil, natural gas, coal) or research and development (R&D)—were initiated and implemented by industry. Government's role as primarily reactive and small-scale, limited to regulating natural monopolies,[1] granting and withholding approval of industry-initiated projects, and funding R&D. The principal exception to this limited government role was the development of nuclear power.

The new public policy emphasis on energy, and the resulting escalation of the government role, has drastically revised relations between the public and private sectors in the energy policy arena. Government is now taking the lead in energy by initiating energy projects and programs that will achieve national energy policy objectives. These objectives, as outlined in *The National Energy Plan*,[2] are (1) in the short term to increase the use of abundant domestic energy resources (for example, coal) in order to moderate the use of scarce, nonrenewable resources (for example, oil) and (2) in the long term to reduce reliance on nonrenewable resources by vigorous expansion of the use of renewable and essentially inexhaustible sources of energy.[3] In order to achieve these objectives, government must enlist substantial support and cooperation from the private sector. At the same time, government must ensure the achievement of private sector goals. This is not a new or unique situation for government, but it is a situation that is new to the energy policy arena.

The Problem

The problem addressed in this chapter is that, given the changes that have occurred relatively recently in energy, neither government nor the private sector has any obviously relevant experience with the role and relationships required to achieve energy policy objectives. Yet the achievement of these objectives depends on the ability of the two sectors to define new roles and relationships that will result in effective cooperation and coordination.

The purpose of this chapter is to determine the changes in public-private relations that are required to achieve energy policy objectives and to examine those changes which have already occurred. To do this, the discussion will focus on one broad facet of joint public-private activity in energy policy—the development and commercialization of new energy technologies, such as solar technologies, which are intended to reduce reliance on nonrenewable resources.

The Example of Commercialization

Commercialization is the current catchword for the process of moving a technology from a status of technical feasibility to a status of acceptance by the marketplace and widespread utilization.[4] In the past, for almost all tasks, this process has been clearly the province of the private sector with government occasionally providing incentives and/or information.

In the wake of the energy crisis, the situation was redefined. Government is now initiating programs to accelerate the development and commercialization of new energy technologies. Government has decided that it is in the national interest to move promising new energy technologies into the marketplace as quickly as possible, and that government must intervene when industry is not developing those technologies at the desired rate. Because most of the promising and "socially profitable" (in terms of reducing reliance on nonrenewable resources and/or providing energy from environmentally acceptable sources) new energy technologies (for example, solar, fuel cells) are not at a stage where industry is willing to invest in the technology and market development required to achieve commercialization, government has acquired a substantial responsibility for commercialization, if government objectives are to be achieved. To perform this task successfully, government must have effective coordination and cooperation with the private sector. Such coordination and cooperation will require the development of a new set of public-private sector roles and relationships.

Organization of the Chapter

With the focus on development and commercialization of new energy technologies, the remainder of this chapter is organized around the following questions: (1) What previous experience has shaped existing public-private roles and relations in the energy policy arena? (2) How do the requirements of the present situation differ from those of previous public-private situations? (3) What kinds of roles and relationships will produce effective coordination and cooperation in the current situation? (4) What is required to develop the new public-private roles and relationships necessary to achieve new energy policy objectives? (5) What additional research and analyses are needed to provide the understanding necessary to make changes and achieve effective public-private sector coordination and cooperation?

Analysis of Previous Experience

Previous experience with joint public-private sector activities for the development and implementation of new technologies includes government funding of private sector R&D for space, national security, and nuclear power purposes; government technology transfer programs; government actions to influence technological innovation by the private sector; and government–private sector cooperation to develop nuclear power.

R&D for Space and National Security Purposes

Where government has sponsored R&D for space and national security purposes, government has been the client for the new technologies developed by the private sector. As the client, government determined the criteria for judging a new technology acceptable. However, the criteria by which those same technologies were considered adaptable for commercial use and judged to be commercially desirable and acceptable were established by the private sector, not the government.

Because of the space and national security emphasis of most government R&D in the past and because of the associated patterns of secrecy, government-sponsored R&D has frequently been cut off from commercial application and implementation activities. Many of the companies heavily involved in these R&D activities have aerospace divisions that have minimal interaction with the company's commercial divisions.[5] In addition, the concerns of government-sponsored R&D have reflected the position of the government as client and end user by emphasizing results that support federal agency missions and thereby neglecting emphasis on commercial market implementation of new technologies. On the other hand, R&D sponsored by the private sector has been, and continues to be, driven by concerns about commercial market implementation of the results of the R&D.

Technology Transfer

Government has been involved since the early 1960s in technology transfer (one notable experience has been with the National Aeronautics and Space Adminis-

tration's Technology Utilization Office), with the purpose of facilitating utilization by the private sector of technologies and capabilities developed in
government R&D for government missions. Federal agencies developed technology transfer programs in order to try to alleviate the problems of availablity
and ease of access of federal R&D results.[6]

Some evaluations of the technology transfer experience indicated that these
programs expended too much of their resources on information dissemination
by means of written reports and too little on dissemination through personal
contact. In an M.I.T. study of the role of federal agencies in technology transfer,
Doctors concludes that "most of the money is spent on routine library functions
. . . little or no personalized transfer is funded."[7] Doctors also laments the
apparent limited mobility of R&D personnel from one sector to the other.[8]

Evaluators of technology transfer programs also concluded that those programs were hindered by a confusion about the proper roles of the public and
private sectors in bringing about secondary applications of technology generated
by public funds.[9] This confusion appeared to be greatest in areas such as technology transfer where responsibility for achieving stated objectives is shared by
the two sectors.[10]

Government Influence on Industry Innovation

Where government has actively sought to stimulate technological innovation in
private industry, the goal usually has been to promote the growth and maintenance of a healthy economy. Government has used a variety of mechanisms to
influence technological innovation in the private sector. Among them are federal
contracts and grants for R&D activities in the private sector, technical information services, education and training support for scientists and engineers, tax incentives, and the patent system.

Other public policies have had decisive, if inadvertent, effects on private
sector innovation: federal regulation, economic and monetary policies, and tax
policies not directly related to R&D. The influence of these policies on private
sector decisions about technological innovation is acknowledged but not well
understood.[11] Policy making in the whole area of technical advance appears to
have suffered from an inability to delineate the proper roles of the public and
private sectors and from a "lack of agreement on criteria for determining when
government programs are justified."[12]

Government–Private Sector Cooperation
to Develop Nuclear Power

The joint venture between government and the private sector to develop nuclear
power provides some experience that is relevant to joint commercialization

efforts. In the nuclear experience, the Atomic Energy Commission (AEC) contracted with a limited number of private organizations[13] to operate its R&D laboratories. At the outset the AEC was charged with controlling the production and use of atomic power in the United States. This mandate encompassed both military and civilian uses and required exceptional secrecy and tight government controls. The aid of the private sector was enlisted to provide managerial and technical expertise, but government assumed all the costs and risks. An unclassified, civilian nuclear industry began to emerge in the 1950s, but to the present it continues to be heavily dependent on direct and indirect government subsidies and heavily regulated and controlled by government, and it is a far cry from a truly competitive industry.[14]

What Is Different Today?

The difference today in public-private sector relations is in the objectives to be achieved by the relationships and in the significantly escalated government role required by those objectives. It is no longer a matter of the government's funding private sector R&D to support the missions of government agencies. Nor is it merely a matter of stimulating private adoption of R&D results originally developed for government agencies under government funding.

It is now a matter of the government's determining which new energy technologies have sufficient potential to warrant taking whatever action is necessary to move them into the marketplace as quickly as possible. Government is no longer the ultimate client for the new technologies developed under government-sponsored R&D, nor is government assuming all the costs and risks. The ultimate clients today are all energy users, and the objective is to solve national energy problems. The private sector still determines the criteria for judging whether a new technology is commercially desirable or acceptable and, consequently, a candidate for private investment. (Criteria such as technical feasibility, economic competitiveness, and potential for market acceptance are commonly used by the private sector to make these judgments.) However, in the current energy policy context, if government determines that a new energy technology should be developed more quickly than the private sector is inclined to do, government may manipulate the criteria to reduce the risk and make the technology an attractive investment (say, by means of tax incentives, loan guarantees, and federal purchases).

In today's energy policy context, government is taking the lead in determining which technologies should be developed and what actions should be taken to effect development. These actions can range from the government's removing barriers to private sector development activities (minimal government involvement) to the government's designing the development and commercialization activities in detail and providing a broad program of incentives and sanctions that will stimulate private sector cooperation. The extent of government involvement and hence the appropriate federal role in the development and commercialization of new energy technologies are policy decisions that have yet to be made by the Department of Energy (DOE).

What Kind of Public-Private Sector Relationships Are Needed Today?

Because the achievement of the new energy policy objectives depends on the effective coordination and cooperation of the public and private sectors, new relationships between the sectors must be based firmly on mutual agreement and understanding of roles and objectives. Each sector must understand the effects of its actions on the other sector, and the effects of the other sector's actions on it. Both sectors must understand the objectives which they share and can therefore pursue jointly and the objectives that are specific to one sector but which must also be realized in the energy policy context. In addition, new relationships between the sectors must be based on a mutually agreed-upon ethic for cooperation that will address their established distrust of each other and minimize the negative effects of that distrust on cooperation.

Effective coordination and cooperation will also require clear definition of the roles, responsibilities, and expectations of each sector, and of the interrelationships of roles, responsibilities, and expectations. These definitions must be acceptable to both sectors and compatible with their mutual and individual objectives.[15]

It is now generally accepted in DOE that implementation and commercialization concerns must drive the overall R&D process. Therefore public-private relationships must be established that will effectively link the early R&D activities to the later development and commercialization procedures. To do this, government R&D must interact with relevant private R&D in the early stages of both. This will require frequent contact between technical personnel of the two sectors and a concerted effort to overcome the separation of government-sponsored R&D from private sector R&D. At the same time, care must be taken to maintain the separation between the two sectors so that government does not become an advocate of industry positions which are not in line with national energy policy objectives.

Effective linking of early R&D with development and commercialization will require that the separation of government-sponsored R&D from commercial application and implementation activities be overcome as well. This may require changes in the methods currently used by government to fund private R&D. Government may have to adopt a private sector perspective on R&D that views R&D outlays for technology development as a series of investments in options to continue to invest.[16] In a recent editorial in *Science,* Carey argues that the fiscal year 1979 R&D budget reflects this perspective and that if it proves to be a new approach to federally funded R&D, "new funding methods may need to be devised and tested as replacements for the 'procurement' approach in supporting R&D."[17] One change might be in the use of level of effort contracts aimed at producing viable products rather than final reports.[18]

What Needs to Be Done to Develop
New Public-Private Relationships?

Government must take the lead to enlist private sector support and cooperation in achieving new energy policy objectives and to develop the new relationships required. These relationships will differ from one energy policy situation to another, and consequently they must be developed or refined to meet the specific needs of a given situation. However, six steps may be employed across situations to arrive at the public-private sector roles and relationships most appropriate for a particular situation:

1. Define explicitly the energy policy objectives to be achieved by public-private coordination and cooperation.
2. Determine what will need to be done to achieve those objectives.
3. Estimate the cost of performing the required activities.
4. Assess the capability of government and the capability and motivation of the private sector to perform those activities.
5. Determine the appropriate roles and responsibilities of the public and private sectors in performing the required activities.
6. Develop a strategy that incorporates specific roles and responsibilities and that includes mechanisms for coordinating the activities of each sector.

The discussion that follows focuses on the application of these six steps to the commercialization of new energy technologies.

In the context of the commercialization of new energy technologies, the definition of energy policy objectives would be in terms of energy to be provided by the technology by specific dates. For example, the Energy Conservation and Production Act calls for the displacement of 1 million barrels of oil per day by 1985 from a combined total of all solar technologies.[19] In order for these six steps to culminate in a workable strategy to develop and commercialize a new energy technology, the policy objectives must be explicitly stated for each of several future dates (for example, displacement of x million barrels of oil per day by 1985, 1990, 1995, 2000).

For the second step, there would be a determination of what kind of industry would be required to achieve the energy-saving objectives (for example, business volume, production capacity, number and types of manufacturers, infrastructure) and what must be done to develop that kind of industry. The latter will involve development of production capacity, infrastructure, and markets, as well as a determination of when these would have to be developed and at what level if the energy-saving objectives are to be achieved.

Third, the costs of performing these activities within the specified time frames must be estimated. Costs would be defined broadly to include capital, labor, and material resources that would have to be expended to achieve the objectives.

The activity and cost estimates must then be compared with existing public and private capabilities. Assessment of capabilities to perform the required activities and absorb the associated costs would address such questions as, What is the current production expansion capacity of the industry within a specified time frame? What is the level of development of the industry infrastructure, and what is the potential for further development without any additional stimulation? What capabilities does government have to promote industry development (for example, procurement to stimulate expansion of production capacity and market development)?

In addition to determining private sector capabilities, private sector motivation must be assessed. The private sector is likely to have some of, if not all, the capabilities needed to achieve the objectives, but it might be unwilling to use them within the time frame judged desirable by the government. If this is the case, government must determine why the private sector is not motivated to move in the desired direction and with the preferred speed and what factors would have to be changed to interest them.

Based on the assessment of capabilities and motivations, government, in consultation with the private sector, must define the appropriate roles and responsibilities for each sector in the development and commercialization processes. Suggested guidelines for determining "appropriateness" of roles and responsibilities are that they make maximum use of the capabilities of each sector; facilitate effective cooperation and coordination between the sectors; provide the private sector with the incentives necessary to enlist their support; provide the means of achieving the energy policy objectives within the specified time frames; are acceptable to both sectors; facilitate the achievement of individual objectives; and minimize the costs to each sector.

Finally, the development of a commercialization strategy will be based on all the previous steps. The strategy will be designed to achieve the energy-saving objectives by performing the required activities with a combination of public and private sector efforts. The strategy will be composed of a set of actions and programs designed to achieve the objectives by providing adequate stimulation to secure industry support. These actions and programs must be based on what is known about the reasons for industry's reluctance to move in the desired direction, and they must take into account the cumulative effects of the total strategy on the private sector. These actions and programs may be tax incentives, loan guarantees, information or technical assistance programs, shifts in monetary or patent policy, or whatever is deemed necessary to get the private sector to cooperate toward achieving national energy policy objectives.

The Need for Further Research

At present there is little understanding of the nature and extent of the interrelationships between the public and private sectors and of how these interrelationships affect the achievement of national energy policy goals. In particular, our lack of knowledge about the process of technological innovation inhibits our ability to design effective mechanisms for public-private cooperation for the development and commercialization of new energy technologies.

Research to address these problems is suggested in the following areas:

1. The effects of government actions—both those that are intended to influence industry innovation and those that are not—on industry decisions concerning R&D and the adoption of technological innovations; especially government regulatory policies, tax policies, monetary policies, patent policies, and R&D policies
2. The effects on effective cooperation between the sectors of personal contacts and personnel mobility across sectors
3. The relationship between social structure and behavior patterns and the implications for relations between the sectors
4. Roles and relationships necessary for successful development and commercialization of new technologies
5. The institutional features and arrangements in energy industries and their influence on dissemination of technological innovations and commercialization of new energy technologies

Notes

1. *Natural monopolies* refer to those energy industries such as natural gas, conventional electricity, and nuclear power where competition would be uneconomical, so government intervenes to protect both the consumer and the industry. See D.H. Davis, *Energy Politics* (New York: St. Martin's Press, 1974), for an extensive discussion of the coal, oil, gas, electric, and nuclear industries.

2. Executive Office of the President, *The National Energy Plan* (Washington: Government Printing Office, April 29, 1977).

3. Ibid., pp. IX–XIV, 25–33.

4. *Commercialization* and *accelerated commercialization* were both defined in the context of contemporary energy policy in Hearings before the Subcommittee on the Department of the Interior and Related Agencies, Com-

mittee on Appropriations, House of Representatives, 95th Cong., 1st Sess., March 1977, pp. 539–540.

5. Samuel I. Doctors, *The Role of Federal Agencies in Technology Transfer* (Cambridge, Mass.: M.I.T. Press, 1969), p. 20.

6. Ibid., pp. 19ff.

7. Ibid., p. 20.

8. Ibid., pp. 17–18.

9. R.L. Lesher and G.J. Howick, *Assessing Technology Transfer* (Washington: NASA, 1966).

10. Ibid.

11. See Lewis M. Branscomb, "Federal Support of Commercially Relevant R&D," *American Scientist* 61 (March–April 1973): 144–151; William D. Carey, "Muddling Through: Government and Technology," *Science* 8, no. 4183 (April 4, 1975): 13; E. Denk, Jr., Chairman, "Priorities for Research Applicable to National Needs" (Washington: Committee on Public Engineering Policy, National Academy of Engineering, 1973), pp. 73–74; and Richard R. Nelson, Merton J. Peck, and Edward D. Kalachek, *Technology Economic Growth and Public Policy* (Washington: Brookings Institution, 1967), pp. 163–168.

12. Nelson, Peck, and Kalachek, ibid., p. 3.

13. Five industrial and two academic contractors—Union Carbide, General Electric, Bendix, Sandia, Du Pont, and the Universities of California and Chicago. See Harold Orlans, *Contracting for Atoms* (Washington: Brookings Institution, 1967), p. 13.

14. Orlans, ibid.

15. See J.G. Wellis and R.H. Waterman, Jr., "Space Technology: Pay-Off from Spin-Off," *Harvard Business Review* 42, no. 4 (1964): 106, for a discussion of role definitions and the importance of industry acceptance.

16. See M.I.T. Energy Laboratory, Policy Study Group, "Government Support for the Commercialization of New Energy Technologies" (Cambridge, Mass.: M.I.T. Press) November 1976) for a description of industry's "investment" approach to R&D outlays.

17. W.D. Carey, "A Policy-Oriented R&D Budget," *Science* 199, no. 4330 (February 17, 1978): 733.

18. Guy Black, "The Effect of Government Funding on Commercial R and D," in *Factors in the Transfer of Technology,* eds. W.H. Gruber and D.G. Marquis (Cambridge, Mass.: M.I.T. Press, 1977).

19. Energy Conservation and Production Act, P.L. 94-385.

12 Bulk Power Supply Reliability and Proposals for a National Grid: Roadsigns in What Direction?

Michael S. Hamilton

Introduction

Proposals for policy change which fail of enactment may nonetheless achieve their ends without legitimation in any duly constituted body. Timely, well-orchestrated public statements and legislative initiatives by key political actors which attract media attention put the general public on notice that change is under active consideration. Repeated introduction of the same proposal in subsequent legislative sessions, perhaps with modifications and a semblance of increased support, educates people interested in a particular issue area about the possibility of impending policy change. Focusing public attention on a problem as defined in a proposed bill and the threat of government action may often be sufficient to stimulate private action calculated to render policy change unnecessary.

This chapter briefly surveys two apparently efficacious, though unenacted, legislative initiatives in what Hughes has lightly termed "the highly charged politics of electric power."[1] Responses of the bulk electric power supply[2] industry to the "reliability"[3] bills advanced in the late 1960s and recent proposals for creation of a national power grid system are discussed. Alternative approaches to the problems identified in these proposals are briefly explored, and an area of potentially productive further research is identified.

Policy Context

Technological Change and Interconnections[4]

The influence of technological change on the electric utility industry in the United States has been pervasive since central station power generation first be-

Portions of the research on which this chapter is based were supported by the Western Interstate Nuclear Board and the Los Alamos Scientific Laboratory. The author is indebted to Henry P. Caulfield, Jr., R. MacGreggor Cawley, and Norman I. Wengert for their review of previous drafts. Unless otherwise noted, responsibility for the content is solely that of the author.

came commercially feasible in 1882. Increases in generator and transmission capacity gradually moved electric supply beyond the neighborhood level where it began, eventually making possible the operation of multistate networks of bulk electric power facilities.[5]

Today these facilities are extensively interconnected in three large networks which blanket much of the North American continent. One is comprised of utilities in the eleven contiguous Western states and parts of Nebraska, South Dakota, Texas, and British Columbia, Canada, which participate in the Western Systems Coordinating Council (WSCC) and maintain total generating capacity of approximately 90,000 megawatts.[6] Firms in the Electric Reliability Council of Texas (ERCOT) serve a second grid with a total generating capacity of nearly 34,400 megawatts, maintaining no interstate interconnections.[7] A third network includes utilities in the remainder of the coterminous United States and parts of Canada with a combined generating capacity of approximately 370,000 megawatts.[8] The WSCC and ERCOT networks remain virtually isolated from the rest of the nation with no major interregional interconnections planned.[9]

Ownership and Interdependence

Ownership of generation, transmission, and distribution facilities in these networks is divided among investor-owned firms, municipalities, state and federal agencies, and rural electric cooperatives. Investor-owned utilities, most of which are vertically integrated,[10] control nearly 80 percent of the total generating capacity of the industry and more than 90 percent of its thermal generating capacity.[11]

Utility companies plan and operate their facilities singly or in groups known as "power pools."[12] Because the large networks are organized on a multisystem[13] basis, with each utility controlling only a part of the network with which it is interconnected, a high degree of technical coordination in design of facilities and in operating procedure is needed if such networks are to function at all.[14] Continuous delivery of electric service at the lowest possible cost to the consumer is a complex task requiring minute-to-minute interchanges of electric power between facilities within a system. Thus, electric utilities in a given geographical area are highly interdependent in both technical and economic aspects of their operations.

Benefits of Interconnection

Development of interconnections between previously separate bulk power systems was fostered by both private initiative and public policy in order to realize certain perceived benefits accruing from coordinated system planning and operations. It has been argued with some eloquence that coordination over a wide geographic area may minimize operating costs and capital expenditures for plant construction, enhance system stability and recovery capabilities during emergency operating conditions, and provide opportunities for reducing total construction—enabling the siting of facilities so as to produce the required amount of power with minimum adverse environmental impact.[15] However, the extent to which these benefits are realized depends on the degree of actual coordination between pooling utilities.

Private Initiative: Consolidation

Investor-owned utilities needed little encouragement to interconnect their facilities. Early competition between utilities within a single city proved burdensome; a tendency toward corporate consolidation led to recognition of electric service as a "natural monopoly" in which prices to consumers would be higher if normal competitive pressures were allowed to exist. Municipal ownership of electric generating facilities and government regulation of privately owned electric service monopolies emerged as alternatives to perceived inefficiencies of competition between companies.

Around the turn of the century, a nationwide controversy was precipitated between advocates of municipal ownership and proponents of regulated private ownership. The conservation movement of President Theodore Roosevelt and Gifford Pinchot was itself divided over which alternative should prevail in government policy.[16] Subsequently two groups of competing federal policies and related institutions developed, one favoring regulated private ownership and the other favoring public ownership or preferential treatment of publicly owned utilities.

The recurrence and intensity of controversy between proponents of these competing policies over the years suggest a tradition of ideological conflict over the proper role of government in the production of electric power. This conflict remains unresolved and is apparent today in attitudes of utility managers[17] and in their responses to legislative initiatives recently set before Congress.

Interconnections in Public Policy

The Federal Power Commission (FPC) was created in 1920 to license hydroelectric developments on interstate streams,[18] and its jurisdiction was extended to wholesale sales of electricity in interstate commerce by the Public Utilities Holding Company Act of 1935.[19] This act also triggered twenty years of "trust busting" by the Securities Exchange Commission, which effectively stalled con-solidations in the electric utility industry for much of that time.

These antitrust actions were directed only toward what were termed *uncon-scionable* business practices, however, and the legitimacy of interconnections was recognized in provisions of the 1935 act which authorized the FPC to "pro-mote and encourage . . . interconnection and coordination"[20] of electric systems. The FPC was further "empowered and directed to divide the country into re-gional districts for the *voluntary* interconnection and coordination of facilities for the generation, transmission, and sale of electric energy."[21] Subsequently, interconnection agreements continued to be made on the initiative of adjacent power companies, and the precursors of contemporary power pools were formed. But efforts of the FPC under this provision prior to 1960 were not impressive.[22]

In the early 1960s the FPC undertook an ambitious effort to estimate the need for increased coordination in the industry. In 1964 it published an exten-sive study of the industry which concluded that closer coordination than then existed was desirable to reduce power production costs.[23]

"Reliability" Legislation

The Northeast Blackout of 1965

The desirability of increased interdependence which accompanies coordination was dramatically put in question by the Northeast power failure of November 9-10, 1965, which left several million people in eight states and parts of Canada without electricity for up to thirteen hours.[24] Bolstered by the occurrence of this massive blackout—which seemed to confirm their assessment of industry planning and operations—the FPC began some prodigious sword rattling which continued for several years.[25] After preliminary investigations into the causes of the blackout, the FPC called for "acceleration of the present trend toward . . . stronger interconnections between systems."[26]

Regional Coordinating Councils

Perhaps seeing the writing on the wall, Northeast utilities moved quickly to form the first regional coordinating council in January 1966.[27] Utilities in other regions were not so quick to act. The FPC then prepared an important follow-up study, *Prevention of Power Failures*,[28] which was released during June and July 1967, and asked Congress for authorization to establish regional planning en-tities and minimum reliability standards, to review construction plans for extra-high-voltage transmission lines, and to require interconnections between bulk power suppliers.[29]

A second major blackout occurred on the Pennsylvania-New Jersey-

Maryland interconnection on June 5, 1967,[30] lending impetus to FPC requests. All told, fifteen similar or identical "reliability" bills were introduced in the 90th Congress, though none were enacted.

The industry responded in 1967 by setting up its own regional organizations, such as WSCC and ERCOT, which now number nine nationwide. An umbrella organization, the National Electric Reliability Council (NERC), was created in 1968.[31] While the actual wording of their statements of purpose varies somewhat, it may be fairly stated that the regional organizations share a common purpose with NERC in being established "to augment the reliability and adequacy of the bulk power supply and transmission network of the electric utility industry in North America."[32]

In considering the role of these regional councils in the industry, it should be borne in mind that they are *voluntary*[33] associations of utilities held together primarily by the mutual determination of participants, who are free to terminate their membership on stipulated terms. Formal agreements concern sharing of information relevant to planning and operating of regional grids, adherence to uniform operating criteria, and administration of the organization. There are no formal sanctions available for use against members who may disregard the terms of these agreements. While they have facilitated better exchange of information on plans for additions to regional grids, the regional councils have not assumed leadership for centralized planning to produce the most efficient systems consistent with reliability standards.

Prospects for a National Grid

It has been suggested that interconnections may be expected to continue to develop until a single national grid evolves.[34] Whether that "evolution"[35] will reflect planning efforts undertaken to best serve the broader public interest or narrower corporate interests of the many utilities involved has recently been sharply questioned. Executives of some engineering firms and electric utilities view current industry planning as limited in scope by the needs of individual utilities and fraught with intercompany in-fighting which may frustrate coordination attempts. They suggest that existing practices may be inadequate to accommodate the planning needs of the future, when construction of energy centers of 25,000-megawatt generating capacity is contemplated.[36]

A National Power Grid Corporation?

An alternative means of ensuring further coordination was proposed in both houses of Congress in 1971, in the form of legislation which would establish a federally owned National Power Grid Corporation and several regional corporations as its marketing agents.[37] Severely criticized by investor-owned utilities in early 1972[38] and ardently defended by advocates of public power later that same year,[39] similar legislation was introduced in later Congresses with lengthening lists of distinguished sponsors.[40] A background study was prepared by the Congressional Research Service in 1976,[41] and the Department of Energy has recently undertaken further feasibility studies for a national grid system.

As proposed, these corporations would be authorized to issue tax-exempt bonds guaranteed by the U.S. Treasury to an aggregate limit of $30 billion. Existing facilities of all federal power agencies except the Tennessee Valley Authority (TVA) would be transferred to the National Power Grid Corporation. TVA would be the regional corporation in its current service area.

Each corporation would be run by three directors: one representative each of consumers, investor-owned utilities, and publicly owned utilities. The National Power Grid Corporation would be responsible for providing all electric power to the regional corporations, which would be obliged to sell power to any electric utility that had given "adequate" notice of its needs, *provided* such utility would permit the use of its excess transmission capacity for "wheeling"[42] power to other utilities.

To meet their obligations, regional corporations would be authorized to purchase for resale surplus power generated by other utilities, to construct generation and transmission facilities, and to acquire by eminent domain any lands, easements, rights-of-way, transmission facilities, or transmission capacity which, in the opinion of the corporation, are necessary to carry out the provisions of the act. They would not engage in retail distribution of electricity to consumers. Power would be marketed at "regional rates" set at the "lowest possible level consistent with sound business principles" and applicable federal, state, and local environmental standards. Each corporation—explicitly including TVA—would be required by law to treat all facility design and siting decisions as significant aspects of land-use planning in which all environmental, economic, and technical issues should be resolved in an integrated fashion, giving "all possible weight to the protection of the environment."[43]

Political Rhetoric

In advancing this proposal, it was said that "the day has passed when the Nation's electrical utilities alone can assure every American an adequate and reliable supply of electricity."[44] Recurring blackouts, controversy over environmental impacts of bulk power production, and utility difficulties in financing investments in additional facilities were cited in support of this assertion.

The sponsors maintain that a National Power Grid Corporation would benefit *all* segments of the industry, helping solve the power supply problems of small, consumer-owned utilities while ameliorating the financing and siting problems of large investor-owned companies.[45] Of primary concern is provision of power to municipals and rural electric cooperatives, the greater number of which are small distributors with little or no generating capacity of their own.

The needs of these utilities in the past were met largely through purchases from federal hydroelectric projects, where accessible, or from neighboring investor-owned firms. Recently growth in demand has outstripped supplies available from power agencies, and difficulties experienced by investor-owned firms in bringing new generating plants online when needed have often been passed along to municipals and cooperatives in the form of curtailed or unrenewed power supply contracts.

Where contracts continue to be made, they reflect escalating fuel prices and construction costs, which in turn may create friction within the membership of cooperatives. Contracts not renewed may prevent municipals and cooperatives from extending service to new customers, which adjacent utilities may then serve directly. Resolving this situation by providing a new source of federal power, on the other hand, might facilitate extension of service into new areas by publicly owned utilities.

Bigger Is Better?

While there is much evidence of concern for environmental quality in this proposal, conservation enters into it primarily in the form of a rationale favoring construction of large-scale generating plants and transmission lines to curb power plant proliferation. The idea is that by building fewer, larger plants the nation will consume less fuel and produce less environmental disruption in the aggregate. Given fuels readily available today, this probably constitutes a built-in bias toward multiunit nuclear or coal-fired energy parks sited at considerable distances from population centers.

"Giant Power" or Voluntary Coordination?

The proposal for a National Power Grid Corporation is the progeny of a long line of "giant power" initiatives advanced periodically since the 1920s by proponents of public ownership of electric utilities. These vary widely in form and origin. Some, like the current proposal, contemplate alternative mechanisms for creation of regional or national publicly owned entities.[46] Others, undertaken by federal agencies, take the form of feasibility studies for generating and transmission networks, on the basis of which subsequent electric transmission and water resources planning could be oriented, and appropriations sought for individual increments of the whole.[47]

In the 1960s FPC activities had the effect of forcing utility managers with conflicting philosophical views to work together in regional and national coordinating organizations, but supporters of the National Power Grid Corporation view these efforts as inadequate and would opt instead for a larger public role in production of electric power. It is not surprising, therefore, that spokesmen for both investor-owned utilities and NERC have taken markedly similar positions in opposition to this proposal, [48] while associations of public power entities have endorsed it.[49]

Although this proposal seemed to gain momentum in the early 1970s, attention was diverted from it in the 95th Congress by President Carter's call for a comprehensive national energy policy[50]—at least until July 13, 1977, when a major power failure in New York City again thrust electric transmission reliability into the national consciousness.[51] As of this writing, hearings have not been held on this proposal in the 95th Congress.

Political Strategy

Raising the threat of a greater federal role in power production may be perceived as sufficient to encourage further interconnection efforts. The late Senator Lee Metcalf, a key sponsor of the bill, hinted as much when he said,

> If the specter of Federal competition causes utilities to do what they should have done anyhow to improve their transmission network, that will be fine with me. But the birchrod can be taken out of the closet [and] the lines can be built by the Federal govenment if that is necessary. . . .[52]

Such statements may lead one to question whether the current proposal was ever expected to be enacted as law.

Experience since initial proposal of both the reliability bills of the late 1960s and the National Power Grid Corporation legislation of the early 1970s— neither of which has been enacted—suggests that the electric utility industry has indeed moved toward greater coordination. The mere *threat* of further government intervention in the industry seems to have borne fruit.

A political strategy for inducing change within the electric power industry might therefore be devised on the basis of "co-optation by invitation," or proposing change through government action which might be accomplished—less painfully for some—via nongovernmental action. Raising the specter of increased federal intervention (in either electric power production or regulation) and an implied shift in the current balance of political power between proponents of private and public ownership should be an integral part of this strategy.

The policy proposed should be sound in itself, susceptible to co-optation, and capable of generating some support from interest groups concerned with electric utility activities. It should provide an acceptable resolution of a problem, whether implemented by government or co-opted by industry prior to enactment.

Alternatives

Consolidation

As an alternative to federal ownership of a national grid system, public policy could be shaped to allow corporate consolidation and merger to "simplify" industry structure.[53] Proponents of this option view large investor-owned utilities as the leading exponents of technological innovation within the industry (ignoring the substantial contributions to industry research and development made by TVA and the Bureau of Reclamation) and point out that large systems under a single ownership are more likely to achieve substantial benefits of coordination than large systems owned in part by several firms.

But fear of the social and political influence which might be wielded by large corporations and doubts as to the effectiveness of regulatory agencies in controlling them[54] militate against policies which favor expansion of large investor-owned utilities. And the well-known resistance of some firms to air and water pollution controls lends some credence to the assertion that their concern for maximizing returns to stockholders may render them insensitive to environmental impacts of their activities.

A much-qualified version of this alternative would attempt to set a benchmark model for a "rationalized" industry structure, thereafter selectively encouraging or discouraging mergers in accordance with specified criteria designed to foster formation of large planning units, which would readily utilize large-scale bulk power technology.[55] This proposal would place more emphasis on multifirm coordination efforts as a prerequisite to merger and would not allow companies to exceed a certain size. It would also impose substantial burdens of information gathering on agencies evaluating merger applications, which they are currently ill equipped to bear.

Status Quo

Maintaining the status quo, which is favored by investor-owned utilities as second best compared to unlimited consolidation (as well as by some publicly owned utilities and NERC), encompasses a variety of contractual arrangements and voluntary coordination efforts. Since coordination efforts frequently spawn mergers, this may constitute a de facto policy favoring further corporate consolidation.

Wholesale specialization is one aspect of the status quo which deserves further consideration. Long practiced by federal power agencies and some associations of rural electric cooperatives, *wholesale specialization* refers to electric utilities which engage only in bulk power supply at wholesale rates to distribution firms.

Investor-owned utilities in New York have recently proposed formation by private action of a similar regional corporation, Empire State Power Resources, Inc. (ESPRI).[56] If this mechanism proves viable, it may provide a means for ameliorating the financial and siting difficulties of large investor-owned utilities, thereby undermining one argument in favor of a National Power Grid Corporation.

Common Carrier

Another alternative would separate ownership of generation, transmission, and distribution facilities, convert the interconnected transmission network into a regulated "common carrier," and encourage competition between generation companies to supply at wholesale the demands of individual distribution systems.[57] It is hoped that, after a drastic restructuring of the industry, this would favor entry of large investor-owned generation companies into competition with existing firms.

Competition as a means of pricing electricity to consumers was generally repudiated at the turn of the century[58] and has survived primarily where protected by public policies permitting formation of municipal and consumer-owned utilities. Whether the potential of this as yet untried form of structured competition would justify the disruption necessary to bring it about seems doubtful. Increased fragmentation of control over planning and operations would likely be incompatible with provision of reliable electric service.

Rate Reform and Regulatory Improvement

Hearings were held during the 94th Congress on a more consumer-oriented alternative[59] that revived many provisions of the reliability bills previously advanced by the FPC, and sought to reform federal electric power policy without restructuring the industry. Provisions expanding FPC jurisdiction, as discussed above,[60] were combined in a proposed, but not enacted, "Electric Utility Rate Reform and Regulatory Improvement Act" with other proposals, including federal standards for state implementation of (1) rate reform based on marginal cost pricing principles, (2) expeditious facility siting procedures, and (3) initiation of load management techniques.[61] However, President Carter's national energy program, which included many similar provisions, took precedence in the 95th Congress and, at this writing, had not emerged from conference committee.

Economies of Scale

All the aforementioned alternatives contemplate continuation of a trend toward introduction of ever-larger bulk power supply technologies. An assumption is made in the power engineering literature to the effect that economies of scale will justify increasingly larger plants and may justify energy parks of 10,000- to 20,000-megawatt capacity in the foreseeable future.[62] Several "diseconomies of scale" have received scant consideration, however.

Diseconomies of Scale

Financial. The extreme capital-intensive nature of bulk electric power facilities and the high proportion of all net private domestic investment necessary to sustain continued electrification through 1985 have been alluded to by Lovins.[63] His analysis reflects concern over the wisdom of pursuing a policy outlined by President Ford[64] which would place heavy reliance on accelerated development of domestic fossil and nuclear resources.

But Lovins does not speak directly to the competitive nature of financial markets or to the difficulties electric utilities continue to experience in raising capital at favorable interest rates. Widely believed to have been in financial crisis in 1974, the industry has only slowly recovered.[65] Whether it could attract its share of the higher proportion of private investment that Lovins envisions being diverted into the energy sector seems highly doubtful. Current difficulties in financing investments in new generating facilities may already be forcing some utilities to forgo certain technological options, including nuclear fission.

Reliability. Larger generating units require larger backup units or spinning reserves[66] in case of unexpected outage, and recently large units have tended to fail more frequently than smaller ones.[67] This is attributed to a general decline in quality of new equipment. However, the consequences of large generator failure are often more severe and widespread than those of small generator failure, even if both fail with the same frequency.

Prevention of blackouts is not merely a matter of avoiding annoyance to the consumer, but is essential in minimizing potentially substantial secondary costs to utilities and people in areas affected. There is always a chance of damage to expensive utility equipment caused by the blackout itself (as distinct from that damage which may trigger a blackout)—an economic burden the consumer must eventually bear. And as events surrounding the blackout of July 13, 1977, in New York City illustrate, substantial economic and social costs may be incurred, including property damage, looting, loss of business, and the like, which fall indiscriminately on individuals and government in affected areas.[68] Aggregate national statistics which show that, on the average, customers have electric service more than 99.98 percent of the time[69] do not reveal substantial losses suffered during severe local disruptions.

Habit. One diseconomy of scale which has received virtually no consideration in the literature to date is inherent in the possibility that bulk electric power facilities are habit-forming. That is, an optimistic bias in favor of large-scale technology on the part of electric utility planners may impede a shift to decentralized energy systems using renewable resources.

Investments in high-voltage transmission networks, once made, encourage use of such facilities. Further investments in large generating facilities may afford opportunities to enhance system stability and operating efficiency, unlike decentralized alternatives (such as residential solar heating and cooling), which do not require high-voltage transmission. Industry planning today is generally geared toward large-scale hardware solutions to energy problems and is slow to incorporate software conservation programs or decentralized technological alternatives. Benefit-cost analyses for current proposals reveal little inclination to assess district heating and cogeneration opportunities forgone in dispersed siting of large plants, as opposed to smaller plants located nearer urban areas.

The electric utility industry is the largest and most capital-intensive industry in the nation today, second only to the federal government in the influence it wields in capital markets.[70] Private investment spent by it now on bulk power facilities may be money that it lures away from new, struggling manufacturers of alternative energy systems. Slowing the growth of these new industries will not facilitate transition to renewable energy resource systems.

Perhaps the cheapest source of electricity today is conservation. The California Energy Commission calculations show that the capital cost per delivered kilowatt of conservation technology averages less than $30. Whether you compare this to the San Diego Gas and Electric estimate of $1,260 per kilowatt (1984 dollars) for the Sundesert I nuclear plant or Jim Harding's estimate of $2,162 per kilowatt (1985 dollars) on the same unit,[71] the differential is striking. Trade-offs evident in our continued heavy reliance on bulk power supply seem a bit lopsided.

Unless electric utilities develop a significant interest in deployment of decentralized alternative energy systems, their activities in pursuit of an electric solution to the energy dilemma may effectively preclude other, potentially more desirable resolutions. With few exceptions, utility managers have resisted consumer efforts to persuade them to expand their planning horizons beyond the single-minded proliferation of bulk power supply facilities to consideration of other means of meeting consumer's energy demands. Traditional patterns of decision making and a history of advances in size of the familiar energy conversion technologies have apparently circumscribed the engineering imagination of many utility managers.

A Modest Proposal

An alternative policy that would involve electric utilities directly in activities which would move the nation toward, rather than away from, a transition to decentralized renewable energy resource systems might be fashioned around low-interest loans for residential installation of approved energy-conserving devices.[72] Federal policy could be shaped so that low-interest loans made to consumers by utility firms could be bought up by the federal government and repaid by consumers through monthly electric service bills, in amounts equal to or less than calculated savings.

There is ample precedent for such policy in provisions of the Rural Electrification Act of 1933[73] which encouraged consumer purchase of electric home appliances in similar manner. Analogous programs are evident in many other areas of federal policy.

This policy could be implemented largely through existing private and public infrastructures. Electricity distribution firms have well-established management, financial, and service departments with the skills necessary to administer such a program. Some have considerable experience in home wiring and electric appliance purchase programs.

The missions of certain federal agencies, such as the Rural Electrification Administration (REA), could be revitalized and expanded to include promotion and administration of this loan program without impairing existing missions, and without creation of additional bureaucracies. Standards for approval of conservation technologies might be developed by REA or in ongoing programs of the Department of Energy, and dissemination of information facilitated by state and federal extension service personnel, as well as through agencies processing loan funds.

This proposal would help "bail out" the electricity consumer rather than the electric power industry. But presumably a considerable amount of the money, if not all, would be returned to the Treasury over time, and the program would be terminated after substantial transition to renewable energy resources is accomplished. Such a program could be audited without disclosure of proprietary information central to the production of electric power.

The aim of this proposal is to provide an incentive for the consumer to purchase energy-conserving equipment and to involve electric utilities of all ownerships in the process. The same program should be available through investor-owned and municipal utilities. The idea is, in part, to induce a learning experience for electric utility managers which will broaden the basis for their planning decisions.

Consumer acceptance could be expected to be high. An extensive recent consumer attitude survey in the Southwest found that government-guaranteed, low-interest loans would convince or encourage 55 percent of the respondents to add insulation to their homes, if needed; more than 66 percent of the sample indicated they would be convinced or encouraged to purchase residential solar equipment.[74] The authors of this study concluded that the "problem seems to be not consumer acceptance, but the lack of a strong program."[75] Other polls have reached similar conclusions.

This proposal is consistent with the emphasis on conservation evident in President Carter's long-delayed National Energy Plan. With the nation struggling to recover from the longest coal miner strike in fifty-six years—on top of slower increases in domestic coal production than was deemed desirable—and under the shadow of an all-too-visible hand in the international oil market, more direct federal action to foster energy conservation seems appropriate.

Conclusion

Precious little rigorous analysis of proposals encompassing near-term widespread adoption of decentralized technological alternatives to bulk electric power supply is yet in evidence. What are the relative merits and demerits of regionwide installation of energy conservation technologies sufficient to reduce future electricity demand by an amount equivalent to that which a large electric power plant might be built to supply; We can guess, but as yet we simply do not know. This chapter has contemplated possible consequences of not asking the question and has tried to extend the dialogue over energy policy into consideration of barriers impeding national transition to renewable energy resource systems.

Notes

1. W.R. Hughes, "Scale Frontiers in Electric Power," in *Technological Change in Regulated Industries,* ed. W.M. Capron (Washington: Brookings Institution, 1971), p. 75, n. 38.

2. Of the three components of electric service—generation, transmission, and distribution—bulk electric power supply refers to the first two.

3. The author was unable to find a precise definition of *reliability* in the literature of power system engineering or public utility regulation. In common usage it clearly concerns maintenance of electric system operating stability so as to avoid prolonged interruption of service to the consumer. Yet *momentary* in-

terruptions are commonplace, though they may go unnoticed by most consumers. The most common method for assessing system reliability is the "loss-of-load probability" method, whereby the probability of loss of generating capacity due to simultaneous outage of facilities is superimposed on the probability of coincidence of this loss of capacity with heavy electricity demands. The generally accepted index of one day in ten years during which a utility may not be able to meet its expected demand with available capacity similarly "is not based on any full scale study of reliability requirements and customer acceptance but has more or less come to be accepted as a convenient measure." N. Savage and L.A. Wofsy cited in Congressional Research Service (CRS), for a Subcommittee of the Senate Committee on Interior and Insular Affairs, *National Power Grid System Study—An Overview of Economics, Regulatory, and Engineering Aspects,* 94th Cong., 2d Sess., Committee Print. (1976), p. 102, n. 17.

4. An *interconnection,* or *intertie,* is a transmission line joining two or more power systems through which power produced by one can be used by the other. Federal Power Commission, *National Power Survey,* 1 (1964): 290. [Hereinafter cited as FPC, *1964 National Power Survey.*]

5. The largest generating unit in 1900 was 1.5 megawatts as compared to 260 megawatts in 1956 and 650 megawatts in 1963; maximum transmission capacity was 60 kilovolts in 1901, 220 kilovolts in 1923, and 345 kilovolts in 1954. See tables at FPC, *1964 National Power Survey* p. 14. This compares with 1,300-megawatt generating units and 765-kilovolt transmission capacity today. Gordian Associates, Inc., *Structural Reform in the Electric Power Industry* (Washington: Federal Energy Administration, 1977), p. 17.

6. Western Systems Coordinating Council, *Western Systems Coordinating Council Ten Year Coordinated Plan Summary: 1976–1985* (Salt Lake City: n.p., 1976), p. 1. National Electric Reliability Council (NERC), *7th Annual Review of Overall Reliability and Adequacy of the North American Bulk Power Systems* (Princeton, N.J.: National Electric Reliability Council, 1977), app. A-3.

7. NERC, *7th Annual Review,* app. A-3. Whether ERCOT utilities will be allowed to continue operating in isolation from utilities with interstate interconnections, presumably in avoidance of federal regulatory jurisdiction, was the subject of proceedings pending before the Federal Power Commission, Securities Exchange Commission, and Nuclear Regulatory Commission in June 1977. "PUC Orders Restoration of Intrastate Power Grid," *Electrical World,* June 1, 1977, p. 28.

8. NERC, *7th Annual Review,* app. A-3.

9. CRS, *National Grid System Study,* p. 100. See also NERC, *7th Annual Review,* app. B-2, B-9.

10. *Vertically integrated,* as used here, refers to those firms which provide generating, transmitting, and distributing services as a single entity or through separate firms controlled by the same holding company. S. Breyer and P. Mac-

Avoy, *Energy Regulation by the Federal Power Commission* (Washington: Brookings Institution, 1974), p. 90.

11. Hughes, "Scale Frontiers in Electric Power," p. 53.

12. A power pool is comprised of two or more electric systems which are interconnected and coordinated to a greater or lesser degree to supply, in the most economical manner, electric power for their combined loads. CRS, *National Power Grid System Study,* p. 223.

13. As used here, the term *system* refers to physically connected generation, transmission, distribution, and other facilities operated as an integral unit under one control, management, or operating supervision. Ibid., p. 225.

14. Hughes, "Scale Frontiers in Electric Power," pp. 46–47. See also S. Breyer and P. MacAvoy, "The Federal Power Commission and the Coordination Problem in the Electrical Power Industry," *Southern California Law Review* 46 (June 1973): 661.

15. Breyer and MacAvoy, *Regulation by the FPC,* pp. 90–93. See also R. Wirtz, "Electric-Utility Interconnections: Power to the People," *Stanford Law Review* 21 (June 1969): 1713.

16. H.P. Caulfield, Jr., "The Living Past in Federal Power Policy," *1959 Annual Report, Resources for the Future* (Washington: Resources for the Future, 1959), pp. 25–33.

17. C. Kroeger and J.R. Rawls, "Managerial Attitudes toward Government Roles in Electricity and Gas," *Public Utilities Fortnightly* 96 (August 14, 1975): 22. See generally Wirtz, "Power to the People,"; M. Hamilton, "Intergroup Conflict and Coordination of Planning and Operations in the Electric Power Industry of the Western United States," Professional Paper, Department of Political Science, Colorado State University, Fort Collins, 1977.

18. 16 USCA 797(e) (1970).

19. 15 USCA 79 *et seq* (1970).

20. 16 USCA 824a (1970).

21. Ibid (emphasis added).

22. Breyer and MacAvoy, *Regulation by the FPC,* p. 89.

23. FPC, *1964 National Power Survey,* 3 vols.

24. Federal Power Commission, *Northeast Power Failure, November 9 and 10, 1965* (1965), pp. 1–17, 43–45.

25. Ibid., pp. 41–45. See also Federal Power Commission, *1966 Annual Report* (1967), pp. 7–8; FPC, *1967 Annual Report* (1968), p. 5; FPC, *Prevention of Power Failures* 1 (1967): 4–5.

26. FPC, *Northeast Power Failure,* p. 43.

27. FPC, *Prevention of Power Failures,* p. 17.

28. FPC, *Prevention of Power Failures,* 3 vols.

29. Electric Power Reliability Act of 1967, S. 1934, H.R. 10727, and others, 90th Cong., 1st Sess. (1967); FPC, *1967 Annual Report,* p. 15.

30. See Federal Power Commission, *Power Interruption: Pennsylvania–New Jersey-Maryland Interconnection, June 5, 1967* (1968).

31. Expectations that private establishment of these organizations would satisfy the FPC may explain a feeling of betrayal voiced by some utility managers when similar legislation was again requested by then-FPC Chairman Lee C. White in 1969. "Shift Set for FPC, White Bows, Nixon Decides to Name John Nassikas, N.H. Lawyer, to Top Regulatory Post," *Electrical World,* May 19, 1969, p. 30.

32. National Electric Reliability Council, *1976 Annual Report* (Princeton, N.J.: National Electric Reliability Council, 1977), p. 2.

33. Voluntarism should not be mistaken for an indicator of enthusiasm, as the "voluntary" efforts of some utilities, power pools, and regional organizations have at times resembled reluctance or exclusivity.

34. CRS, *National Grid System Study,* p. vi; T.J. Nagel, "The National Grid—A Misconception," *Public Utilities Fortnightly* 89 (January 6, 1972): 31.

35. Since the electric power industry is hardly an organic entity and past development of interconnections has often been artificially stimulated by external political pressures and public policy, it is not, strictly speaking, an evolutionary process, and claims to this effect should be carefully scrutinized.

36. CRS, *National Power Grid system Study,* pp. 287-290, 302-303.

37. The National Power Grid Act of 1971, S. 2324 and H.R. 9970, 92d Cong., 1st Sess., 117 *Congressional Record* 26343, 26481 (July 21, 1971).

38. See Nagel, "The National Grid—A Misconception."

39. Ken Holum, "National Power Grid Would Meet the Test of Public Interest—Voluntary Power Pools Fall Short of Meeting the Challenge of the 1970s," *Public Power,* October 1972, reprinted at 119 *Congressional Record* 5559 (February 27, 1973).

40. National Energy Resources Improvement Act of 1973, S. 1025, (H.R. 1110, H.R. 4998), 93d Cong., 1st Sess., 119 *Congressional Record* 5558 (February 27, 1973); National Electrical Energy Conservation Act of 1975, S. 1208, 94th Cong., 1st Sess., 121 *Congressional Record* 6883 (March 17, 1975); National Electrical Energy Reliability and Conservation Act of 1977, S. 1991, 95th Cong., 1st Sess., 123 *Congressional Record* S. 13444 (August 3, 1977).

41. CRS, *National Grid System Study.*

42. *Wheeling* is the transmission of electricity from one utility by a second company over its lines to a third utility. FPC, *1964 National Power Survey,* p. 292.

43. National Electrical Energy Reliability and Conservation Act of 1977, §201(b)(2), at 123 *Congressional Record* S. 13446 (August 3, 1977).

44. Congressman Robert Tiernan, 117 *Congressional Record* 26481 (July 21, 1971).

45. Senator Lee Metcalf, 119 *Congressional Record* 5558 (February 27,

1973). For a guide to the literature on these problems, see M. Hamilton, *Power Plant Siting (With Special Emphasis on Western United States),* Exchange Bibliography no. 1359-1360 (Monticello, Ill.: Council of Planning Librarians, 1977.)

46. Gifford Pinchot and Morris Llewellyn Cooke, *Report of the Giant Power Survey Board* (1926); Leland Olds, "Giant Power for the American People," Paper presented to the Western States Water and Power Conference, Salt Lake City, Utah, May 11, 1957; H.P. Caulfield, Jr., "Federal Electric Power Policy," Paper presented to the annual meeting of the American Political Science Association, St. Louis, Missouri, September 4-6, 1958; H. Zinder and Associates, Inc., *A Study of the Electric Power Situation in New England, 1970-1990* (New England Regional Commission, 1970).

47. Note the frequency with which these were prepared in regional agency offices during Republican administrations or near the end of Democratic Presidential terms, perhaps in response to perceived or expected shifts in discretionary executive policy. See U.S. Department of Interior, Bureau of Reclamation, *A Study of Future Power Transmission for the West* (1952); U.S. Department of the Interior, *Transmission Study 190,* Steering Committee Report (1968); U.S. Department of the Interior, *North Central Power Study* (1971); U.S. Department of the Interior, Federal Task Force Study Management Team, *Southwest Energy Study,* Draft (1972).

48. Compare Nagel, "The National Grid—A Misconception," with National Electric Reliability Council, *An Assessment of the Proposed National Power Grid Act* (Princeton, N.J.: National Electric Reliability Council, 1973, and Edison Electric Institute (EEI), *Position of the Edison Electric Institute on the Need for a National Grid* (New York: Edison Electric Institute, 1974).

49. American Public Power Association, "Codification of APPA Resolutions" (Washington: American Public Power Association, 1977), pp. 6, 20; National Rural Electric Cooperatives Association, "Continuing Resolutions: No. 25, Tennessee Valley Authority; No. 75, Interregional Reliability Interties," *Rural Electrification,* April 1977, pp. 78, 82.

50. President Jimmy Carter, "National Energy Program" *Presidential Documents* 13 (April 20, 1977): 566.

51. "National Power Grid Proposed as Protection against Power Blackouts," *Public Power Weekly Newsletter,* August 22, 1977, p. 5.

52. 123 *Congressional Record* S. 13445 (August 3, 1977).

53. Nagel, "The National Grid—A Misconception," p. 38.

54. T.G. Moore, "The Effectiveness of Regulation of Electric Utility Prices," *Southern Economic Journal* 36 (1970): 365; Breyer and MacAvoy, *Regulation by the FPC.*

55. Hughes, "Scale Frontiers in Electric Power," p. 74.

56. Gordian Associates, *Structural Reform,* p. 60.

57. L. Weiss, "Antitrust in the Electric Power Industry," in *Promoting Competition in Regulated Markets,* ed. A. Phillips, (Washington: Brookings Institution, 1975).

58. Caulfield, "Federal Power Policy," p. 31.

59. *Electric Utility Rate Reform and Regulatory Improvement,* Hearings on S. 1666, S. 2208, and others before the Senate Committee on Commerce, 94th Cong., 2d Sess., ser. no. 94-77 (1976); *Electric Utility Rate Reform and Regulatory Improvement,* 2 vols., Hearings on H.R. 12461, H.R. 2633, and others, before a Subcommittee of the House Committee on Interstate and Foreign Commerce, 94th Cong., 2d Sess., ser. nos. 94-127 and 94-128 (1976). [Hereinafter cited as House, *Rate Reform and Regulatory Improvement.*]

60. See text at n. 30.

61. As defined in this proposal *load management techniques* include any procedure or equipment designed to reduce maximum kilowatt demand on an electric utility. House, *Rate Reform and Regulatory Imrpovement,* pp. 20-21.

62. D. Jopling, "Large Capacity Plant Sites: Problems and Opportunities" *Power Engineering* 80 (January 1976): 36. But see "Energy Parks Could Create Problems," *Electrical World,* March 1, 1976, p. 23.

63. A. Lovins, *Soft Energy Paths: Toward a Durable Peace* (Cambridge, Mass.: Ballinger Publishing Company and Friends of the Earth International, 1977) pp. 30-31.

64. President Gerald Ford, "State of the Union Address," *Presidential Documents* 11 (January 15, 1975): 45-53.

65. Gordian Associates, *Structural Reform,* pp. 25, 57.

66. *Spinning reserves* are operating generating units with capacity which is not currently in use but ready for use. FPC, *1964 National Power Survey,* p. 291.

67. CRS, *National Power Grid System Study,* p. 129.

68. "The Blackout," *Newsweek,* July 25, 1977, pp. 16-30; Federal Power Commission, *Staff Report on July 13-14, 1977, Electric System Disturbance on the Consolidated Edison Company of New York, Inc., System,* 2 vols. (1977). See also FPC, *Northeast Power Failure.*

69. EEI, *National Grid Position,* p. 3.

70. Gordian Associates, *Structural Reform,* p. 20.

71. Jim Harding, "Sundesert: California's Fiscal Mirage," *Not Man Apart,* mid-March 1978, pp. 4-5.

72. Energy-conserving devices include, but are not limited to, residential solar heating, cooling, and hot-water systems; onsite wind or biomass conversion and utilization systems; retrofit cogeneration projects with residential district heating; more efficient home appliances and improved home insulation and weatherization.

73. 7 USCA 905 (1970).

74. W.H. Cunningham and S.C. Lopreato, *Energy Use and Conservation Incentives: A Study of the Southwestern United States* (New York: Praeger, 1977), p. 98.

75. Ibid.

13 Energy Policy and Social Equity

Lenneal J. Henderson, Jr.

The distribution and pricing of America's energy resources raise serious social equity issues. Past and present unemployment, underemployment, racism, inflation, and economic recession limit the incomes of the poor, racial minorities, the elderly, and the handicapped. As a result, these groups suffer inferior access to energy resources. Petroleum, natural gas, and electricity prices grow more rapidly than the incomes of these socially disadvantaged groups. Moreover, few energy policymakers come from or represent these groups. Federal and state energy policies are therefore key determinants of the energy futures of the poor. Whether social equity will be a basic principle in national energy policy depends on the nature of governmental intervention.

The Policy Context

The Arab petroleum embargo of 1973–1974, subsequent price increases imposed by the Organization of Petroleum-Exporting Countries (OPEC), a major economic recession characterized by an unprecedented combination of inflation and unemployment and continuous increases in consumer energy demand dramatically changed the U.S. energy context. Electric utilities began to request substantial rate increases from state public service and utility commissions. "Between 1969 and 1974, consumer prices for fuel oil, natural gas, electricity and gasoline increased more than any other item on the consumer price index except food."[1] (See table 13-1). Since 1974, when the "energy crisis" became a pervasive national public policy concern, increases in energy prices have surpassed food price increases by more than 10 percentage points.

These precipitous price increases are causing severe hardship for poor and minority communities. Utility costs, whether paid directly by these households or indirectly through rent and other service charges, are the most conspicuous, continuous, and essential energy costs poor and minority households face. In 1975 the Federal Energy Administration (now part of the Department of

This chapter was made possible by a fellowship from the Moton Center for Independent Studies. My warm thanks to Dr. Broadus Butler, President of the Center. This chapter does not represent the views of the U.S. Department of Energy or any of its employees.

Table 13-1
Fuel Price Increases in the Consumer Price Index, 1969–1974

Consumer Price Index	up 34%
Electricity	up 40%
Gasoline	up 58%
Fuel oil	up 100%
Food	up 49%

Source: Dorothy Newman and Dawn Day, *The American Energy Consumer* (Cambridge, Mass.: Ballinger, 1975). Copyright 1975, The Ford Foundation. Reprinted with permission of Ballinger Publishing Co.

Energy) found that "low- and fixed-income families have been under increasing pressure as they pay for electricity and natural gas which consumes an increasing proportion of their income despite their efforts at conservation."[2] Eunice Grier argues that

> in the aggregate, direct household energy costs for American households mount well into the billions of dollars. Still, for the average household they are . . . relatively small compared to incomes at this time. For low-income households, however, the financial burden created by rising energy costs is not a minor one. Furthermore, each unit of energy they consumed in their homes cost them more, on the average, than U.S. households of all income levels in both 1973 and 1975. This was largely as a result of pricing policies which rewarded larger consumers with lower per-unit prices.[3]

Utility rate increases combined with other increases in energy costs, threatened social service institutions serving nonwhite and poor communities and households.[4]

This observation underscores three critical dimensions of the impact of energy costs on the poor and minorities. First, rising energy prices profoundly affect the price of other essential commodities and services needed by the poor. Corporate and industrial institutions pass on increased utility costs to consumers in the form of higher prices for their goods and services. The result is a sharply increased overall cost of living for minority and low-income households, a declining capacity to generate sufficient income to meet the current cost of living in these households, and a consequent decline in the quality of life enjoyed by minorities and the poor.

Second, energy costs impact not only on low-income and minority households but also on community-based and social service institutions which serve these households. If the services which these institutions provide are significantly impaired by rising utility and other energy costs, then existing social inequities are exacerbated. Reductions or terminations of essential services provided by a variety of employment, youth, health, welfare, housing, and other agencies mean personnel retrenchment, reductions in the quality and quantity of services (particularly remedial services) needed by minorities and the poor, and a consequent inability of poor and minority households to face rising energy and other costs.

Third, the impacts of energy policies vary with the type of energy in the marketplace. Although natural gas, petroleum products, electricity, coal, and other fuel sources cost consumers more each day, prices increase differentially. Also, the policy arena varies with each energy form. Social equity issues must therefore be related to each energy form.[5]

These three dimensions of price impacts among low-income people are paradoxical when low-income energy consumption patterns are considered. Although studies of energy consumption patterns strongly suggest that the poor use energy primarily for bare essentials, they continue to pay more per unit for the energy they consume. Regressive utility rates reward higher-volume users with lower per unit costs. This consumption/cost relationship existed even before the OPEC oil embargo. For example, a 1973 RAND study of electricity use by income in Los Angeles from 1960 to 1961 found an inverse relationship between income and the percentage of income spent for electricity (table 13-2).

Similarly, a study of low-income household expenditures in the Detroit area found that an average inner-city household paid eleven times as much of its income per month per unit of electricity as does a family in a wealthy suburb.[6] Both the Los Angeles and the Detroit case studies were developed before the 1973-1974 energy crisis.

Grier's recent study compares 1973 and 1975 (pre- and postembargo) energy consumption rates in low-income households (table 13-3). Says Grier:

> Both in 1973 and in 1975, low-income households consumed less energy in their homes and paid lower total amounts for household energy . . . their average consumption of natural gas and electricity was considerably lower in 1975 in terms of millions of BTUs than the average for all U.S. households combined; and their per-household expenditures for these two primary forms of energy were lower also.[7]

Table 13-2
Electricity Usage as a Percentage of Income, Los Angeles, 1960–1961

Average Los Angeles residential	1.3%
Average Western United States (1960–1961 study)	1.4
Los Angeles: below $2,000	4.04
$2,000–3,900	2.51
$4,000–4,900	1.67
$25,000 plus	0.70

Source: Rand Study, *The Impact of Electricity Price Increases on Income Groups: A Case Study of Los Angeles* (Santa Monica, CA.: Rand Corporation, 1963).

Table 13-3
Current Utility Rate Design Proposals

Proposal	Nature of the Proposal	Theory of the Proposal
Lifeline rates	Establishes a minimum service at low rates for low-income persons.	Relief to small and low-income energy consumers for whom energy is indispensible but high prices are prohibitive.
Time of day/peak load pricing	Design of rates to assign fixed costs to consumers who use electricity during peak hours.	Consumers should bear a cost burden for using energy during peak periods. Peak charges will encourage consumption during nonpeak periods.
Rate flattening and inversion	Eliminates cost differentials between consumers. Charges a flat rate to all consumers.	Flat rates reform inverted utility rate schedules and encourage energy conservation by eliminating discounts to high energy consumers.
Marginal costing or long-run incremental costs	Rate design-based anticipated future costs with reduced rates to designated consumers so that revenues will not exceed revenue requirements.	Fixed rates on this basis will assure the most economical construction by utilities by giving the customers signals as to the impact of increased usage.

Source: Adapted from Louis Flax and Mark Drazen, *Current Proposals for Changes in the Design of Electric Utility Rates* (Washington, D.C.: National Association of Manufacturers, 1976).

To restate, although per household expeditures for natural gas and electricity were relatively low in low-income households, the proportion of the budget spent on these energy resources remained greater than that spent by other households. That fact, combined with the impact of utility costs on commodities and services needed by the poor and institutions serving the poor, generates profound social equity problems for utility policymakers. These cost/equity relationships are diagrammed in the simple model in figure 13-1.

Social Equity Concepts in Energy Policy Making

Given these cost/equity problems, three social equity concepts seem germane to energy policy making: (1) equitable access and representation of socioeconomic minorities in energy policy making (input generation), (2) integration of social equity principles into national and state energy policies (equitable policy outputs), and (3) effective monitoring of energy policy impacts on the socially disadvantaged (policy outcomes). These concepts suggest that government intervention and energy policy *accommodate* the socioeconomically needy while *compensating* for the adverse effects of past energy policies.

However, equity concepts also require articulation with systemic social con-

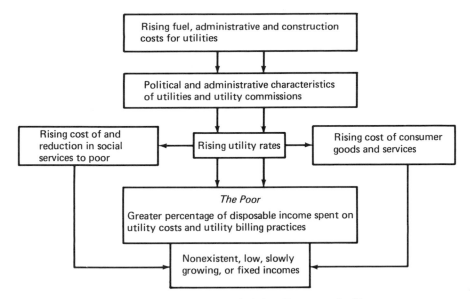

Figure 13-1. The Impacts of Utility Rates on the Poor.

cerns. Artificial separation of the needs of socioeconomic minorities from overall energy needs may be counterproductive. For example, a separate energy consumer "bill of rights" for residential consumers and low-income consumers is less helpful than a single "bill of rights" which includes low-income consumers. Moreover, special and remedial energy programs for the needy should *reduce* dependency on government while achieving energy conservation, efficiency, and economic goals. When government intervention is necessary, it should be efficacious, cost-effective, and administratively efficient to preclude burdens on other consumers or on industry and commerce.

Social equity in the generation of energy policy inputs requires that socioeconomic minorities have as much opportunity to influence energy policy as other interests. However, given traditional participatory barriers, interest group aggregation and advocacy for the energy needy require stimulation as well as availability. For example, at the federal level, community action agencies (CAAs) and other implementing Community Services Administration (CSA) weatherization programs must establish Project Advisory Committees, a majority of whom must be poor. Similarly, the Department of Energy (DOE) weatherization regulations require *state* program advisory committees, most of whom must be poor. In addition, the DOE recently funded the Minority Energy Technical Assistance Project (METAP), conducted by the Center for Urban Environmental Studies (CUES). Led by Maryland legislator Larry Young, METAP stimulates energy advocacy among minority elected officials through training and information dissemination. Also, the DOE Office of Consumer Affairs vigorously encourages low-income consumer advocacy through public hearings and newsletters.

Executive Order 12044, "Improving Government Regulations," issued by President Carter in March 1978, encourages public participation by "publishing advanced notice of proposed rule-making, holding conferences or public hearings, sending notices of proposed regulations to publications likely to be read by those affected and notifying interested parties directly." These programs stimulate interest group aggregation and coordination among socioeconomic minorities in both overall energy policy and policies directed at the needy.

At the state level, access to public utility regulation is the principal equity issue. Residential consumers generally enjoy less representation in utility rate hearings than industrial or commercial consumers. Socioeconomic minorities are underrepresented in the regulatory process. "Traditional regulatory theory lacks a social equity dimension. The hardships of low-income and minority consumers are considered a tragic but unavoidable consequence of the utility's efforts to do its job. When social equity is included, it really arises from *ad hoc* processes."[8] For example, eighteen states have developed consumer advocate units or "people's counsels" within their public service or utility commissions. These units exclusively represent residential consumers in utility rate-making cases. In most instances, these units are subsidized by assessing the utilities. Generally, these units have small staffs, small budgets, and few resources. They are more responsive to well-organized consumer interests than to socioeconomic minorities. But many "people's counsels" are experimenting with various ways and means of developing effective low-income utility advocacy.

Equity and Energy Policy Options

Equitable energy policy outputs and outcomes are inseparable. Public utility policy is the best example. Price-setting procedures are the source of most equity problems in public utility actions. Three practices addressed in the 1978 National Energy Act, particularly the Public Utilities Regulatory Policies Act of 1978, deserve particular attention: (1) average cost pricing, (2) declining block rates, and (3) the fuel adjustment clause. Frank Camm argues that

> current regulation of gas utility profits requires that the price charged for gas be an average of the historical prices of all contracts from which that gas is obtained. Hence, the price that utilities charge for gas is lower than the cost to the utility of obtaining new gas: average cost pricing of gas leads to a price lower than the *marginal* cost of gas. This subsidy has two effects. First, it encourages gas consumers to use too much gas. Second, the subsidy discourages gas users from switching to other energy sources that could provide them with the same amenities at a lower cost than the real cost of the gas they use.[9]

Average cost pricing thus poses a dilemma for utility decisionmakers. Continuation of average cost pricing for gas service may provide low-income households with cheaper natural gas per unit while extracting higher total charges for more natural gas consumed. Stated differently, marginal cost pricing will raise the cost of each 1,000 cubic feet of natural gas for residential consumers (including the poor), forcing low-income consumers to conserve or pay higher utility bills. Since the poor generally use gas for essentials, where and how will they conserve? If they do not conserve, how will they pay for higher-priced gas? A trade-off between natural gas conservation and rate relief for the poor lies at the root of the dilemma.

A shift to marginal cost pricing gives utilities "excess profits." "Lifeline rates, gas stamps, excess profit taxes, and franchise fees have been posed as alternatives means of extracting profits and returning them to consumers."[10] However, with few exceptions, such measures have not been fully adopted. When adopted, their impact on poor households is poorly evaluated. The potential for effective redistribution of excess profits to the poor via marginal cost pricing is yet to be realized.

Utility companies have traditionally applied "declining block rates," allowin the largest users to receive the largest discounts. The most common rationales for declining block rates are that the different prices reflect actual costs of service to different users, that by selling larger volumes of energy the costs are lowered for all users, and that such rates allow electricity to be more competitive with natural gas. This rationale reflects an early recognition by utility decisionmakers that the more energy a customer consumed, the more "elastic" was that customer's demand, that is, the more control the customer could exercise over the amount of consumption and the type of energy consumed. Also, the largest customers had the possibility of direct wholesale buying or self-generation. The declining block rate structures discouraged such alternatives by rewarding higher users of energy with a progressively larger discount as more gas and electricity were consumed.[11] Lower per unit energy consumers pay noticeably more than those who consume greater quantities of energy. The effect of the declining block rate structure is therefore to subsidize higher-volume energy consumers with the higher rates charged to lower-volume energy consumers. In other words, low-income communities subsidize affluent consumers.

Both the structures (which reflect the utility costs of various types and classes of consumer *relative to one another*) and the absolute price levels which individual minority and poor households pay promote higher energy use among the affluent at the expense of the poor. The result is a serious social equity question.

A third issue which arises under the theory of regulation is the utility fuel adjustment clause. A fuel adjustment clause is a provision in a utility's tariff that permits the utility to bill customers for increases in the utility's stated or, in some cases, projected fuel costs without the utility having to file for a rate increase. Fuel clause proponents argue that fuel clauses are essential for the financial health of the industry and that utilities should not be required to await the completion of a formal rate-making procedure to recoup their increased fuel costs.[12] The Subcommittee on Oversight and Investigations of the House Committee on Interstate and Foreign Commerce reported in 1975 that fuel adjustment costs were a substantial part of the $8 billion increase in the price of electricity in 1974.[13] The Committee also concluded that fuel clauses deprive utilities of incentive to minimize fuel costs and to oppose petroleum industry efforts to decontrol and increase the price of oil and natural gas. The Committee concluded as well that automatic fuel adjustment clauses threaten the basis of utility regulation to the extent that their use encourages the adoption of similar "automatic adjustment clauses" encompassing other key aspects of utility regulation.[14] The effect of these clauses on consumers, particularly low-income consumers, is to accelerate cost increases for electricity and natural gas, contributing to the inability of consumers to keep pace with utility rate increases.

However, both utility rate structures and fuel adjustment clauses reflect historical and contemporary regulatory policy. Rate structures were institutionalized in a period of cheap and available energy. Conversely, fuel adjustment clauses came into use largely as periodic shortages in fuel occurred, as prices for fuel sharply increased, and as fuel-associated costs increased. Both rate structures and fuel adjustment clauses are designed to ensure a "fair rate of return" on utility investments. Often, consumer groups question fair-rate-of-return concepts which excessively burden customers. This trade-off between social and corporate equity is an adamant dilemma.

Equity: Utility Policy Options in the National Energy Plan

President Carter included utility rate reform in the National Energy Act (NEA). The Public Utility Regulatory Policies Act of 1978 establishes eleven rate reform and load management initiatives. These rate-making standards must be considered by state regulatory authorities and nonregulated utilities. They include (1) time-of-day rates; (2) seasonal rates; (3) cost-of-service pricing; (4) interruptible rates and load management techniques; (5) prohibition of declining block rates which are not cost-justified; (7) lifeline rates; (8) master metering; (9) review of automatic adjustment clauses and information to consumers; (10) advertising; and (11) termination of service. These provisions are less stringent than those originally introduced by the administration, which would have set mandatory requirements for rate reform and load management initiatives. Moreover, some of these proposals are designed specifically for low-income consumers. Others are more broadly based policies which are likely to affect low-income consumers. Other proposals were initiated at the state level prior to or subsequent to the President's package. But each proposal has obvious

relevance to the energy futures of low-income households (table 13-3). Thus, through the Public Utility Reform Act, President Carter seeks "to establish national minimum standards for electric rate-making to encourage efficient use of electric energy by insuring that electric utility rates are designed to encourage energy conservation by minimizing energy consumption."
It also provides for greater consumer representation of electric consumers in regulatory proceedings. The act also required the restructuring of utility rate schedules to standardize per unit energy charges paid by most consumers. Moreover, the act prohibited any utility rate increases not subject to rigorous evidentiary hearings and required a review of automatic adjustment clauses every two years.

Following congressional scrutiny, however, reform of utility rates by state commissions was made largely voluntary rather than mandatory. Although many states have or are now considering rate reform, there will be no minimum federal standards for such reform.

Perhaps the most popular proposal for bringing about rate relief for low-income energy consumers is "lifeline rates." Lifeline rates establish both a minimum number of kilowatthours required for the subsistence of utility consumers on low or fixed incomes and a special low or discount rate for these kilowatthours. This rate is based on the theory that utility services are essential to certain disadvantaged consumers who cannot afford regular utility rates.

The origin of the term *lifeline rates* is unclear, but, to reiterate, it refers to a minimal amount of power provided at a reasonable rate. It must be emphasized, however, that each "lifeline" must be viewed specifically in the context within which it is proposed. Some critics of lifeline rates avoid this approach and erroneously contend that all lifeline proposals are merely income transfers rather than economically efficient rate systems.[15]

The California Public Utilities Commission established lifeline usage prior to January 1, 1976. On September 21, 975, the Commission adopted lifeline gas usage at 75 therms for Pacific Gas and Electric Company in Decision No. 84902. Later in the year, the same lifeline gas usage was also adopted for Southern California Gas Company and San Diego Gas and Electric Company. With regard to electric service, in Decision No. 84902, the Commission also adopted lifeline electric usage of 300, 400, or 500 kilowatt hours per month, with the amounts varying according to Pacific Gas and Electric Company's rate areas. Once these lifeline usages were established, no rate increases have been authorized for lifeline usage.[16]

Although California's experience with lifeline rates suggests that the most needy are helped, those who exceeded the requirements for lifeline eligibility but nevertheless suffered economic hardship could not take advantage of the lifeline rates. Fundamentally, the lifeline concept is an emergency concept which is aimed less at the incorporation of a basic social equity principle in utility pricing than at providing an emergency service to the needy at less than normal cost.

A second proposal for utility rate reform is time-of-day, or peak-load, pricing. The purpose of this pricing scheme is to spread energy demand as evenly throughout the service day as possible by charging consumers more per unit for consumption during periods of high demand. A customer would be charged more for using electricity during that part of the day when demand for electricity throughout the utility system is highest. Conversely, the customer could expect a lower per unit charge for electricity consumed during "off-peak hours," or hours in which system demand is low.

Few studies have examined the impact of peak-load pricing on low-income or minority energy consumers. Whether utility consumption patterns in low-income and minority households significantly deviate from patterns throughout the system has yet to be empirically examined. It is clear, however, that consumers wishing to take advantage of this pricing strategy not only must be willing to alter their consumption patterns but also must control temperature and thermostat gages and home appliances which use energy. Many of the homes of the minorities and the poor are without thermostats, making participation in cost savings from peak-load pricing a problem. It is important to stress that the ultimate intent of peak-load pricing schemes is economic rather than social. There are no explicit provisions for standardizing per unit energy costs or for relieving the impact of these costs on poor and minority households. The focus is on tying costs to consumption in a more direct and conspicuous way.

A third proposal for reforming utility rates is the flat rate proposal. Newman and Day recommend that "state public utility commissions introduce a flat rate structure supplemented by a system of peak load pricing for electricity, as a matter of equity and national energy conservation."[17] Although they do not make clear what their recommendation is based on, it is clear that a flat rate pricing system would effectively reform inverted utility rate structures. Low-income consumers would pay less for energy because they actually use less. However, Newman and Day incorrectly assume that peak-load pricing would tend to reduce overall electricity consumption and lead to an eventual reduction in power plants needed to serve consumers. Peak-load pricing does less to reduce overall consumption than to distribute it more evenly throughout the service day or service week. In fact, consumption could increase as consumers make costly adjustments in their lifestyles and consumption patterns.

Lifeline rates and flat rate proposals offer the best short-term policy instruments for addressing social equity considerations. As mentioned earlier, lifeline is oriented more to emergency than to social equity in that it reserves sufficient energy at low cost for low-income and fixed-income subsistence. However, flat rate proposals are much more related to social equity considerations. First, they do not penalize income-based low energy consumption. The poor would pay less because they use less. Second, more minorities and the poor would be reached by flat rate pricing. Since the pricing scheme is presumably applicable to all customers rather than those considered eligible for lifeline rates, the positive impact of flat rates would be greater. Third, flat rates are more likely to be institutionalized into the utility rate-making process than other reform proposals. Moreover, flat rates would also help the other income groups who benefit little from lifeline or other short-run utility rate innovations.

Regardless of what rate innovations are adopted (or whether they are short-term or long-term), more rigorous, continuous, and comprehensive assessment of their consumer impact is needed. Few utility commissions can authoritatively describe how lifeline, flat rate, or other innovations impact on the variegated residential consumer class. Nor can they detail innovation impacts by city or rural area.[18]

Utility rate innovations suggest several strategies for advocates of poor and minority energy interests. (1) The socioeconomic impact of federal and state rate innovations must be continuously analyzed and monitored. Analysis and monitoring must stem from grass-roots, regional and national consumer, and low-income advocacy organizations as well as from government. However, analysis and monitoring should be coordinated with people's counsels and other consumer units within state regulatory commissions. (2) Utility rate innovations should reward conservation in low-income communities with lower per unit rates. Existing declining block rates penalize the poor for energy conservation. Thus, advocate organizations must be particularly vigilant about rate/conservation trade-offs. (3) Poor and minority communities must participate more effectively in rate hearings and other outlets for public participation. Implementation of utility rate reform will benefit the poor little if they fail to maximally participate. Some states, like California, Wisconsin, and New York, are ahead of federal standards; most are woefully behind. Whether a state is ahead or behind, implementation of federal standards affords the poor unique opportunities for participation. For example, Executive Order 12044, "Improving Government Regulations," expands opportunities for public participation in the development of federal regulatory guidelines for utility rate reform. Now is the time for maximum input of the poor in the creation of these guidelines. (4) Advocates of the poor should appropriately differentiate strategies by type of fuel. Utility decision making about gas, electricity, solar, and other fuel types not only differentially affects the poor but also arouses different industries and interest groups. Advocacy strategies should be sensitive to differences in types of utilities and the equity issues they raise.

Thus, the basic objective of utility reform should be social as well as corporate equity. Ideally, social and corporate objectives should be compatible rather than competitive. Although rate reform is an instrument of *short-term* distributive and redistributive policies, the *long-term* impact of these programs should reduce low-income dependence on government intervention. This would support the insistence of gas and electric utilities on capable customers and minimal government while promoting social equity.

Thus, public utility rate making illustrates the need to interrelate social equity to energy policy inputs, outputs, and outcomes. Socioeconomic minorities must participate throughout the energy policy-making process. Although social and corporate equity must be constructively balanced, although equity and national energy goals must be made compatible, no *national* energy plan can afford overlooking the needs of the nation's poor and minorities.

Notes

1. See Dorothy K. Newman and Dawn Day, *The American Energy Consumer* (Cambridge, Mass.: Ballinger, 1975).

2. Federal Energy Administration, *Fact Sheet: Utilities and Energy,* May 1975.

3. Eunice S. Grier, *Colder . . . Darker: The Energy Crisis and Low-Income Americans: An Analysis of Impact and Options* (Washington: Community Services Administration, June 1977), p. 9.

4. Lenneal Henderson, "Energy Policy and Socioeconomic Growth in Low-Income Communities," *The Review of Black Political Economy,* Fall 1977.

5. See David Howard Davis, *Energy Politics* (New York: St. Martin's Press, 1977).

6. J. Musial, *Public Utilities and Price Discrimination: The Need for Non-promotional Electric Rates in Detroit Edison's Domestic Service Classification before the Michigan Public Service Commission,* No. 3910, January 19, 1972, chap. 6, pp. 6-7.

7. Grier, *Colder . . . Darker,* pp. 9-10.

8. Lenneal J. Henderson, "Energy, Public Utilities and Social Equity: A Review of the Salient Issues," in *Energy and Social Equity* ed. Ellis Cose (Washington: Joint Center for Political Studies, 1978).

9. Frank A. Camm, Jr., *Average Cost Pricing of Natural Gas: A Problem and Three Policy Options* (Santa Monica, Calif.: Rand, July 1978), p. 1.

10. Ibid., p. 2.

11. Elliot Taubman and Karl Freiden, "Electricity Rate Structures: History and Implications for the Poor," *Clearinghouse Review,* October 1976, p. 432.

12. National Economic Research Associates, Inc., *The Fuel Adjustment Clause* (Raleigh, N.C., 1975).

13. *Electric Utility Automatic Fuel Adjustment Clauses* (Washington: House Subcommittee on Oversight and Investigations, 1975), pp. 1-2.

14. Ibid., p. 2.

15. Elliot Taubman and Neal Rauch, "Recent Decisions on Rate Structure Reform: A Survey with Emphasis on Lifeline Rates," *Clearinghouse Review* 10 (October 1976): 612.

16. California Public Utilities Commission, Utilities Division, *Report to*

the California Legislature on the Miller-Warren Energy Lifeline Act P.U. Code Section 739, February 1, 1977, p. 1.

17. Newman and Day, *The American Energy Consumes,* p. 195.

18. Ellis Cose, *Energy and the Urban Crisis* (Washington: Joint Center for Political Studies, 1978).

**Part III
Energy Policy: A
Laboratory for
Political Scientists**

14 Congress and the Making of Energy Policy

Charles O. Jones

On October 13, 1977, President Carter held a news conference in which he criticized the oil companies for excess profiteering in the current energy crisis. While the oil merchants were the subject of Presidential abuse, however, the remarks were targeted to senatorial ears, for on Capitol Hill the Senate was dismantling much of the President's energy program. The clear implication of the President's comments was, of course, that the Senate had submitted to pressure from the oil lobby. Carter wanted to leave that impression with the media and the general public. Still that point could not be made outright. Rather, in speaking about the Senate, the President displayed the kind of restraint that eventually causes "executive gastritis."

> The package that was presented to the Congress in April is fair. It is well balanced. . . .
>
> It is absolutely important that the legislation be passed. The House has done a good job. They have come forward with legislation I can accept.
>
> It is up to the Senate. I have confidence in the Senate. And I believe that we will come out of this legislative session with a reasonable policy established for our country. . . .
>
> I think that Senator Russell Long is working long and hard to come up with an acceptable energy package. And my own hope is that before this year is over legislation at least equivalent to what the House passed will be in its final version.[1]

This chapter treats the matter of Presidential-congressional relations in the development of energy policies. The basic contention is that those who have stakes in and pay attention to this set of interactions have differing concepts of the role of Congress. I will identify the more important of these concepts, the values they represent, and the reform proposals which follow in their wake. Finally, I will refer to recent examples of each concept as realized in congressional action on energy and draw conclusions about the future of Congress in energy policy making.

Three Concepts of the Role of Congress

In their most interesting book on congressional reform, Davidson, Kovenock, and O'Leary point out that "implicit in most of the recent writing on congressional reform are concepts that can be categorized into reasonably distinct theories of the proper functions of a legislative body."[2] First is a "literary theory" of legislative supremacy. By this view, Congress is first in the Constitution and ought to remain so. Second is the "executive-force theory" which stresses policy leadership emanating from the President and the bureaucracy. And third is the "party-government theory" where weight is given to the legislature's responsibility to respond to the "national party constituency."[3]

This set of perspectives can be usefully adapted to an understanding of how various policy actors view the role of Congress in energy policy development. The three concepts are modified here to suit what I observe to be happening in this important issue area. The idea of contrasting congressional roles leading to differing demands remains, however.

First is the role of Congress as *initiator* of comprehensive energy policies. By this view Congress should produce its own energy policy, either as an alternative to what is offered by the President or in the absence of Presidential action. Typically this concept imagines that Congress can, and should, somehow act independently of either the executive or "special interests" or both.

In strong contrast is the view that Congress should build support for and then ratify a program proposed by the President and the bureaucracy. Lacking the expertise in such a complex issue area, Congress should, by this attitude, encourage and endorse the proposals developed by technicians seeking to achieve the goals established by the President as "chief interpreter of the public interest." I will refer to this as the *silent partner* role for Congress—seen but not heard.

The third concept identified here is that of Congress primarily as a representative body, reflecting all the special and public interests associated with a complex issue area. The results may be, and usually are, modification or rejection of the President's program. In this role, Congress is the *facilitator* of all opinions—public and private—so that the full range of effects might be known.

The first two concepts are based on very much the same value set. That is, those holding these views normally have definite substantive biases in favor of particular energy programs. They believe in making, coordinating, and implementing coherent plans. Policy analysis is a very definite "good." The public interest is served when the work of independent analysts and planners is approved and implemented. How does the difference in expectations of Congress come about? It is determined by the extent to which the actor involved influences the policy plans of the President. If the actor is successful, then Congress is expected to be a silent partner; if unsuccessful, the Congress should be the initiator of alternative proposals.

Those picturing Congress as a facilitating institution generally favor the political over the planning process. A plan is the beginning, not the end, of policy making. All voices must be heard—not just those of the expert, technician, and planner. Those holding this view do not believe for a moment that the analysts will have adequately accounted for the diversity of interests in the pre-legislative stage. The public interest, therefore, emerges from representing all viewpoints, of which the President's is but one (important though it is acknowledged to be). Unquestionably those with this third point of view also have substantive biases which they judge to be served by a high degree of access for all interests. And it probably goes without saying that proponents of one set of proposals over another may well adjust their concepts of Congress to suit their estimate of which will more likely provide success.

It follows that a set of organizational expectations accompanies each concept. Those who picture Congress as initiating energy programs expect the legislature to demonstrate an independent capacity for policy analysis and planning. It is the responsibility of leadership to build and support this analytic capability, to see to its effective implementation, and to facilitate the passage of the legislation which it produces. Andrew S. Carron, a staff aide to Senator Thomas Eagleton (D-Missouri), expressed it this way in his critical review of "Congress and Energy":

> The greatest institutional need . . . seems to be for policy analysis. There are too few experts on energy policy associated with Congress, and what experts there are may be unavailable or mistrusted. Policy analysts could be helpful in eliminating many of the limitations that currently afflict the congressional handling of energy policy. . . .
>
> Policy analysts are needed to help Congress *develop* potential energy solutions. . . .
>
> Lack of leadership seems primarily responsible for Congress's inaction on energy lesislation and for its failure to develop the necessary capabilities for conducting first-rate analyses of various policy alternatives.[4]

Presumably this need for independent analysis results from executive incapacity to analyze the problem and develop proposals and/or the production of "wrong results" by the executive. As will be noted later, results from the congressional perspective may be "wrong," by definition, when a President of one party (say, Richard M. Nixon or Gerald R. Ford) offers energy proposals to a Congress with a majority from the other party. Thus, the Congress-as-initiator model may be said to assume an organizational contretemps between the two branches, resulting from substantive or partisan considerations or both.

The silent partner role for Congress requires a cooperative legislative leadership which is respected and followed. Congressional committees and staff are to build support for the program by displaying its features before the public. The most that Congress should do, by this view, is to provide suggestions for refinement and improvement of a basic program designed by the executive, much in the manner of a parliament. Naturally associated with this set of preferences is a party-responsibility concept by which the President works with party leaders in Congress. Presumably this model is preferred by President Carter and the architects of his energy policy. That is understandable. It also is very likely what the authors of the 1974 Ford Foundation study *A Time to Choose* had in mind.[5] At least that would seem to be a reasonable inference, given the fact that the authors of the report hardly even mention the Congress, let alone discuss its role in energy decision making.

In commenting on the ideology of the Ford study, Riker nicely outlines the principal expectations of this school:

> The primary element of this ideology is the belief that the federal government can make a coherent national policy on an extremely complex subject like energy and will in fact do so. . . . At the outset the authors deplore "the lack of a coherent national policy" on energy-related problems. Throughout the book many alleged mistakes are blamed on the absence of a "coherent" policy. And in the end, having stated their precise goals of usage and conservation, they propose an Energy Policy Council "with responsibility for developing and coordinating national energy policy" . . . whose "guidelines" would be "mandatory" at the federal level. It is true that for the record, they deny that they are proposing an energy czar, but a "coordinator" with the powers and duties they propose is indeed a czar under another name. So strongly, apparently, do the authors believe in coherence that they are willing to impose a substantially dictatorial policy maker, to ensure that the authors' version of good policy is in fact carried out.[6]

While it is not altogether clear how President Carter views the congressional role in this sphere, there is evidence in his remarks to suggest that he expected Congress to assume the silent partner stance. And it is, perhaps, no slight coincidence that the director of the Ford Foundation energy policy project, S. David Freeman, was also influential in the development of the President's energy proposals in 1977.[7]

The third (facilitator) concept assumes an incompleteness of policy analysis and planning, whatever its source. Those supporting this view expect an essentially porous and permeable legislative organization—one with multiple points of access. The committee structure, in particular, should encourage reaction and response by affected groups and individuals, but other stages of the legislative process should also be open to expression of interest (for example, legislative markup sessions, the floor, and conference proceedings). Not too suprisingly, one does not find very many people actually espousing this facilitative model. As we have been told over and over, supplying, distributing, and using energy are all highly complex and technical processes. Public knowledge is assumed to be relatively low, and interest group reactions are judged to be highly prejudicial. Thus most of those active in energy policy development and implementation tend toward the silent partner or policy initiator models of congressional involvement. Riker offers one of the few conceptual summaries of the facilitator model —and his comments are not directed solely at the role of Congress:

> It is, of course, astonishing that anyone should expect or even seek coherence on such a multi-faceted subject as energy policy. . . .
>
> There is . . . a good reason why public policy is not coherent on complicated subjects concerning which citizens have many different interests and values. Liberal democratic government is based on the notion of making public policy out of the desires of citizens. Thus, if these desires are not themselves consistent, when policy makers add up the individual desires to make a social policy it may well happen that the policy is not coherent in the way that an individual person is coherent. . . .
>
> Democratic governments make policy by compromise and cannot be expected to be coherent where complex subjects are concerned.[8]

The whole image of the energy policy process changes markedly if one accepts this pluralistic ideology as legitimate. Proposals are floated precisely to get reaction so that a basis for compromise may be identified. Coherence is expected to emerge through time and testing (if it appears at all), not to be produced *de novo* by technicians for endorsement by elected representatives.

A partial explanation for this widely divergent set of concepts might well be that policymakers at all levels of government and across all public institutions are seeking to develop new programs with significant impacts on society. Not even the boldest advocate is prepared to guarantee success either of a method of decision making or of a substantive outcome. We may expect to find, then, cases where each of these three models "lives" in the real and complex world of energy policy development. And further it is likely that the conglomeration of decisions that will some day be called our energy policy will have derived from a mix of congressional styles and structures.

Three Roles of Congress

If one rises above the recriminations over who did what wrong today in energy policy and politics, it is possible to observe the evolution of an energy policy apparatus over the past three years. Important organizational changes have been made, a number of programs have been set in place, and important public and private decisions have been made which directly or indirectly impact on energy supply and consumption. We have witnessed Congress accommodating to these new demands and the changing political circumstances in which they are made. In fact, one can identify the three roles cited earlier—Congress as initiator, silent partner, and facilitator.[9]

Congress Tries to Initiate under Ford

The Arab oil embargo in the fall of 1973 found the national government ill prepared to cope with the impending crisis. There was no Department of Energy in the executive, no Committee on Energy in either house of Congress, little knowledge or understanding of the issue in government, and a mounting crisis of confidence in the Nixon administration. The several months following the embargo were among the most tumultuous in American history. It is not unreasonable to conclude that the erosion of Presidential authority seriously delayed the organizational and programmatic adjustments to the new energy imperatives.

Several events in 1974 were significant as context for energy policy making. First and foremost, of course, was the Nixon resignation and the elevation to the Presidency of Gerald R. Ford, whose legitimacy was traceable not to election but rather to approval by Congress under the Twenty-fifth Amendment. Second, congressional Democrats were increasingly pressured by the media and the public to take policy initiatives where a collapsing executive could no longer act effectively. And the 1974 elections provided further encouragement for congressional initiative as the Democrats emerged with a two-to-one majority in the House of Representatives and a comfortable margin in the Senate.

Third, certain executive reorganizations (for example, the creation of the Federal Energy Administration, the Energy Research and Development Administration, the Nuclear Regulatory Commission, and the Council on Energy Resources) offered the potential for a more coherent policy development apparatus than had existed in the past. A fourth condition for energy politics in 1974 was more in the manner of a nonevent—that is, the failure of Congress to reorganize effectively either to initiate policy or to manage the policy initiatives of others.

The first two sets of events ensured that congressional Democrats would prepare their own energy program in 1975. The second two made it unlikely that this effort would be successful. That is, the Democrats were moved by reason of a weak executive and their own electoral success to produce an alternative to the President's proposals. Yet the emerging executive organization and the lack thereof in Congress were likely to give President Ford the advantage.

Knowing that the President would reveal his energy proposals in the State of the Union Message on January 15, House Democrats announced their intention to reveal their program on January 13. President Ford, in turn, upstaged the Democrats by addressing the nation on television and radio on that same day— January 13. Reactions generally favored the clarity and coherence of the President's offerings over those of Speaker of the House, Carl Albert (D-Oklahoma), for the Democrats.

The manner in which congressional Democrats sought to take initiative in this important issue area is most interesting and well worth brief description. Lacking an integrated committee structure on energy issues (one count showed twenty-three committees and fifty-one subcommittees dealing with some aspect of energy),[10] party leaders were forced to rely on ad hoc arrangements. In the House the work was done by a Democratic task force chaired by James Wright (D-Texas). While important enough in the party, Wright did not chair any of the major substantive committees or subcommittees concerned with energy. The House group was responsible for the proposals offered by Speaker Albert on January 13. In the Senate an ad hoc committee chaired by Senator John Pastore (D-Rhode Island) prepared an economic and energy package for consideration by the Democratic Policy Committee and Caucus. Pastore's principal energy-related experience was in chairing the Joint Committee on Atomic Energy.

The two groups met in February and eventually announced a joint plan on the 27th of that month. The reactions by the two committee chairmen with major responsibility for action on the energy program, Senator Russell Long (Committee on Finance) and Representative Al Ullman (Committee on Ways and Means) ranged from patronizing comments by Long ("Let Pastore have his day") to lukewarm endorsement by Ullman (whose committee was actively developing other proposals at the time). Little else was heard about the Democratic program from that point on.

Several legislative realities made it difficult for congressional Democrats to initiate a comprehensive energy program as a viable alternative to that proposed by the President. First, however advantageous bicameralism may be in serving other purposes, it makes it extremely difficult for Congress as a whole to develop comprehensive plans for complex and technical issues. Second, the committee structure adjusts slowly to new large-scale demands which cross-cut jurisdictions—partly because no one knows for sure how the demands will develop over time and partly because committees naturally compete for the larger shares of power associated with such an issue. Third, party efforts to develop substantive policy proposals are frequently threatening to the integrity of the committee system. Thus, unless these efforts are carefully managed by party leaders, the impact of such moves will be severely limited. And finally, even an unelected President can upstage Congress at almost any time because of greater media attention.

Having identified these many major hurdles to successful congressional policy initiative, it is important to point out that the effort itself was innovative and had several possible effects. The President moved to back his program more strongly than he might have otherwise. Members of Congress were made more aware of the issue and their structural and political inadequacies for coping with it. And possibly in the same fashion that James L. Sundquist observed for Democrats during the Eisenhower years, congressional Democrats appear to have prepared themselves for policy action on this issue pending the return of a Democrat to the White House.[11]

The House as Silent Partner for Carter

President Carter presented his energy program in a series of public appearances during the week of April 18-22, 1977. He first spoke to the nation and made references to members of Congress as "my partners" in acting on what the President referred to as the "moral equivalent of war." At midweek the President spoke directly to Congress, outlining the details of his program and calling on the members to "act now." And on Friday, the President held a news conference to explain the program further.

Speaker of the House Thomas P. "Tip" O'Neill believed strongly that it was time for Congress to act. Thus, he set about establishing a procedure to facilitate passage of a bill before the August recess. O'Neill created an extraordinary committee as a means for giving himself tighter control. The decentralized committee structure has long been the bane of party leaders' efforts to develop coordinated legislative action on complex issues. Typically an integrated program proposed by the President is disassembled and distributed among several committees (for example, Ways and Means, Interstate and Foreign Commerce, Interior and Insular Affairs, Science and Technology, in the case of energy). Whether it comes back to the floor in one piece is problematic, to say the very least. Standing committees work at their own pace and in accordance with their individual styles and procedures.[12]

A forty-member Ad Hoc Select Committee on Energy was the Speaker's device for overcoming the uncertainty of the more normal process. Established just for handling the President's energy program, the Committee was chaired by party stalwart Thomas L. Ashley (D-Ohio) and included the most important House members involved in energy policy. Five committee and fifteen subcommittee chairmen were on the Speaker's committee. Included were the chairmen of Ways and Means, Interstate and Foreign Commerce, and Interior and Insular Affairs, as well as the chairmen of the major energy-related subcommittees from Science and Technology. Eighteen of the twenty-two standing committees had representation on the Select Committee, but the committees with principal jurisdiction were most heavily represented. (See table 14-1). The Speaker's sensitivity to the regional nature of energy problems was also demonstrated by the geographical distribution of membership. (See table 14-2) The Speaker appointed both the Democratic and Republican caucus chairmen to the Com-

Table 14-1
House Committee Representation on the Ad Hoc Committee on Energy

Committees	Number of Members		
	Demo-crats	Repub-licans	Total
Banking, Finance, and			
Urban Affairs	3	2	5
Government Operations	2	4	6
Interior and Insular Affairs	6	1	7
Interstate and Foreign			
Commerce	8	3	11
Merchant Marine and Fisheries	4	–	4
Rules	2	1	3
Science and Technology	2	2	4
Ways and Means	7	3	10

Note: Figures exceed the total number of members on the Ad Hoc Committee because of multiple committee memberships. Also, only committees with substantial representation are listed here.

Table 14-2
Regional Representation on the Ad Hoc Committee on Energy

Region	Number of Members		
	Demo-crats	Repub-licans	Total
East	7	3	10
Midwest	7	4	11
South	6	4	10
West	7	2	9
	27	13	40

mittee—Thomas S. Foley (Washington) and John B. Anderson (Illinois), respectively. He also included a sprinkling of junior members. Seldom has a committee been so carefully constructed to accomplish a specified purpose. Even given the controversial nature of energy proposals, if this group could approve a program, chances were good that it would pass the House.

The President's energy bill was introduced by Majority Leader James Wright (D-Texas) on May 2, and various sections were referred to five different standing committees (Ways and Means; Interstate and Foreign Commerce; Banking, Finance, and Urban Affairs; Government Operations; and Public Works and Transportation). A deadline of July 13 was set by the Speaker for these committees to report out legislation. The Ad Hoc Committee held its own hearings on the whole range of energy problems during the early summer. They then simply awaited the work of the standing committees (it would have been difficult to do otherwise since most of the members were engaged in the frantic effort to meet the Speaker's deadline in their regular committees). Confounding the critics, four of the five committees completed their work on schedule. Interstate and Foreign Commerce was one day delayed.

The Ad Hoc Committee now took over to prepare the legislation for floor consideration. While the Committee members could not amend the bill itself, they could offer amendments on the floor. It was at this point that the careful attention paid earlier to Committee membership paid off. Most of the members had already been through major sections of the bill. The principal standing committees with interest and expertise in the legislation had acted, and those responsible in each case were also present in the Ad Hoc Committee to lead the way. Further, since Speaker O'Neill was determined to win within his own party, he had appointed a majority of Democrats loyal to him. Success for the President's program in the Ad Hoc Committee was virtually ensured. Finally the Committee on Rules had powerful representation on the Ad Hoc Committee in the person of Richard Bolling (D-Missouri). His presence plus that of House Democratic Caucus Chairman Foley ensured that the legislation would move once it emerged from the Ad Hoc Committee.

Thus, though the bill had 113 separate provisions, it was processed quickly by the Committee, which acted "largely as a Democratic Forum":

> Democratic members on the panel, basically working as an arm of the party leadership that named them, established an unshakable majority to protect President Carter's energy program.
>
> They operated principally through private caucuses they held the day before each committee meeting to agree among themselves on specific amendments they would allow the next day.
>
> The pattern prevailed throughout the week with the agreed-upon amendments easily approved and others easily rejected—mostly along party lines. The actions produced howls of protest from Republicans who said they were being frozen out of decisions on national energy policy.[13]

The Committee did propose some amendments for floor consideration, and great care was exercised to prevent eventual defeat by debate and delay on the House floor. Working with Bolling, the party leadership obtained a modified closed rule to limit debate. Much to the chagrin of the Republicans, only certain amendments were allowed. Their own energy package could be introduced as a substitute, but it had to be voted on in *toto* rather than section by section, thus guaranteeing its defeat.

Given such masterful orchestration, it was not surprising that the bulk of the President's energy program was passed by the House. Only the gasoline tax was soundly defeated (it did not even survive the standing committee stage). The bill passed August 5—right on schedule. The vote on final passage was 244 to 177 with 82 percent of the Democrats and only 9 percent of the Republicans voting in favor. Key votes occurred on an amendment to end price controls on natural gas (defeated 199 to 227) and on the motion to recommit the bill to the Ad Hoc Committee with instructions to delete the crude oil equalization tax (defeated by the narrow vote of 203 to 219). Of the eight amendments adopted by roll call votes, five were introduced by the Ad Hoc Committee. Only one Ad Hoc Committee amendment was defeated on a roll call vote—an effort to enact a portion of the President's gasoline tax increase.

It is, of course, an exaggeration to depict the House as a silent partner to President Carter in the passage of the energy bill in 1977. The members involved in meeting Speaker O'Neill's tight schedule would rightfully resent any such characterization. They would argue that certain provisions were rejected (say, the gasoline tax), improvements were made, and opposition voices were permitted to be heard. Comparatively speaking, however, the process was certainly controlled and reserved, if not altogether silent.

How is it that the House accomplished this feat on such a complex and controversial national program? Much of the credit has quite rightly been assigned to Speaker O'Neill.[14] But what did he do? Above all, he correctly appraised the strengths and weaknesses of his own leadership position and then made important moves to capitalize on the former and reduce the effects of the latter. In particular, he made effective use of his party's majority in the House—Democratic support for a Democratic President on a major national issue. He accepted President Carter's statement of urgency and used it to justify speedy action in the House. Understanding the traditional weakness of House party leaders in relationship to the standing committees, he devised an effective means for bringing committee leaders together in an arena he had created—the Ad Hoc Committee. Thus he was able to accomplish what so many party leaders find impossible to achieve—coordinated legislative action on a major program within a time limit. Put bluntly, O'Neill was successful in managing existing processes and creating new ones where necessary to achieve legislative goals.

It is important for our purposes to observe that a number of conditions facilitated O'Neill's realization of the partnership role for the House. As noted earlier, the House and the Senate had taken initiative in this area, and thus neither the problems nor various proposed solutions were as new to the membership as in 1973-1974. This point was made several times when the Speaker found it necessary to justify the deadlines he had imposed. Second, both the President and the Speaker were new to their jobs. This condition could, of course, work to the disadvantage of both. In this case, however, the special combination of a President with virtually no Washington experience and a Speaker with many years of congressional service appeared to facilitate action. O'Neill urged his Democratic colleagues to assist the new President in this most urgent issue area. And the Speaker had two advantages: (1) he had several new responsibilities as a result of the many congressional reforms during the previous five years, and (2) he had succeeded Carl Albert, a Speaker generally acknowledged to be weak and ineffective.

A third condition favoring the partnership role for the House was that the many taxing provisions in the bill required that the House act first. Combined with the confidence and clarity of direction which characterized the Speaker's action, this condition resulted in postponing many of the conflicts inherent in this policy issue. Quite simply, many lobbyists preferred to do battle in the Senate rather than in the House. They judged that Speaker O'Neill had effectively reorganized the process in the House so as to favor the President's program. This is not to say that the lobbyists (in particular, the oil industry) were absent on the House side—indeed Speaker O'Neill at one time shouted to the House, "Never have I ever seen such an influx of lobbyists in this town as from big oil . . ."[15]— but rather that they saved their strongest push for the Senate, where the process would be more accommodating to their interests.

In summary, the Carter administration's expectations of Congress as a silent partner were nicely accommodated by several favorable conditions in the House in 1977. Whether similar results can be achieved in the future—particularly given the imbroglio in the Senate—is highly problematic.

The Senate as Facilitator of Energy Interests

Following several defeats for his energy program in the Senate, President Carter attacked the oil industry: ". . . as is the case in time of war, there is potential war profiteering in the impending energy crisis. This could develop with the passing months as the biggest ripoff in history."[16] Many senators smarted over this attack, which, by implication, was directed at them. Senator Floyd Haskell (D-Colorado) expressed this view: "As far as I am aware, they [the administration] didn't consult with any member of the Senate. . . . I think, by and large, where they made their mistake was to present something and then tell the Congress, 'Adopt it.'"[17]

In strong contrast to Speaker O'Neill, Senate Majority Leader Robert C. Byrd (D-West Virginia) doubted that legislative action could be completed on all parts of the program in 1977.[18] In a statement following the President's address on April 20, Byrd said, "I hope all of us would give it [the President's plan] the consideration it deserves. There is always time down the road to say no."[19] Whatever else might be said, the President's energy program did not lack "consideration" in the Senate.

Each of these statements suggests that Senate action was quite different from that in the House. There was no clear statement of strategy and timetable from Senator Byrd. In fact, the Majority Leader had little to say at all on the subject of the energy program—either to the general public, or, apparently, to his fellow senators. Rather the statements came from the standing committee chairmen with principal responsibility for the legislation as well as other individual senators espousing special points of view.

The procedure in the Senate for acting on the President's program was that which O'Neill sought to avoid with his Ad Hoc Committee innovation. The legislation was referred to the Committee on Finance (chaired by Russell B. Long, D-Louisiana) and the new Committee on Energy and Natural Resources (formerly the Committee on Interior and Insular Affairs, chaired by Henry M. Jackson, D-Washington). No effort was made to reconstruct the legislation as one bill. Rather, several bills were reported out for Senate floor action.

It did not take lobbyists very long to identify the merits of this more disjointed method of acting on the President's energy package. There were ample appeal points should any one special interest lose out along the way. Oil interests had a strong ally in Chairman Long who argued consistently that incentives to produce were needed. And lacking a strong and resourceful ally in the Senate (that is, a counterpart to O'Neill in the House), the inexperienced White House staff could be expected to lose control of the situation, and they surely did.

What actually happened in the Senate approached the bizarre. All the more traditional legislative techniques were employed, and one or two new methods were introduced. By no means can the full account of Senate action be recounted here. That must be the subject of a book someday. The most that can be done is to review highlights which establish Senate action as meeting the conditions of the facilitator role.

The two committees—Energy and Natural Resources, and Finance—operated quite differently. The first sent legislation to the floor in several different pieces. The least controversial bills—coal conversion and energy conservation—were passed by mid-September.[20] Then Senator Jackson acknowledged that his committee was deadlocked on natural gas pricing, 9 to 9, and he was, therefore, sending the legislation to the floor. When it became apparent on the floor that the supporters of deregulation had a majority, Senators James Abourezk (D-South Dakota) and Howard M. Metzenbaum (D-Ohio) began an unusual filibuster by amendment.[21] The two were remarkably successful; and yet while their tactic prevented passage of a bill deregulating natural gas prices, it likewise disrupted the progress of the entire Carter energy package. The filibuster continued for nine days before Senator Byrd teamed up with the Vice President to stop it. Byrd called up the many Abourezk-Metzenbaum amendments, and Vice President Mondale ruled them out of order. The Senate was in an uproar as senators objected to the procedure used to kill the filibuster. It appeared as though the Carter administration was, itself, permitting deregulation of natural gas to be enacted into law. Senator Byrd was the subject of considerable criticism on the floor of the Senate, and he lashed back at his critics. When it was all over, the

deregulation bill did pass, 50 to 46, guaranteeing that the House-Senate conference would be faced with fashioning a compromise between seemingly irrecon-
cilable positions.

A fourth bill to encourage energy conservation by utilities was also reported
out by the Committee on Energy and Natural Resources. The legislative provisions were not nearly as strong as had been asked for by the Carter administration. The weaker bill passed the Senate, 86 to 7.

The Committee on Finance fashioned a single bill on energy taxation—
paying little or no heed to what was asked for by President Carter. In fact, the
approaches of the Long and Carter bills were quite different—Long favoring tax
credits and other incentives for production, Carter favoring the use of taxes to
reduce consumption, with rebating provisions to return the money to the U.S.
public. Senator Long also wanted the Senate to permit maximum flexibility in
the bill so that Senate conferees would be in a good bargaining position with
House conferees. Long got very much what he wanted. His committee's bill
passed, 52 to 35.

It is difficult to imagine more of a contrast with the House action. Where
leadership was exercised, it was typically in opposition to rather than supportive of the Carter program. It proved extremely difficult for the Majority Leader
even to maintain the flow of the normal process. Many senators were involved in
legislation action, both in the debate and in offering amendments—not just those
from the committees with jurisdiction. A total of 73 roll call votes were taken
on the five bills, exclusive of the 109 votes associated with the filibuster. As a
consequence, two quite different legislative packages were brought to the
conference—a single House bill that gave the President most of what he wanted
and five Senate bills that differed dramatically from the President's requests
on several major issues (see table 14-3).

Why did the Senate play a role more accommodating to the many private
interests touched by this issue? As with the House and its role, this question is
important since the answer reveals the conditions favoring the facilitator role.
First, consider the manner in which the legislation came to the Senate from the
House. As noted earlier, the President's program survived the House almost intact
and was sent to the Senate as a single bill. This, of course, elated the administration, but the program still represented a coherent target for those opposed to
various sections. Had the House made more changes—say, satisfying this or that
special interest—the legislation might have been less susceptible to comprehensive criticism. Further in this connection, the momentum built up in the House
was halted with the August recess. Opponents to the program had a full month
in which to make contacts and develop strategies. Meanwhile the Carter administration became embroiled in, possibly even preoccupied with, the Bert Lance
affair. Thus, as with the other cases, legislative and political context is important.

Second, the program itself was vulnerable both substantively and politically.
The first is understandable. It would be difficult, indeed, to prepare an energy

Table 14-3

Congressional Action on the President's Energy Proposals, 1977

Proposals	House	Senate
1. Tax credits for home insulation	Approved	Approved
2. Increase in gasoline tax	Rejected	Rejected
3. Tax on gas-guzzling car	Approved	Rejected; banned their production
4. Rebated of "gas guzzler" tax to buyers of gas-saving cars	Rejected	Not considered
5. Mandatory energy efficiency standards for home appliances	Approved	Approved
6. Extend controls on natural gas prices, with higher ceilings	Approved	Rejected; ended price controls for new gas
7. Crude oil tax	Approved	Rejected
8. Tax on utility and industrial use of oil and natural gas	Approved with changes	Approved with further changes
9. Coal conversion	Approved	Approved with changes
10. Electric utility rate reform	Approved	Rejected

Source: Adapted from a chart in *Congressional Quarterly Weekly Report,* November 5, 1977, p. 2357.

program over which there was not basic substantive disagreement. The second, political vulnerability, is traceable perhaps to the fact that the President and his aides were unfamiliar with the congressional terrain. Whatever the reason, senators were dissatisfied with how the program was put together and sold.

Third, the President lacked a strong advocate in the Senate—one of the stature of Speaker O'Neill. A Lyndon B. Johnson as majority leader might have provided the kind of resourceful party leadership required for moving the President's program through the Senate (though it is worth noting that Johnson did not serve under a Democratic President). As I have noted elsewhere, however, "It may be dangerous to draw too many conclusions about what is possible or likely from a study of the leadership style of Majority Leader Johnson. We may never see his like again."[22] Certainly Robert Byrd was not prepared to attempt anything like the political tour de force of Speaker O'Neill.

Fourth, with a lack of supportive leadership in the Senate, the inexperience and ineptitude of the White House stood out in bold relief. Soon senators normally supportive of the administration were critical of both style and substance. At one point, Senator Abraham Ribicoff (D-Connecticut) said, "I am just wondering . . . if the President shouldn't admit that his energy program is a shambles."[23]

Bad timing, substantive and political vulnerability, lack of leadership, inexperience, inept style—these are the conditions which led to access and influence for many of the interests opposed to the President's program. In Neustadt's

terms, President Carter failed to protect his sources of power, notably "his reputation in the Washington community," and no one in the Senate was prepared to
protect them for him.[24]

Conclusions

At this writing the House-Senate conference on the 1977 energy legislation has
not completed its work. The conferees finally gave up trying to fashion acceptable compromises, and the first session of the 95th Congress ended. As expected,
the failure to enact a law resulted in recriminations all around.

While we all have a personal interest in the outcome of the current debate
and process of compromise, it is not necessary for actions to have been completed in order to accomplish the purposes of this chapter. Attention here has
been directed to exploring the various expectations of Congress in the development of energy policy. Not surprisingly, these hopes derive from a set of preferences about what ought to be done, given differing political conditions. The
major conclusions from this exercise are as follows.

1. Much in the manner of the original Davidson, Kovenock, and O'Leary
formulation, one can identify three roles or sets of expectations for Congress in
the development of energy policy: Congress as initiator, as silent or reserved
partner, and as facilitator of access and influence for affected interests.

2. Specific values are associated with the expectations of Congress in energy
policy development, and specific political conditions are associated with the
realization of these expectations. Although much more rigorous work is necessary to establish details, suffice it to say at this point that comprehensive
planning and policy analysis values appear to be associated with the first two
congressional roles (as initiator or partner). "Preferential pluralism" and political
analysis values tend to be associated with the third (that is, as facilitator). In the
cases examined here, the following political conditions were associated with
each role: split party control (Congress and the White House) and perceived crisis with the initiator role; accommodating, resourceful congressional leadership
and an acceptable rationale for altering the normal process with the partner role;
a vulnerable proposal weakly justified and a strong concentration of opposing
forces with the facilitator role.

3. It is worth special mention that many of the structural features of Congress make it difficult for that institution to initiate large-scale policy programs
(for example, bicameralism, decentralized committee system).

4. A number of organizational changes have been made in Congress to adjust
to the emergence of the energy issue as a priority item on the national agenda
(for example, committee reorganization, increased staff and policy analysis
capability, development of ad hoc mechanisms for treating special problems).

The institution is better prepared to play any of the three roles than it was in 1973.

One cannot escape the influence of personal preferences and values in assessing recent performance and future behavior of Congress on this important issue. I suspect that in strict process terms most evaluations will divide along a fairly traditional planning versus politics line. Those favoring the former will not be pleased with what has gone on and will be quite pessimistic about the future. Those favoring the latter will have been relieved by the Senate's more aggressive role in untracking the Carter program. Those who want a comprehensive energy policy *now* will inevitably be disappointed in lengthy congressional debate and compromise. Those who doubt that a comprehensive energy policy can be effectively implemented without attention being paid to all affected interests expect the process to be deliberate.

These evaluations will also likely divide on the estimate of legislative capability to cope with a highly technical issue. The planners doubt that Congress can or should be deeply involved in decision making on such issues. Even Congress as initiator should, by this view, accept the recommendations of its own policy analysts. Congressional involvement in all issues is an article of faith for the more politically oriented. For them, *technical* is a relative term and denial of jurisdiction on one issue leads directly to congressional impotence.

In actual practice, it is our tradition not to resolve such disputes but rather to benefit or suffer from the resulting conflicts. Recent energy policy development has been very much in this heritage. Some people would, therefore, argue that it is being constitutionally derived and thus all is well. That may not be very satisfying to those anxious about where the next Btu is coming from. But it is how we have normally handled the public business in this country.

Notes

1. Presidential News Conference, October 13, 1977.

2. Roger Davidson, David Kovenock, and Michael O'Leary, *Congress in Crisis: Politics and Congressional Reform* (Belmont, Calif.: Wadsworth, 1966), p. 17.

3. Ibid., pp. 17-37.

4. Andrew S. Carron, "Congress and Energy: A Need for Policy Analysis and More," *Policy Analysis,* Spring 1976, pp. 293, 295, 296.

5. Energy Policy Project of the Ford Foundation, *A Time to Choose: America's Energy Future* (Cambridge, Mass.: Ballinger, 1974).

6. Institute for Contemporary Studies, *No Time to Confuse* (San Francisco: Institute for Contemporary Studies, 1975), p. 146.

7. S. David Freeman, *Energy: The New Era* (New York: Vintage, 1974).

8. Institute for Contemporary Studies, *No Time to Confuse,* pp. 146, 147, 155.

9. Concentration here on comprehensive energy packages is not meant to overlook the many other policy relationships between the President and Congress in this field. Two major types of policy action of continuing importance are authorization of ongoing energy research and development and attending to the energy-related impacts of other legislation (for example, economic, environmental).

10. Charles O. Jones, *An Introduction to the Study of Public Policy* (North Scituate, Mass.: Duxbury, 1977).

11. James Sundquist, *Politics and Policy* (Washington: Brookings, 1968).

12. This conclusion is slightly less applicable than in the past as a consequence of the new budgetary process in Congress. A much more serious effort is made now to establish and conform to a legislative timetable.

13. *Congressional Quarterly Weekly Report,* July 23, 1977, p. 1487. Particularly heavy reliance was placed on these reports for recounting congressional action in 1977.

14. *New York Times,* August 1, 1977; January 2, 1978.

15. *Congressional Record,* August 3, 1977, p. H8417.

16. Presidential News Conference.

17. *Congressional Quarterly Weekly Report,* October 22, 1977, p. 2236.

18. *Congressional Quarterly Weekly Report,* May 21, 1977, p. 957.

19. *Washington Post,* April 21, 1977.

20. In order to facilitate meeting in conference, the Senate attached their individual bills to insignificant House bills (for example, the Senate coal conversion bill was attached to a House bill providing duty-free entry of bobsleds and luges).

21. Cloture had been invoked on September 26, and thus debate was limited to 100 hours. Quorum calls and votes on amendments submitted in advance of cloture are not counted in the 100 hours, however. Abourezk and Metzenbaum had filed 508 amendments and intended to call for a vote on each one.

22. Commission on the Operation of the Senate, *Policymaking Role of Leadership in the Senate* (Washington: Government Printing Office, 1976).

23. *Congressional Quarterly Weekly Report,* October 8, 1977, p. 2121.

24. Richard Neustadt, *Presidential Power* (New York: Wiley, 1960), p. 179.

15 The National Energy Plan and the Congress

Alfred R. Light

The year 1977 was in many ways a year of energy politics. It began with an un-believably rapid response to a Presidential initiative on emergency natural gas allocation.[1] A kind of rapidity was to characterize energy politics for the re-mainder of the year, but congressional rubber-stamping of Presidential proposals was not in the cards. Curiously, the President received simultaneous criticism for his slowness and for his haste in moving on energy policy in 1977. But adminis-tration spokesmen admitted throughout it all that energy was *the* top priority for President Carter's first year and that it would be fair to judge Presidential performance on the fate of the energy proposals.

The President's first three months in office were ones of largely symbolic leadership. His call-in talk shows, attendance at town meetings, frequent press conferences, and so on lent legitimacy to his Presidency but contributed little of policy substance. Many issue-oriented supporters grew restless. In April, how-ever, the energy policy push began as the President declared a "moral equivalent of war" on the nation's energy problems. He announced a comprehensive energy policy complete with objectives, timetables, motivating principles, and proposed government programs. James Schlesinger, the future first Secretary of the Department of Energy, and his analysts had used the three "symbolic months" to draw up a carefully balanced National Energy Plan for the nation.[2] Literally thousands of individuals had responded to Dr. Schlesinger's March request for public comment regarding national energy policy.[3] In some respects, the White House was slow because it tried to get everybody in on the act.

By autumn of 1977, however, many important congressmen complained that the original National Energy Plan had been hastily prepared and ill conceived and was therefore a political disaster. After a series of setbacks for the Carter program in the Senate Finance Committee in October, Abraham Ribicoff mused publicly, "I'm just wondering if President Carter shouldn't admit his energy pro-gram is a shambles" and suggested that the administration energy planners go back to their drawing boards to devise a new program.[4] Legislative drafting appeared shoddy under scrutiny. Testimony in the Senate Energy Committee, for example, indicated a good deal of skepticism about the language used in the utility rate reform proposal. Divisions of responsibility between the national and state governments were so vague that many senators simply voted against the proposal.

Both friend and foe of the administration claimed that the President had not touched base with the key forces needed to ensure passage of his energy program. Some claimed that the National Energy Plan was drafted in secret by Schlesinger's staff and that it had not been circulated widely even within the executive branch. Energy tax proposals had not been checked by the Treasury. Key committee chairmen like Russell Long saw portions of the package only days before the package was released. Was the overt openness of the plan's drafting a facade? Critics claimed that the administration compounded its error by imposing an end-of-the-year deadline for congressional passage of a package which "had some real ragged edges."[5]

Although final action on the National Energy Plan dragged on through 1978, the administration has already learned some lessons from its experience. Perhaps energy served as a first indicator of trouble to come for the administration's policy efforts on taxes, welfare, national health insurance, urban affairs, and a number of other reforms. The history can also inform this administration and later ones about better and worse means of developing future energy policies and programs.

Useful political lessons emerging from the National Energy Plan's history have come in at least four major areas. First is the ironic nature of the energy issue itself. A second involves the cross-pressured complexity of interest group positions on energy proposals. Another concerns the key role of organizational politics for the prospects of congressional adoption of comprehensive plans or programs. Finally, President Carter might discern from his experiences in the energy arena some of the tensions, dilemmas, or inconsistencies in his basic philosophy of governance. At the conclusion of this chapter, I suggest a few conclusions which the former Georgia governor might well keep in mind in his future interactions with Congress and with the nation concerning energy policy.

The Ironic Nature of the Energy Issue

It is not very surprising that Jimmy Carter decided to move first in his development of comprehensive reform proposals in the area of energy. For several years the Washington energy policy arena has been characterized by a kind of "comprehensive" planner-style mentality. In 1972 Congress began its attempt to cope with the future repercussions or impacts of new energy technologies with its establishment of an Office of Technology Assessment. It wanted to "equip itself with new and effective means for securing competent, unbiased information concerning the physical, biological, economic, social, and political effects of [technology] applications."[6] Clearly, the call was for comprehensive assessments. When the Federal Energy Administration (FEA) was created in response to the

1973-1974 energy crisis, the new agency received two missions: to handle the mandatory fuel allocations program in the event of recurrence of shortages and to do a comprehensive energy policy analysis, specifically to plan for independence from foreign energy sources.[7]

The FEA's approach to policy analysis clearly fell into the tradition of the Ford Foundation's Energy Policy Project and "the Project on the Predicament of Mankind."[8] A basic policy tool was a massive econometric model. From model outputs the agency built scenarios of alternative energy futures dependent on "national" policy choices about energy. J. Friedrick Weinhold, a chief designer of the FEA model, had been involved in the same kind of operation as a senior engineer with the Ford Foundation project. The formats of the energy policy scenarios in the Ford and FEA projects were macroeconomic, or "big picture," constructions, resembling Department of Defense (DOD) scenarios of future wars around which DOD bases its force structuring and sizing. The DOD style of top-down policy analysis and planning so prevalent in Washington since the PPBS (Planning Programming, Budgeting System) days began to dominate energy policy analysis and planning in the early 1970s.[9] This analytic style contrasts with the fragmented, disjointed, and incremental style of policy development that characterized the politics of coal, oil, natural gas, and electric power generation prior to the 1970s.[10]

Political scientists have always been skeptical of systems analysis and comprehensive planning approaches to public policy making. Such approaches may be impossible in a real-world context and therefore may be ill conceived. FEA staff conceptualized the problem of energy shortage and hypothesized alternative solutions. They constructed models based on assumptions about the sensitivity of supply, demand, and prices of various goods to changes in energy prices and to resource constraints at national and regional levels. Manipulation of policy variables produced outcomes based on these assumptions. The major myth may be that "we" can find a correct national energy policy, make a once-and-for-all decision about where "we" want to go as a nation, manipulate those policy variables, and get there. Weiner and Wildavsky recently explored the potential error in such an attitude in an article entitled, "The Prophylactic Presidency."[11]

In the real world, thousands of individuals make energy production and consumption decisions each day. "Analysis and evaluation are disjointed in the sense that various aspects of public policy and even aspects of any one problem are analyzed at various points, with no apparent coordination and without the articulation of parts. . . ."[12] The Ford Foundation, FEA, and National Energy Plan approaches to policy making attempt to fight the disjointed and incremental nature of the process. As Rose put it, "An adequate national energy policy must of course rise from basic decisions made by or on behalf of the country as a whole, decisions concerning national security, costs, the present and future quality of life, and so on. When these decisions have been made, a planner can set down tentative desiderata. . . ."[13] Jimmy Carter calls himself a planner. Downs calls this planner mentality a superman syndrome.[14]

Riker has labeled the superman syndrome as it applies to U.S. energy policy as undemocratic and un-American.[15] Where scenarios and macropolicy dominate, government control of U.S. energy supply and utilization is a serious topic of debate.[16] Even if the approach is moral and patriotic, however, the realities of fragmentation and incrementalism overwhelm the very thought of implementing a comprehensive national energy policy in the view of many political scientists.

There are additional ironies in recent national efforts to analyze and plan energy policy beyond the fact that the enterprise may be undemocratic or, lacking that, impossible. These other ironies involve the specific employment of economic theory and econometric methodology to the assessments of various energy policies. Not only may "big" energy choices be impossible to make, but economic methods may also fail to inform us on precisely those aspects of energy policy where the most difficult problems occur. The economists' "hidden hand" and the econometricians' "black box" have always held a mystical quality. A theorist may rely on market forces distorted by public policy-induced incentives and disincentives to achieve desired outcomes. But there are usually missing links in the theoretical chain because of assumptions about the behavior of individuals. One has only to look at the horrendous implementation problems associated with the "controlled" experimental studies on income maintenance and housing allowance to discover how silly simple economic concepts can look when confronted with the complexity and subtlety of a social context.[17] Economic approaches leave some important policy implementation questions unanswered because they ignore them.

Cross-pressured Complexity of Group Interests

The President does not have the luxury of ignoring cross-pressured group interests. A key implementation problem deals with the likely positions of interest groups. Assessments of interest group influences and positions is sometimes called force field analysis.[18] Public administration scholars seek to incorporate in the training of MPAs some sensitivity to political and interest group calculations in shaping recommendations for policy actors. But even where attempts at such inculcation of the political nature of policy problems are made, often it does not sink in until after politicians have critiqued, or ignored, an administrator's proposals.[19] "Pure" economic or scientific analysis may imply politically silly conclusions.

President Carter's analysts in 1977 operated from a relatively knowledgeable position in framing the National Energy Plan. Schlesinger sought a balanced, fair plan in political as well as economic and technical senses. In his balancing act, the President could rely on a very recent history of a number of energy proposals in Congress. For example, Congress had approved a gradual rise in oil prices in 1975 but had also voted to retain price controls. Carter's National Energy Plan likewise sought to retain controls but to boost prices with a wellhead tax.

President Ford, with the encouragement of William Simon, had sought a large federal tax on gasoline. Although Congress had killed the idea, it had mandated fuel efficiency standards for new cars. President Carter sought to enact a gasoline tax on a standby basis only; this seems to be a middle ground. The tax would have taken effect only if congressionally mandated efforts and other programs did not actually reduce gasoline consumption. A "gas guzzler" tax proposal similar to the President's had been defeated in 1975, but Congress had approved civil fines for makers of inefficient automobiles. By 1977 Congress had already acted in the areas of tax credits for energy conservation, also. The previous year it authorized grants to states for development of incentives to insulate. Other legislation that year authorized HUD to develop energy efficiency standards for buildings subject to Congress's setting of penalties for failures to meet those standards. In a variety of areas, the President's National Energy Plan appears to have been only an incremental adjustment to directions in which Congress already was moving by 1977. Looked at in this way, it contrasted with the Ford Foundation, and, to a lesser extent, the Project Independence study.

Other of President Carter's proposals, although untried at the national level, had been experimented with at the state and local levels. Studies of time-of-day or peak-load pricing for utilities had been conducted in several states. The Central Vermont Public Service Commission had tested, on a voluntary basis, various rate designs that involved cost incentives, penalties, and physical controls affecting time and magnitude of electric energy consumption. Connecticut and New Jersey have studied public acceptance of peak-load pricing. Several Georgia towns have experimented with mandatory peak-load pricing. By 1977 California had ordered major utilities to provide time-of-day rates for large consumers. New York had even ordered all major utilities to file time-of-day rates where utilities had or could obtain the necessary metering devices.[20] Utility reform seemed a coming idea in early 1977.

Despite the rich congressional and state-local track record on energy, the President's planners seem to have miscalculated on many key issues concerning the center of gravity among the relevant interest groups. Furthermore, the Administration failed to involve interest groups in the initial framing of proposals, and tried to balance administrative interests against those of others without their participation. In doing so, the administration may have changed inadvertently the balance of power on some issues. For example, the National Energy Plan proposed to raise the interstate price of natural gas from $1.46 to $1.75 per million cubic feet. However, gas association lobbyists and their advocates in Congress (for example, Congressman Krueger or Senator Bentsen) were not involved in the decision. This "concession" to gas lobbyists without their application of pressure may have whetted the lobbyists' appetites for still higher prices. Some consumer lobbyists attributed the victory for deregulation forces in the Senate to this early administration admission of vulnerability on the gas pricing issue. A little hard-headed negotiation between the administration and deregulation advocates in Congress might have resulted in proposals similar to the President's and might have co-opted the opposition.[21]

Another interesting aspect of interest group positions on the National Energy Plan involves the President's "friends." Interests one normally expects to find in the Democratic column did not endorse all segments of the plan. The AFL-CIO, for example, continued its strong endorsement of the breeder reactor during 1977. Labor groups opposed the President's crude oil equalization tax as a burden on the workingman despite the rebate and tax credit components of the proposal. Consumer groups also opposed some taxes while endorsing price controls on oil and natural gas. Columnists Evans and Novak went so far as to attribute the President's energy setbacks in the Senate primarily to those Democratic pressures rather than to the oil industry lobby, which they claimed was relatively invisible during the critical fall 1977 decision-making period.[22]

Interest group pressures in energy politics are remarkable for still another reason. Energy policy impacts are often geographically limited. The environmental repercussions of coal strip mining, of the siting of nuclear or conventional power plants, and of the development of many other energy sources are localized. The regional implications of gas deregulation and of the increasing reliance of particular regions on imported petroleum sources have become all too obvious in the last few years. The organization of Congress along geographical lines reinforces the geographical cleavages existing in energy policy. The Western states contain the lion's share of the nation's remaining energy resources. Even the more exotic new sources of energy such as solar and geothermal favor the West. However, most people do not live near these remaining resources.

The human misery exacted by a producer state's exorbitant coal severance tax is far removed from the concerns of that state's Congressional delegation. New England's geographical, political, and economic distance from Texas led it to seek cheap foreign sources of oil. Texas congressmen obtained relief through protective import and pricing policies. Peculiarities in the natural gas regulatory system coupled with these oil import policies led New England and Texas to distinctively different patterns of gas consumption. When the gas system began to produce shortages where gas was sold cheaply, New England obtained federal relief in Congress with a priority allocation system to specifically favor residential consumption of scarce gas at controlled prices. When the Organization of Petroleum-Exporting Countries raised the price of crude oil, New England's representatives fought for and got price controls on domestic crude oil. There is little wonder that congressional energy battles are often called a new "War between the States."[23]

Organizational Politics in Congress

The administration's experience with the National Energy Plan surely sensitized it to another dimension of the legislative process not quite as visible as the cross-pressured complexity of interest group activities. Organizational manuevering was a key factor in the strategies designed to pass and to oppose the plan. In retrospect, it is difficult not to admire Speaker O'Neill's skillful navigation of the complex set of energy proposals through the House of Representatives.

For a number of months before Carter introduced the proposals, O'Neill had been involved in a struggle with House committee chairmen who had energy-related responsibilities. In 1977 the Speaker compromised; he dropped his proposal for a permanent energy committee in return for a series of stringent deadlines to be set for House consideration of Carter's energy proposals. The House created a special Ad Hoc Select Committee on Energy for the sole purpose of review and coordination of President Carter's energy package. After an initial set of presentations to the Ad Hoc Committee, parts of the package were reviewed by various normal standing committees, with firm deadlines for reporting the legislation back to the Ad Hoc Committee.

Speaker O'Neill personally chose almost all the members of the Ad Hoc Committee who were Democrats. The Democratic members were selected with a view for giving the President's plan a friendly reception. *Congressional Quarterly*'s analysis of the Ad Hoc Committee Democrats found that "a solid majority have in the past supported higher taxes on gasoline, continued regulation of prices on oil and natural gas, stringent controls over strip mining, and similar proposals that indicate a philosophical compatibility with the President's approach to energy policy."[24] Speaker O'Neill's Ad Hoc Committee took only five days in July 1977 to "reconcile and harmonize" the plan's titles as reported by the standing committees. In the Rules Committee, the Speaker sought and received a modified closed rule, limiting opponents to a few selected proposals for amendment on the floor. He successfully protected the plan from significant weakening on the floor after Texas proponents and opponents of gas deregulation reached a comparomise to raise prices but maintain controls.

On the other hand, Robert Byrd, the Senate Majority Leader, and Henry Jackson, Carter's Senate energy floor leader, were not able or did not try to ramrod the National Energy Plan through the upper chamber. While Speaker O'Neill skillfully had managed to reassemble House-passed versions into a single omnibus piece of legislation, Senator Byrd split the plan into at least six bills. Despite the creation of a comprehensive Committee on Energy and Natural Resources under Senator Jackson early in the year, authority over the plan was divided. Without the mechanism of an Ad Hoc Committee, the President's package could never be reassembled in the Senate. With the entire Senate voting on various fragments of the program, opponents of the President had many more opportunities to take shots at the package.

Perhaps even more significantly, neither Senator Byrd nor Senator Jackson supported the plan wholeheartedly. Byrd testified against aspects of it in the Senate energy committee. Each Senator voted against parts of it. During the gas deregulation dispute in the Senate, Byrd almost faced a mutiny. A loophole in the Senate's cloture rule allowed Senators Abourezk and Metzenbaum to force the Senate to take separate votes on each of 500-odd amendments filed to the gas deregulation bill. Despite Byrd's holding of the Senate in round-the-clock sessions, the two senators had an almost unbeatable filibuster. When the majority leader ended the filibuster with some parliamentary razzledazzle, Senate decorum broke down. Amid shouts of "dictator" and worse, Byrd called up amendment after amendment, which Vice President Mondale ruled out of order under the cloture rule which states that "no dilatory motion or dilatory amendment or amendment not germane shall be in order."[25] Only by invoking the Senate custom requiring the presiding officer to recognize party leaders when they are among several senators seeking recognition, in conjunction with a ruling that Mondale could "take the initiative" in ruling the amendments out of order, was the filibuster ended.

Senator Russell Long, who fought Carter tooth and nail on deregulation, engineered an organizational strategy to help the President resurrect energy tax proposals which the Senator could not get out of his Finance Committee. Unable to reach accord on the crude oil tax, gasoline tax, and taxes on utilities using oil and gas, the Finance Committee had dismantled the centerpieces of Carter's plan. Faced with a lengthy floor fight on any taxes the Committee might recommend to the Senate anyway, Long chose to have his Committee send the Senate a noncontroversial bill with only tax credits. Thus the Senate did not delay getting its proposals to the House-Senate Conference Committee. This maneuver helped push the legislative process along but ultimately did not work. The energy tax conference adopted the proposal for tax credits only as its own and was unable to resurrect any energy taxes which Long's committee had abandoned.

The House and Senate leadership tried to devise a general organizational strategy for the Conference to grease the tracks for the President's program. While the Senate chose different conferees for different parts of the plan, the House appointed the same conferees for all the plan's titles. House conferees were all selected from the Ad Hoc Committee initially. Once all the bills came out of conference, O'Neill would seek a rule allowing the House to vote on the entire package of legislation in one vote. Despite the Senate's fragmentation of the plan, the House thus would be able to reassemble it again. The President, however, would receive the package of proposals in several pieces, any of which he could veto.

Again, the Speaker was able to make use of special House rules to enhance chances for passage of any compromises reached in conference. But this strategy could not help matters in the Senate. After intense wrangling over natural gas pricing, the Conference did work out a delicate compromise. But the institutional problems of the Senate's Rule 22 remained, and Abourezk was again able to stall that element of the plan on the floor during the fall of 1978.

Conclusions

Whatever history's judgment of President Carter's "moral equivalent of war" for a comprehensive national energy policy, the energy controversies during his first year illuminated significant problems in the implementation of major reform proposals. How these problems are solved during the remainder of his administration may determine history's judgment about his general effectiveness. A central issue revolves on the President's ability or inability to marshal political resources for a comprehensive approach to social problems.

The President faces the ubiquitous dilemma that he himself can never be totally certain of the propriety of the policies he advocates but must nevertheless demand the loyalty of his subordinates and supporters in pressing for a comprehensive program. The President claimed when he announced the National Energy Plan that he recognized the problem: "The Plan is complicated. I am sure that many people will find some features of it they will dislike along with features they can support. But it is a carefully balanced Plan, which depends for its effectiveness on all of its major parts."[26] If President Carter believed in this interrelationship, it was a mistake for him to tolerate the insubordination of his own people. Administration forces cannot be among the "many people" chipping away at the President's proposals. Carter's people were too quick to compromise on key features of the energy plan. If Schlesinger, the Energy Department, the Treasury Department, and so on are not committed to the complete policy, failure is likely. Within the administration, in the future Carter should be more determined to get everybody in on the act of policy making earlier; but once committed to a course of action, his Cabinet should be as one. However, President Carter believes in Cabinet government. His department heads maintain much discretion in their spheres of influence. Is the hierarchy necessary for waging a "moral equivalent of war" necessarily too rigid for the open democracy and independence of thought the President desires for his Cabinet officers?

A related problem arises in President Carter's reliance on public and other "outside" support to pressure Congress and the special interests toward his point of view. The fickle finger of fate strikes often at Presidential popularity. The effectiveness with which the President can mobilize outside pressure on Congress varies enormously over time. During a cold winter immediately after his election, the President's proposals had a much better chance than during an idyllic summer with the news dominated by Bert Lance's troubles. Gas deregulation forces in the Senate have seized opportunities to press forward whenever they saw an opening. President Carter might have exploited opportunities more effectively had his legislative timetable been somewhat more flexible, not so commited originally to a December 31, 1977, deadline.

Election years have advantages, too. The opposition then is more consolidated. A major advantage of Speaker O'Neill's House strategy was the inability of his opponents to concentrate their efforts on weak points rather than to fight the energy plan as a whole. Senate critics, on the other hand, were able to get away with negativism. In the Finance Committee, after totally demolishing President Carter's energy tax proposals, some senators did sheepishly suggest that perhaps they ought to propose some alternatives. But the Senate had no Senate energy plan. If President Carter would have found one, he might have done a better job in advocating his own proposals. The President had to fight a guerrilla war on energy rather than a conventional (that is, electioneering) one.

Several important lessons we might draw from the 1977–1978 energy history can be summarized as follows:

1. The President must maximize "real" policy-making participation in the early stages to enhance the probability of ultimate success.
2. An administration divided against itself cannot stand.
3. A President needs flexible timetables to exploit the political opportunities which occasionally present themselves.

Notes

1. The House held hearings on a Friday, marked the President's bill up on the following Monday, and voted it through, 367 to 52, the next day. Robert Byrd bypassed relevant committees and took the bill straight to the Senate floor. After a 91-to-2 favorable vote, the two houses took less than a day to compromise on their two versions. On Wednesday, the bill arrived on the President's desk for his signature. He signed it the same day, and the Emergency Natural Gas Act of 1977 became law less than a week after the President proposed the legislation.

2. Executive Office of the President, Energy Policy and Planning, *The National Energy Plan* (Washington: Government Printing Office, 1977).

3. *Federal Register,* March 2, 1977.

4. *Congressional Quarterly Weekly Reports* 35, no. 43 (October 22, 1977), p. 2121.

5. *Congressional Quarterly Weekly Reports* 35, no. 41 (October 8, 1977), p. 2062.

6. P.L. 92-484, Technology Assessment Act of 1972.

7. P.L. 93-275, Federal Energy Administration Act of 1974.

8. Ford Foundation Energy Policy Project, *A Time to Choose* (Cambridge, Mass.: Ballinger, 1974); and Donella Meadows et al., *The Limits to Growth* (New York: Potomic Associates, 1972).

9. Albert Shapero, "Planning, Programming, Budgeting System: A Concise Introduction to PPBS," in *Whatever Happened to State Budgeting?* ed. Kenneth Howard (Lexington, Ky.: Council of State Governments, 1972).

10. David Howard Davis, *Energy Politics* (New York: St. Martin's Press, 1974).

11. Sanford Weiner and Aaron Wildavsky, "The Prophylactic Presidency," *Public Interest,* Summer 1978, pp. 3-19.

12. David Braybrooke and Charles E. Lindblom, *A Strategy of Decision* (New York: Free Press, 1970), pp. 105-106.

13. David Rose, "Energy Policy in the United States," *Scientific American,* January 1974, p. 1.

14. Anthony Downs, *Inside Bureaucracy* (Boston: Little, Brown, 1968).

15. William Riker, "The Ideology of *A Time to Choose,*" in *No Time to Confuse* ed. Institute for Contemporary Studies (San Francisco: Institute for Contemporary Studies, 1975).

16. Congressional Research Service, *Resolved: That the Federal Government Should Control the Supply and Utilization of Energy in the United States* (Washington: Government Printing Office, 1973).

17. See, e.g., Peter H. Ross and Sonia R. Wright, "Evaluation Research: An Assessment of Theory, Practice, and Politics," *Evaluation Quarterly* 1, no. 1 (February 1977): 1-52.

18. Richard Todd, Jonathon Raymond, and Theresa Marton, "An Approach to Planning Organizational Transition," *Public Administration Review* 37, no. 5 (September/October 1977): 520-527.

19. James L. Garnett, "Bureaucratic and Party Politics in an Intergovernmental Context," in *Intergovernmental Administration 1976,* eds. James D. Carrol and Richard W. Campbell (Syracuse, N.Y.: Maxwell School of Citizenship and Public Affairs, 1976).

20. Council of State Governments, *Energy Conservation: Policy Considerations for the States* (Lexington, Ky.: Council of State Governments, November 1976), p. 23.

21. *Congressional Quarterly Weekly Reports* 35, no. 41 (October 8, 1977): 2062-2063.

22. Rowland Evans and Robert Novak, "Carter's Energy Package: Problems with Tactics," *Washington Post,* September 30, 1977.

23. American Enterprise Institute, *Energy: A New War between the States?* (Washington: American Enterprise Institute, 1976).

24. *Congressional Quarterly Weekly Reports* 35, no. 29 (July 16, 1977): 1436.

25. Senate Rule 22.

26. Executive Office of the President, p. ix.

16 Pluralism and Energy: Carter's National Energy Plan

David Howard Davis

When President Carter denounced the oil and natural gas lobbies for blocking congressional passage of his National Energy Plan (NEP), accusing them of "war profiteering" and seeking the "biggest ripoff in history,"[1] he was echoing a common political science criticism of interest groups. The pluralist model of U.S. politics points out, as President Carter so dramatically did, the iron triangles forged among interest groups, congressional committees, and administrative agencies. These closed subgovernments leave large segments of the population unrepresented in the group process because they are not organized due to diffuse interests (for example, consumers), lack of political skills (for example, Mexican-Americans), lack of resources (for example, the poor), and so forth. This leaves the political arena for the organized, the politically skilled, and the wealthy.

But is the pluralist model, harking back to James Madison and Arthur Bentley, still valid in the end of the 20th century, an era of big government and complex technologies? Pluralism might have been a satisfactory explanation for Pendleton Herring writing about the business-dominated 1920s or David Truman writing about the government-sponsored cartels of the New Deal and World War II,[2] but is pluralism still valid in the 1970s when government is so much larger and longer established? The classic group model explains how interest groups, working with sympathetic congressional committees, impose their will on federal agencies, all too eager to comply in order to ensure their budgets and authority. Thus, for example, cotton farmers organized as the National Cotton Council, with the alliance of the House Agriculture Committee's Subcommittee on Cotton, control the U.S. Department of Agriculture's Commodity Credit Corporation target prices for cotton—a tidy triangle forming a private subgovernment. Still, this view presents the government agencies as passive vehicles of private and congressional power. It belittles agencies' roles as innovators and leaders. It counters political science assessments that the executive branch bureaucracy has come to dominate policy making, not just implementation.[3]

Using the National Energy Plan to Test Group Theory

Recent events in energy policy test the group model. Is the traditional picture true that interest groups dominate policy formation, or is it more accurate to give greater prominence to the role of the bureaucracy? President Carter's National Energy Plan, presented so boldly in an address to Congress on April 20, 1977, offers a case study. Convenience suggests four phases for analysis: initiative, lobbying, congressional process, and results.

Initiative

Initiative came entirely from within the executive branch. James Schlesinger headed an Energy Task Force in the Executive Office of the President. This team became the leadership of the Department of Energy upon its official establishment on October 1, 1977. The NEP's genesis was remarkably closed even within the executive branch. Carter and Schlesinger were obsessed with secrecy. This secrecy allowed Carter to package a multitude of decisions about energy (many of which the Nixon and Ford administrations had considered) into a single, dramatic policy. Schlesinger's task force developed the NEP with minimal direct input from other government agencies and virtually none from congressional and business leaders. Only by forcefully demanding their rights to be consulted were the Treasury, the Office of Management and Budget, the Council of Economic Advisors, and the National Security Council allowed to participate in the final stage of the drafting.[4]

The NEP's early stages were highly technical, based on a computer model—the Project Independence Evaluation System (PIES). PIES was an econometric simulation of the United States that forecast the energy consequences of changes in production, consumption, and so on. Based on PIES, Schlesinger's task force decided the optimal levels of prices, taxes, imports, or whatever.

Schlesinger presented the tentative plan to a marathon meeting of the Cabinet on April 6 and 7, during which the most Draconian measures were moderated. Carter delayed many decisions until the last moment. As late as April 16, 1977, the President was still contemplating natural gas deregulation. Even after the NEP was in its final form, no one besides Schlesinger could explain the total package. That no one else could explain the program was to prove an impediment to educating Congress and public.

Carter's self-imposed deadline of presenting a comprehensive energy plan 90 days after his inauguration had both supporters and critics. S. David Freeman, a member of the task force, favored it, saying that "without a deadline we could easily have spent the Summer and Fall [drafting the plan] and come up with a watered down project" that would have been "nickeled and dimed to death."[5] On the other hand, this was precisely the NEP's fate. It was nickeled and dimed to death in Congress. Would it not have been better for the Energy Task Force to have resolved more of the conflicting interests in the comparative privacy of the executive branch where at least the President's reputation would not have been at stake?

Lobbying

Vindicating pluralist theory, lobbying in Congress on energy policy was intensive in 1977. Table 16-1 summarizes the activity. Most notable was the magnitude of the effort. For 36 percent of business lobbyists to focus on energy was a significant increase over prior years. Oil and natural gas companies predominated. Perhaps more impressive is that 67 percent of the state and local governments which registered did so for energy issues. These registrants were chiefly municipally owned public utilities, thus more like private utility companies than their government categorization would imply. Not surprisingly, environmental groups were highly concerned with energy (41 percent). The percentage of citizens groups concerned with energy would have been much higher except that the total number of registrants was inflated by numerous antiabortion groups organized at the congressional district level. That only 15 percent of trade associations registered sought to influence energy legislation was low compared to the other categories.

As this 15 percent points out, simply counting the number of registrants is only the first step in assessing their power, [6] for this last category includes the

Table 16-1
Lobbyists Registering During 1977

Lobby Category	Total	Energy	Percentage
Business	492	178	36%
Energy subcategories:			
Oil		62	13
Natural gas		51	10
Public utilities		21	4
Coal		8	2
Automobile		6	1
Miscellaneous		30	6
Trade associations	385	56	15
Labor unions	31	4	13
State and local governments	33	22	67
Environmental	29	12	41
Citizens associations	92	12	13

Source: *Congressional Quarterly Weekly Report* 35, nos. 12, 13, 17, 24, 26, 34, 43, 45, 48 (1977); 36, nos. 1, 8 (1978).

potent American Petroleum Institute (API) and the Independent Petroleum
Association of America (IPAA). Additional factors include size, cohesiveness,
access, and money among others. The API and IPAA would rank high in regard
to all such characteristics. In the business category, six of the seven major oil
companies registered. Both the nuclear and automotive industries are oligopo-
listic, so there are only a few firms involved; virtually all lobbied.

Congressional Process

This phase yields a mixed verdict as to the utility of the pluralist theory, largely
because the House and the Senate responded so differently. Under Speaker Tip
O'Neill's firm hand, the House passed the NEP in three months. To do so, O'Neill
appointed an Ad Hoc Energy Committee, set step-by-step deadlines, and guided
the bill through floor debate under a modified closed rule designed to avoid
amendments. The result was that the bill passed on August 5 with hardly any
changes from the President's proposal.

The NEP's reception in the Senate was far different. First, the Senate split
the House bill into five separate bills. The Finance Committee so gutted the
President's tax program that Chairman Russell Long had to patch together a
crude facsimile to take to conference. Natural gas deregulation aroused even
more controversy. From September 23 until the acrimonious climax on October 3, Senators Abourezk and Metzenbaum filibustered to block deregulation,
finally losing 50 to 46. On October 18, a conference began to reconcile the
House and Senate versions. From December through May, the conference committee deadlocked on natural gas deregulation. Senator Long of Louisiana, a
staunch supporter of his state's petroleum industry, held hostage the tax provisions under the jurisdiction of his Finance Committee until the conference
reached an acceptable compromise. Finally on May 24, 1978, the conferees
narrowly agreed to a complex six-year plan for deregulation.

These Senate machinations conformed to pluralist theory. For example,
David Truman writes of the advantage of defending the status quo over seeking
change.[8] Truman also notes that the Senate's representation by state rather than
by population benefits states with small populations[9] such as Louisiana that
happen to produce natural gas. Yet this institutional factor should have also
aided Senator Abourezk since he, too, comes from a small state. And the argument that defense enjoys an advantage should mean that the advantage would be
just as accessible in the House of Representatives.

Indeed, the contrasting fate of the NEP in the House and Senate is a serious
challenge to the pluralist analysis for if interest group pressure explains the Senate action, then party and technocracy explain the House action. In the 1976
campaign Speaker O'Neill had promised that his Democratic majority would
show people in the United States how effective the House could be if a Demo-

cratic President were elected. His strong leadership in guiding the NEP to an expeditious passage fulfilled his pledge. The Democratic leader in the Senate, Robert Byrd, displayed much less partisan loyalty to President Carter.

O'Neill was able to place party above interest groups in part because James Schlesinger had set forth a technocratic plan that fit Democratic party ideology. Like previous Republican approaches, in the NEP high prices would dampen consumer demand, but, unlike Nixon and Ford proposals, energy producers would not gain "windfall profits." The added costs were to be returned to consumers through a complex series of taxes on gasoline and crude oil; tax rebates on solar, geothermal, and conservation activities; and expanded regulation of natural gas and electricity. This was distinctly Democratic rather than Republican economics. Republicans would have been more comfortable with a free market solution in which energy producers gained the profits, presumably stimulating production as well as dampening demand. The House and Senate votes on natural gas deregulation illustrate this fact. In the House on August 3, Republicans voted to deregulate, 127 to 17, while the Democrats voted to keep regulation, 210 to 72 (Phi = .59). On October 4, the Senate voted similarly: Republicans favored deregulation, 34 to 3, while Democrats opposed it, 43 to 16 (phi = .62). Thus the outcome was that the Senate voted 59 to 46 to deregulate while the House did the opposite, 199 to 227. Likewise House Democrats voted to keep Carter's crude oil tax, 216 to 66, while Republicans voted against it, 137 to 3 (phi = .85)

Results

The conference committee formal vote on May 24 to approve the secretly negotiated natural gas compromise marked the climax of the bargaining within Congress, thus completing the phase in which interest groups are most potent.[10] Assessing the results at that juncture shows the extent to which special interests modified Carter's NEP. The score card indicated President Carter lost on most issues.

The conference's agreement to deregulate natural gas prices by 1985 was the most notable NEP defeat. It reversed a forty-year policy established in the Natural Gas Act of 1938. The President himself had been less firm. While occasionally promising to deregulate *new* gas, he had never publicly suggested deregulating *old* gas, and at several times he spoke very forcefully against any deregulation, denouncing "special interest lobbyists" and threatening vetoes. While by its complexity and seven-year time span the conference compromise mitigated immediate shocks, nevertheless it clearly was deregulation of both new and old gas. Moreover, the conference leaders met secretly to negotiate their settlement. The secrecy so offended the House of Representatives that it voted on April 13 that the clandestine meetings must cease; all the sessions should be public. The House's protest was ignored.

Electric rate reform was another NEP proposal that failed to get through Congress. Carter asked the federal government to regulate intrastate electricity by establishing national rate standards, thereby preempting state public utility commissions. For example, Carter asked Congress to outlaw declining bloc rates for industry. The utility companies preferred the existing system of state regulation. The companies were like prisoners who had learned to love their chains. David Truman suggests a similar case. At the turn of the century the insurance industry sought regulation at the federal rather than the state level because it chaffed under state commissions. But after a 1944 Supreme Court decision altered the legal doctrine, it held the contrary position because it then believed state regulation would be more lenient.[11]

Like natural gas deregulations, the NEP's tax proposals took a severe drubbing in the Senate. Except for the 50 cent per gallon tax on gasoline, the House approved the NEP's tax on crude oil, "gas guzzling" automobiles, and industrial and utility use of oil. The Senate Finance Committee rejected all these. Furthermore, to harden its position, it instructed the Senate conferees that if forced to compromise, no tax revenues could be rebated to the public as the NEP proposed. The Senate, like the House, rejected the 50 cent per gallon gasoline tax. No matter what Dr. Schlesinger's PIES computer model showed, Congress was not about to intervene that extensively with the American's love affair with his automobile.

The President's most serious loss was more general: his failure to secure the prompt enactment of his legislative proposal. Carter has staked his reputation on the NEP, addressing Congress and a national television audience when he introduced it, defending it vigorously (even emotionally), and dramatically postponing a foreign trip to be available at what he hoped would be a critical period of the conference. As the months dragged on, the stalled plan became an embarrassment.

The first three examples discussed—natural gas, electricity, and taxes—represent victories for energy interest groups. The fourth, the NEP's slow progress through Congress, represents not an interest group victory but only a defeat for the Carter administration. Two interest group victories were defensive. Electric utilities sought to ward off national standards, and oil producers and consumers sought to avoid new taxes. Natural gas deregulation was offensive. After decades of regulation producers moved to end the system that had distorted the market severely. This came about because the industry had access to enough senators, in particular to Senator Long. Led by Long, the Senate concocted a deal just barely palatable enough to end the filibuster, pass the full Senate, and win a narrow margin in the conference committee. Carter's failure to gain enactment of his NEP conferred no benefit to any interest groups. No single group wished for the NEP's total demise. Indeed, many favored 90 to 95 percent of it. They wished only to protect their own small corner. Yet the entire structure inexorably crumbled as each removed a few bricks.

Assessment of Pluralism in the Energy Context

Reviewing the four phases—initiative, lobbying, congressional process, and results—permits an assessment of the extent to which interest groups determine policy, and thus of the pluralist model.

Interest groups had minimal influence initiating the NEP. Schlesinger and his staff drafted the plan in isolation from industry, members of Congress, and even other executive branch agencies such as the Treasury. The NEP presumably included particular provisions in anticipation of various interests, but not as a result of direct input. The plan was bureaucratic and technocratic in this first phase.

Even before President Carter solemnly unveiled the plan to Congress, lobbying picked up. Besides the NEP, Congress was considering the Department of Energy Organization Act, an additional reason to lobby. That more than one-third (36 percent) of all business registrants were lobbying on energy shows the extent of these interest groups' mobilization. Concern with energy picked up in other categories as well. Moreover, a number of lobbyists reregistered to add energy matters. Thus once the NEP left its White House nursery for the congressional arena, interest groups began to loom large.

The NEP's schizophrenic reception from Congress points to party as the explanation in the House of Representatives and interest groups in the Senate. Speaker O'Neill's taut discipline moved the bill to expeditious passage with few modifications. In the Senate Democratic party loyalty was weaker. Majority Leader Byrd did not share O'Neill's fealty. Structure and personality converged differently. In the House, tax provisions went to the Ways and Means Committee chaired by Al Ullman, a liberal from an energy-consuming state. In the Senate they went to the Finance Committee, chaired by Russell Long, a conservative from a petroleum-producing state. In the House, O'Neill appointed an Ad Hoc Committee for the nontax provisions while in the Senate they went to the Energy and Natural Resources (formerly Interior) Committee, dominated by Western senators. In the more open Senate, party discipline gave way to special pleading and immobility, immobility being a victory for the energy status quo. The conference committee repeated the immobility of the Senate situation.

In terms of the conference committee results, interest groups were the victors, largely because they defended the status quo. Defeat of the NEP proposals for standardized national electricity rates and the various taxes were illustrations. The deregulation of natural gas was not a defense of the status quo. Credit goes primarily to Senator Long. It goes as well to forty-nine other senators, thirty-four of them Republicans whose party is philosophically opposed to regulation. Furthermore, recall that the oil and gas industry had long cultivated the Senate while largely ignoring the House. During the 1950s when Lyndon Johnson, along with Robert Kerr, dominated the Senate, Texas, Oklahoma, and Louisiana petroleum interests contributed to the campaigns of many Senate candidates from nonpetroleum states, thereby earning their gratitude. With so many friends in the Senate, oil and gas men had little need to cultivate the House of Representatives as well

In conclusion, it may be stated that pluralism is alive and well and living on Capitol Hill. At least this is what the analysis of President Carter's struggle to secure passage of his National Energy Plan shows. Before presenting it to Congress on April 20, the administration did manage to avoid interest group influence in formulating the NEP; yet all the secrecy and discipline in formulation proved of little value once Congress began debate. Schlesinger's Energy Task Force had ignored the conflicting interests that soon tore apart its intricate handiwork.

This raises several questions. Did lack of a strong department hurt? The Department of Energy (DOE) was not formally established until October 1. Even then it had to undergo a shakedown period before it could function well. Would the NEP have fared better had a well-organized bureaucracy stood behind it? Or would an established DOE merely have sold out to the very groups it was supposed to counterbalance? Experience in the DOE's predecessor agencies shows many examples of industry capture. The Department of Interior's Bureau of Land Management and the National Petroleum Council were good friends of the petroleum industry. The Atomic Energy Commission was notorious as a promoter of the nuclear industry. Thus a strong bureaucracy might have hurt the NEP rather than helped it.

Once passed in whatever form, will control of the NEP revert to the executive branch? Carter's chief successes in energy policy have been administrative. The DOE's Energy Information Administration now collects and analyzes data on oil and gas reserves that private industry associations (API and AGA) had provided previously. The President also renounced plutonium as a fuel for nuclear reactors. He rejected funding for the Barnwell, South Carolina, reprocessing plant. Later he vetoed the authorization for the Clinch River fast breeder plant and vowed to spend money appropriated for Clinch River to terminate the project. These examples indicate Carter's willingness to use his executive power even in defiance of Congress and interest groups.

Finally, there remains the question of whether energy is an issue which can evolve into a unified national goal. Is there a public interest as opposed to the sum of all private interests? The national defense aspects clearly call for coordinated national policies such as controlling nuclear weapons proliferation and immunity against another oil boycott like that of 1973–1974, but what further reasons exist for national government intervention? State public utility commissions (PUCs) are capable of regulating natural monopolies to protect consumers (assuming the PUCs chose to do so). A competitive market is the traditional means of allocating consumer goods in nonmonopolistic situations. Has market failure really occurred, or is it merely flight from the market? Where does the public interest lie? These three questions, along with many others, will transcend the narrower issues of the degree of interest group influence on the NEP's legislative history.

Notes

1. *New York Times*, October 14, 1977.

2. Pendleton Herring, *Group Representation before Congress* (Baltimore: Johns Hopkins Press, 1929); David B. Truman, *The Governmental Process* (New York: Knopf, 1951).

3. Cf. Dwight Waldo, *The Administrative State* (New York: Ronald, 1948).

4. *Washington Post*, April 23, 1977.

5. Ibid.

6. Lester M. Salamon, and John J. Siegfried, "Economic Power and Political Influence," *American Political Science Review*, September 1977, pp. 1026-1034.

7. Cf. John M. Bacheller, "Lobbyists and the Legislative Process," *American Political Science Review*, March 1977, pp. 252-263.

8. Truman, *The Governmental Process*, p. 353.

9. Ibid., p. 323.

10. John Ferejohn, "Who Wins in Conference Committee?" *Journal of Politics*, November 1975, pp. 1033-1046; Gerald S. Strom and Barry S. Rundquist, "A Revised Theory of Winning in House Senate Conferences," *American Political Science Review*, June 1977, pp. 448-453.

11. Truman, *The Governmental Process*, p. 323.

17 The States' Response to the Energy Crisis: An Analysis of Innovation

Patricia K. Freeman

The energy shortage of the 1970s was one of the most serious problems confronting the states in several decades. All government jurisdictions were faced with a multitude of problems: the shortages in supply, rapidly increasing energy costs, dependence on foreign imports, and the possibility of mandatory allocation programs. The states, however, were forced to assume the major responsibility for policy development in the area of energy. This was because the federal government provided only a minimum of policy leadership, thus leaving the states with the task of initiating, enacting, and implementing policies that would alleviate the problems induced by the shortages.[1]

The action that was taken at the federal level in the two years after the onset of the 1973 oil embargo was at best ineffective and at worst created additional problems. The states experienced considerable difficulty not only in interpreting federal programs, but also in dealing with the federal structure engaged in energy policy.[2] In short, throughout 1974, 1975, and much of 1976 the states not only were facing a number of energy-related problems of growing proportion but also had to cope with the indecisiveness and fragmentation of federal policy.

This chapter examines the states' response to the energy crisis by analyzing innovation patterns in the adoption of legislation. Specifically, we will examine (1) where the policies were developed (that is, were there "national leaders" among the states that were involved in the creation of much of the energy legislation as well as its early adoption?), (2) the diffusion patterns across states to determine whether there are certain states within regions that serve as leaders (that is, are they the first adopters of legislation?), and (3) the impact of the federal government's involvement on innovation in the states.

Where Did Policy Solutions Originate?

In discussions of innovation a distinction is frequently made between the adoption of an idea originated elsewhere and the actual creation of a policy or object.[3] Nevertheless, the definition of *innovation* generally used—the adoption of a means or ends that is new to the adopting unit—completely obscures the distinction. In this study each process wil be examined separately. Legislation will be considered as being created by a state if (1) the state is the first to enact that type of legislation and (2) the legislation had not been suggested by a professional organization prior to the state's enactment. To determine adopting patterns, we compared the legislation enacted from 1973 to 1977 that dealt with energy policy in each of the fifty states[4] and compared the enacted legislation with the "model" legislation suggested by professional organizations.[5]

The energy conservation measures enacted by the states contain a significant number of programs that are original responses to the problems created by the energy shortages. Among the most significant of the legislation and the states in which it was originated are:

Provision of incentives for solar energy use	Arizona
Appliance energy efficiency standards	California and New York
Energy efficiency standards in buildings	California
Development of a permanent energy office	California, Minnesota, Louisiana, North Carolina, Connecticut
Funding for home insulation programs	California

Because of the small number of policies examined, it would not be wise to overstate the importance of the conclusions that can be reached from these data. This legislation does represent, however, the significant state responses to a problem of considerable magnitude and thus provides important indicators of how the states respond when faced with a crisis.

What is immediately obvious is the extent to which large, industrialized states lead the nation in the initiation of policy responses. Of the five programs, California was in the forefront for four of them. California's predominance in the development of legislation is not surprising, given Walker's and Gray's finding that when a scale score is assigned to the fifty states regarding the time elapsed before adoption of a number of policies, California ranks in the top five states, along with other large, industrialized states.[6] These top-ranking states, California and New York in particular, are described by Walker as national leaders. In addition to being early adopters, this analysis indicates that these states are also actively engaged in policy development.

The larger, more highly industrialized states, however, do not always lead in the creation of policies. Arizona's development of legislation granting tax incentives for solar energy attests to this (Arizona ranks in the lower half of the Walker and Gray innovation scales). In the development of a permanent energy agency, Louisiana, North Carolina, Connecticut, and Minnesota responded as rapidly as California and more quickly than the other national leaders. This legislation, along with the other policies initiated by states generally considered to be low on innovation (Florida, for example, was the first state to institute life-cycle cost analysis in buildings), supports the thesis that the acceptance of innovation is issue-specific.[7] That is, some states may be more apt to adopt innovations than others and may do so more rapidly. However, past innovation behavior does not provide an adequate basis for predicting the creation or acceptance of any one innovation.

Diffusion of Energy Legislation

From whom do states take cues regarding energy policy? Walker asserts that, in addition to national leaders which compete with one another for recognition as being innovative, there are a number of regional leaders. There are, he writes,

> . . . a set of pioneering states linked together in a national system of emulation and competition. The rest of the states would be sorted out along branches of the tree according to the pioneer, or set of pioneers from which they take their cues.[8]

Walker identifies New York and Massachusetts as being regional leaders in the East (with Connecticut also ranking high), Michigan and Wisconsin in the Midwest (with Minnesota also ranking high), California dominates the Far West and Colorado the Mountain region. Louisiana and Virginia lead the South.

In investigating the diffusion patterns of the five policies discussed above, fairly clear regional patterns appear. Legislation providing tax incentives for the use of solar energy was adopted first by Arizona; Indiana followed in 1974. In 1975 of the ten states enacting property tax exemptions, two are regional leaders (Colorado and Massachusetts) and two rank very high on Walker's innovation scale (Oregon and Illinois). The emulation that is occurring within the region is perhaps most readily apparent when the legislative provisions are compared. Most of the Eastern states provide only that localities may adopt these standards; the program is not implemented at the state level as in other regions.

As noted above, the first adopters of appliance efficiency standards were California (prohibiting gas pilot lights) and New York (prohibiting TV energizing units). Adoption by Arizona occurred in 1976 (the text is almost identical to California's), and in 1977 Minnesota followed.

Invention by national leaders with subsequent adoption by regional leaders is the pattern with building efficiency standards, as with most of the legislation considered in this analysis. California initiated the legislation, but enactment in Colorado, Minnesota, and New York occurred within the same year. Maryland

and Maine also passed efficiency standards, but with voluntary compliance. In 1975 three Western and Northwestern states (Oregon, Washington, and Nevada, plus Texas) passed similar legislation; in 1976 Ohio followed.

The pattern created by the diffusion of legislation creating a permanent energy office is similar, except that rather than invention occurring in one or two states and diffusing to regional leaders, invention occurred simultaneously in several states, in national and regional leaders. Diffusion to other states within the respective regions occurred in subsequent years.

Finally, as with the other four policies examined, after invention the enactment of loans for home insulation occurred first in states that are regional leaders. Colorado and Minnesota followed California's passage in 1976. Virginia and two other Southern states plus Vermont followed in 1976.

This general overview of the diffusion pattern of five energy policies clearly confirms Walker's thesis regarding the existence of national and regional leaders among the states. The dominance of California and Minnesota in the energy field indicates the significance of some factor or factors which facilitated a rapid response to the energy crisis. The energy-related problems confronting these states were not as severe as in other states, most notably those in New England, where 80 percent of the oil is imported from a foreign source. Yet their legislative responses, both in the invention of policies and in rapid emulation, exceed those of the rest of the nation.

The importance of states being able to copy the legislation developed elsewhere cannot be overstated—particuarly when states are confronted with a complex problem requiring an immediate solution. The average diffusion rate for legislation, according to Walker,[9] is twenty years for adoption by twenty states. Energy legislation, because of the immediacy of the problem, spread at an accelerated pace. The initial responses to the Arab oil embargo demonstrate the extent to which states look to other states for legislation. Statewide gasoline allocation plans spread to fourteen states in forty days. Legislation granting emergency powers to the governor and franchise protection enactments also diffused at a phenomenally high rate.

One component that should not be overlooked in this rapid dissemination of information is the role of professional organizations—in this case, the Council of State Governments, the National Governors' Conference, the National Conference of State Legislatures plus various regional organizations. Besides offering "model legislation," these groups held seminars, conducted research, and facilitated interaction among the states. In this study it is impossible to delineate the role that they played; whether states would have become aware of certain policies without their activity cannot be determined. It seems likely, however, that these groups are becoming increasingly important, given the growing complexity of the issues and the number of issues requiring a rapid state response.

Involvement of the Federal Government: Who Emulates
Whom and the Federal Impact on State Innovation

Federal involvement in states' energy policy began in December 1975 with passage of the Energy Policy and Conservation Act (EPCA). The legislation was designed to reduce the demand for energy through the establishment of policy guidelines and financial and technical assistance for the development and implementation of state conservation programs. To qualify for financial assistance under the act, the states were required to enact five energy conservation programs. The mandated measures, which had to be adopted by January 1, 1978, are (1) lighting efficiency standards for public buildings; (2) promotion of carpools, van pools, and public transportation; (3) energy efficiency in procurement practices of the states and their political subdivisions; (4) mandatory thermal efficiency standards and insulation requirements for new and renovated buildings; and (5) adoption of right turn on a red stoplight.

Much of the discussions regarding the states' role in the federal system generally delegates the states to a subsidiary position. Rose, for example, maintains that the normal pattern of state action is "mild innovation and legitimacy" and when confronted with a serious problem requiring immediate action, "it is unlikely . . . (that) states could institute major changes in the required short period of time."[10]

The growth of federal grant assistance to states is cited as a factor that is further limiting the states' influence. Sundquist writes that

> The federal grant is conceived as a means of enabling the federal government to achieve its objectives. . . . As a matter of administrative convenience, the federal government executes the program through state or local governments rather than through its own field offices, but the motive force is federal, with the states and communities assisting—rather than the other way around.[11]

Thus, the dominant theme of most discussions of state activity is that of a nearly impotent, frequently backward unit with nearly complete dependence on federal guidance.

Examination of the five mandated policies indicates a reverse pattern: not only did the states initiate action with the onset of the oil embargo, but the federal government also emulated the states in its development of federal directives. States have had the authority to mandate thermal efficiency standards and lighting efficiency standards, and legislation has been passed allowing a right turn at a red stoplight in several states prior to the establishment of federal guidelines. Life-cycle costing has been the dominant response to achievement of energy efficiency in procurement practices, and this, too, was developed at the state

level. Promotion of public transportation and vehicle pooling is the only program that did not receive substantial attention at the state level before federal
involvement.

Since the federal government has become actively involved in the area of
state energy conservation, the question which arises is whether there will be a
curtailment of state innovation. It is too early to answer with certainty, but
from all indications to date this does not seem to have occurred. A 5 percent
reduction in energy consumption in each of the states is mandated by the EPCA
by 1980. The five required programs fall far short of achieving the necessary reduction; only an estimated 15 percent of the total energy reduction predicted
by 1980 will result from these programs.[12] The rest comes from a variety of programs developed by the states, many of which continue the innovation shown in
the past. As examples, New York and Florida are proposing residential energy
audit programs while Tennessee is planning on using infrared photography to
assess insulation needs. Michigan has enacted a system to recycle oil. The states,
at least in the field of energy, have fulfilled their function as "laboratories of
democracy."

An examination of the states' response to the energy shortages of the 1970s
substantiates many of the conclusions reached by Walker regarding the existence
of national leaders which strive to be early adopters and appear to be, very
often, the initiators of policy. The research also supports findings regarding the
pattern of legislative enactments within regions and, more generally, the important role that emulation plays in state policy formation. Finally, the analysis
points to the key role that states have played and continue to play in energy
conservation in the United States.

Notes

1. This is the assessment of reports issued by the Federal Trade Commis-
sion in 1974 and the Council of State Governments. See Council of State Gov-
ernments, "The Energy Crisis," in *The Book of the States* (Lexington, Kentucky:
The Council of State Governments, 1974–75), pp. 505–514. Also see Alfred R.
Light, "Federalism and the Energy Crisis: A View of the States," *Publius*
(Spring 1976), pp. 81–96.

2. For a discussion of the problems involved in obtaining information
from federal officials see Light, ibid.

3. Lawrence B. Mohr, "Determinants of Innovation in Organizations,"
American Political Science Review, March 1969, p. 112; and Jack Walker, "The
Diffusion of Innovation among the American States," *American Political Science
Review,* September 1969, p. 880.

4. The 1973 and 1974 legislation comparison was compiled by the South-

ern Interstate Nuclear Board; the 1975, 1976, and 1977 legislation was collected by the National Conference of State Legislatures.

5. Model legislation was suggested by the Council of State Governments and the National Governors' Council.

6. Walker, "The Diffusion of Information"; Jack Walker, "Innovation in State Politics," in *Politics in the American States,* 2d ed., eds. Herbert Jacob and Kenneth N. Vines (Boston: Little, Brown, 1971); and Virginia Gray, "Innovation in the States: A Diffusion Study," *American Political Science Review,* December 1973, pp. 1174-1185. The top five states in Walker's scale are New York, Massachusetts, New Jersey, California, and Michigan. Gray's scale is the same except Wisconsin replaces Michigan.

7. Mohr, Gray, ibid.; Dondal D. Menzel and Irwin Feller, "Leadership and Interaction Patterns in the Diffusion of Innovations among the American States," forthcoming in the *Western Political Quarterly,* 1978; and Kenneth Warner, "The Need for Some Innovative Concepts of Innovation: An Examination of Research on the Diffusion of Innovation," *Policy Sciences,* December 1974, pp. 433-451.

8. Walker, "Innovation in State Politics." See also Ira Sharkansky, *Regionalism in American Politics* (Indianapolis, Ind.: Bobbs-Merrill, 1970).

9. Walker, "The Diffusion of Innovation."

10. Douglas D. Rose, "National and Local Forces in State Politics: The Implication of Multi-Level Policy Analysis," *American Political Science Review,* December 1973, pp. 1162-1173.

11. James L. Sundquist with David Davis, *Making Federalism Work* (Washington: The Brookings Institute, 1969).

12. Connie B.Q. Laughlin, *Energy Conservation: The State of the States* (Washington: National Governors' Association, Center for Policy Research, 1978).

18 Accommodating Energy Needs and Public Values: Open Planning as a Process for Mutual Cooperation

Dennis L. Thompson

Energy Conservation as a Public Ethic

The current watchword in energy consumption is *conserve*. Efforts are being made by industry, transportation, and homeowners to decrease their consumption of whatever energy source they use. Use is to be more efficient, and the results of the use are to be more effective—more erg for the calorie. The argument is made to the energy producers[1] that their responsibility is not to growth, but to limiting growth. Oil companies should discourage driving and purchase of automobiles, and public utilities should discourage population influx into their service areas. Yet energy is not the only independent variable acting on consumption. Population increases or at least shifts location, and vehicular use increases for numerous reasons. Thus the demand for energy increases, and the energy producers attempt to meet that demand. It is argued with vigor that their ultimate responsibility is to enforce conservation by not increasing production, thus requiring that the current available supply be reallocated. In a situation of acute scarcity where there is not enough new resources for an incremental increase in consumption, or of total scarcity where the supply does not even meet immediate demands, this would have to be the case.[2]

However, barring these conditions, energy producers respond to energy users' demands. They do market their product and attempt to induce greater utilization and sales, or at least they used to. In general, they provide energy within their marketing area as needed, or, in the case of a national market, they count on a fairly fixed share of the market—whether they are integrated, primary, or secondary producers.

It can easily be argued that energy producers have a public responsibility to meet public demands. In the case of public utilities, they are required to provide services on demand. This is enforced by the states' public utilities commissions. For example, in the *Colorado Revised Statute* we read the following with respect to the definition of a public utility:

> To fall into the class of a public utility, a business or enterprise must be impressed with a public interest and those engaged in the conduct thereof must hold themselves out as serving or ready to serve all members of the public, who may require it, to the extent of their capacity.

209

The nature of the service must be such that all members of the public
have an enforceable right to demand it. . . .

And it is well settled that those words "supplying the public" mean all
of the public within its capacities—it means indiscriminately.

This, of course, does not obligate the energy producer to provide service in an
area which it has not agreed to serve. But everyone *within* its service area has an
equal demand on the company's product.

In times of stringency where there is a short or fixed supply, the energy producer is not apt to encourage growth (economic, industrial, or population) in its
area of activity because that would exacerbate the situation. But while most
energy producers do encourage conservation, they have not taken the step of
limiting public consumption of energy by not supplying current demand.

A constant increase in energy demand in the United States (except for 1973
and 1974) has led to the need for increased energy-producing facilities. The increase from 1960 to 1978 was from about 23 million barrels per day of oil
equivalent (MB/DOE) to nearly 40 MB/DOE, or an average increase of 4.1 percent per year. And the energy demand is forecast to increase to 51.5 MB/DOE
by 1990, or an average annual increase of nearly 2.4 percent. Thus while the rate
of demand is slowed, the projected actual increase in energy consumption is
.95 MB/DOE per year from 1978 to 1990 compared to an actual increase in
energy consumption of .94 MB/DOE per year from 1960 to 1978.[3] Thus the
demand for new energy production facilities over the next decade will continue
at about the same rate which we have experienced over the past two decades.
This demand comes at a time when the obvious locations for such facilities are
already being used, though by many criteria, in the past not all energy facility
siting has been done wisely or obviously. This new development must take place
in the face of an increased environmental concern and an increasingly vocal
public.

One should not expect or desire the energy producers to determine social
or economic policy. If growth is to be curbed, population controlled, or energy
allocated, governments should make the decisions. In the face of no alternative
policy, the energy producers should be expected to perform as usual. Therefore
the energy producers must build new facilities or expand old ones at about the
same rate as they have been doing if the present policy of responding to demand
is continued.

The Planning of Projects Affected with the Public Interest

Without a significant policy change, we are led to a logical position that the
energy producers must be planning for increased production capacity. Their
alternatives are to (1) increase current production facilities, (2) build new ones,

or (3) change to alternative sources of energy supply which, in turn, would also require new facilities.

The nature of planning requires rational prognostication. It is oriented toward the future. Planning for the past or present makes no sense. And in planning for energy supply, even the near future is an inadequate time period. Thus future needs must be divined, sources chosen, and facilities planned and built far ahead of the time when the need is self-evident to avoid significant disruptions or even crises.

The usual procedure for planning public projects in the United States is to plan internally, announce the plan, and then defend the plan. This is not to imply that external interests are not taken into consideration—they may be. But the identification of factors and values and their subsequent weighting and influence in the plan take place within the performing organization. After a public announcement of intent is made, a public hearing is held at which the organization becomes both an advocate and a protagonist for the policy which it already has developed and subscribed to. Once a public position has been taken, it becomes much more difficult for the agency to back down or alter plans which it has already approved. And it is rare in contemporary society that a proposed public project is universally assented to in any given format.

The ultimate cause of differences is values. In the planning process numerous value judgments are made. It is obvious wisdom to recognize the presence of value judgments in the planning process and of competing values relating to the problem, as well as that these values and judgments inherently impose subsequent implications on policy decisions. There are numerous values to which most interested parties could give common consent and thus upon which there is little basic disagreement. It is well to remember the foundations of common purpose, because in many altercations one gets the impression that there are no common interests. It is the remainder of the value judgments, those which are not commonly held, around which controversy swirls. Naturally the planning organization most easily identifies with, and finds credence in, those values which fortify its interests and concerns.

Few will seriously argue that there are not multiple values and interests which should be met in public programs, or that it is well to provide for the input of responsible public concerns. Neither can it be argued that one group or set of values has the only legitimate demand on governing energy or any other programs. Yet some organizations have planned as though providing for their own interests were all that was necessary. Neither corporate, nor governmental, nor environmental values should be presumed to be dominant.

In the past decade numerous laws and regulations have been imposed which require either that agreement be generated for proposed public projects or that various processes be undertaken to enable the expression of extant values and concerns. And many procedures which have been developed have been designed to respond to the demands of protesting interest groups. Yet, too often the procedures show little evidence that anyone was listening; thus even minor accommodations are not made to satisfy competing interests.

In our society diversity of interests strengthens our processes, programs, and policies as well as engendering support.

Citizen Involvement in the Planning Process

There is disagreement as to the procedures for incorporating diverse interests into the policy process.[4] However, the democratic aspiration which has been most widely ascribed to in the United States has been "citizen involvement." Although there is theoretical opposition to this concept, there has not been much debate as to whether there should be greater citizen participation in broadly determining public policies. This is a widely shared ideal as old as the republic.[5] In fact, it is the lack of citizen involvement that has been the cause of most concern.

Norman Wengert has identified a number of ways in which citizen participation is perceived by its advocates:

Participation as policy—a vague, normative choice that it is good policy to involve people

Participation as strategy—a way of getting things done, often including unstated objectives unknown or unrecognized by the citizen participants

Participation as communication—a procedure for providing information inputs into decision-making processes

Participation as conflict resolution—a way to reduce tension by increasing understanding and decreasing mistrust of other participants

Participation as therapy—a means of relieving the distress caused by alienation resulting from other factors such as poverty or discrimination[6]

There are numerous types of programs which have provided for citizen participation. They are generally categorized as community-based, agency-based, or problem-based. Community-based programs usually are concerned with the total activity in the community rather than one or two issues. The most common focus is on neighborhood councils. An agency-based program provides for citizen involvement in the planning or decision-making process of a public agency. These programs normally provide for citizen advisory committees and/or public hearings.

The interest-based program originates with a group of citizens who seek to influence public institutions concerning specific group interests. These types of programs create their own forum if none is available, including resorting to litigation. The problem-based program is a problem-specific version of community-based involvement. Ad hoc citizen groups, often neighborhood- or locale-oriented, form to provide input or action on specific decisions which are impacting them. They usually disband when the issue has passed.

Energy-related decisions could be acted on by all four types of participatory programs, but most often they have been engaged in by interest-based and problem-based groups. This implies narrow or specific interests being represented, whereas the democratic ideal calls for broad-based citizen participation.

The public interest involves many sources. There is the public sector composed of elected and administrative officials of established governmental institutions at whatever level. They, of course, have an inherent advantage in getting their values injected into the policy process.

The private economic sector composed of businesses, unions, and associations which operate the economy generally provides for its interest representation and in addition is often delegated the decisional responsibility which normally rests with the public sector.

The institutional sector is composed of independent citizen-supported organizations, such as churches, colleges, private health and welfare agencies, cultural institutions, and so on, which serve a broad community interest. For some purposes utility companies are seen as being in this sector, but for energy issues they must be viewed as belonging to the previous category.

The media sector reports on, analyzes, and publicizes events and problems (although on problems affecting their own industry they would also be viewed as a component of the private economic sector).

The citizen interest sector, composed of organizations and associations formed by citizens to promote and protect particular interests, ranges from social groups to primarily politically activist organizations. They are organized to keep informed and to represent their interests.

An ad hoc sector is coincidental with problem-based programs as they are temporarily organized to act on any issue of immediate importance.

There is also a hidden sector which is composed of individuals who are not influential in any of the aforementioned sectors but who are often sought out and usually listened to by other sector leaders. Their position of influence is achieved because of previous positions held, experience, acquaintance with decisionmakers, possession of wealth and property, or some combinations of these which has given them residual influence.

Then there is the silent sector, a numerical majority, but usually ill informed, unconcerned, or disaffected. However, this does not mean they have no interests or values to consider.

It is argued that when there is no mechanism to induce the public to participate and scrutinize questions of value from the perspective of societal well-being, the responsibility often passes to special interest groups and to individuals by default.[7] The object of a citizen participation scheme is to provide for representation and ingress for all these sectors, not merely those which have automatic responsibilities, access, or strong interests. To provide only for these latter groups is to leave the process to nature.

Obtaining Citizen Involvement in Planning

Efforts to induce citizen participation usually have not been successful. Numerous federal programs have required citizen input and have failed to get it. In a well-known case of an attempt to get citizen involvement, it was reported that the government would not act without having public acquiescence, even if that meant delaying action and if the acquiescence had to be bought with public funds. When the necessary public was not organized, the government organized them. There finally was citizen influence in the planning of Fort Lincoln, but the process of "taking citizen interest into account" became quite distinct from that of "achieving citizen participation."[8] (Fort Lincoln was a federal housing project which was to be built in Washington, D.C. It was supposed to show the way for a national program for the development of surplus federal land. President Johnson ordered it built in 1967 as a priority Presidential project, yet by 1970 almost no construction had occurred.) Neighborhood councils have had some limited success in providing for broad-based participation as they provide for a forum, act as advocates, and serve as channels to two-way communication between local governments and a community of citizens. But their applicability is limited to small communities or neighborhoods.[9]

Programs calling for citizen participation have often abandoned any meaningful public participation for numerous reasons: difficulty of getting adequate representation, unwillingness of citizen leaders to continue to work within the system, cost in terms of time and money, and the basic insecurity of the government agency.[10] Those with authority and access have tended to resist yielding the power to propose solutions to problems and determine their realization. In these instances the stalemate discourages the participants, and the result is the designation of citizen advisors who serve as a buffer and sounding board, but without any authority and little influence. Here citizen participation defeats the instrumental goals of policy reform and implementation.[11]

When citizen participation fails, the norms for decision making are provided by the formal decisionmakers, the public administrators, and influential members of the public. They are all properly involved, but their interests are not necessarily coincidental to the public interests. Jennings has reported that even the administrators tend to be bound by the norms attached to their various positions, while the influentials have a greater mobility across various issues and issue areas; thus any integration of issue resolution and policy has a greater possibility of coming from the influentials. There is also ample evidence, Jennings reports, that the two groups form alliances and coalitions. The implications for decision making are that these policy-involved incumbents are apt to have their opinions and behavior shaped and modified by their interactions.[12] Thus the pluralism which may appear to exist in policy formulation is in reality unitary.

When extant values are perceived as not being sufficiently manifest in the policy decisions, the public often belatedly responds. Sometimes this occurs at a point when the newly declared interests can be incorporated into the policy, but usually the policy as stated is defended to stand as announced. This has led to a further strategy of citizen participation—litigation. This has been particularly common with respect to environmental issues where the administrative agencies have been seen as unable to accommodate newly recognized ecological perspectives into the development and management of natural resources. The government agencies which are supposed to be protecting the public interest are often cited as defendants in these actions. Private initiatives are sometimes needed to provoke, and at times to displace, administrative agencies charged with protecting the public interest. In short, the import of most citizen-initiated litigation is the charge, bluntly put, that agencies are not to be trusted to effectuate the public interest.[13]

Litigation, as an adversary process, does not provide for discussion, compromise, inclusion, or accommodation. The process results in winning or losing, but not cooperation. Thus decision and action are often delayed.

Citizen Involvement in Energy Planning

In responding to increased energy needs, a mechanism must be found to allow decisions to be made and implemented expeditiously. Citizen involvement appears to be necessary because of widespread concern over various aspects of energy generation processes. To ignore public interests engenders antagonism at best and crucial delays at worst. Two important factors have been identified which must be present to encourage enduring citizen participation:

1. The process must convince competing groups that their needs have been fairly considered.
2. Participation requires that actual influence over the content of decisions must be granted to those people who are affected by those decisions.[14]

These factors obviously have not always been present in public policy presentations, nor have they been perceived to be evident in citizen participation programs.

An approach to promoting widespread involvement in a particular policy area which incorporates these critical factors is variously called "open planning," "public planning," or "fishbowl planning."

In 1969 the U.S. Corps of Engineers attempted "to air critical technical decisions and value conflicts by means of local information workshops, public forums and other citizen-planner dialogues" in its formulation of a complex river basin plan for the Susquehanna River.[15] Their major objectives were "(1) to formulate alternative development and management strategies and present these to the public for *preliminary* consideration and (2) to incorporate preferences (and even additional suggestions) of the 'recipient' citizenry in plans to accommodate the present and projected water-related needs, concentrating on the next ten to fifteen year period."[16]

Even though the public participants were impressed with the technical competence and responsiveness of the agency personnel and felt that they had had a significant opportunity to express their ideas and possible solutions, they often felt that they had not received all the information available and were only "moderately confident" that their preferences would be incorporated into the final plan.[17]

Then in 1971 a minority report to the National Academy of Engineering Study on Power Plant Siting advocated "new forums" to bring the public into the plant siting process at the beginning, along with the utilities and the government regulatory bodies. The report said that the utilities "must come to these forums recognizing their validity and freely surrendering the perogatives of unilateral decision-making."[18]

The concept of open planning depends on agreement on some basic assumptions; but if the basic assumptions are not readily identifiable to the participating parties, then the first task of the process is to create agreement on those basic assumptions. For example, it is necessary in an energy siting decision to agree that increased energy output be made available. If there is disagreement over the need for increased energy production, then there is no need to proceed to the task of choosing the site of whatever kind. Once it is agreed that increased energy output will be provided, there then needs to be a basic agreement on the source of energy which will be made available. This end, to some degree, is open to alternative policy decisions, but the opportunities available will be fairly restrictive in most instances. Then the process of planning for how and where can be addressed.

A variation of open planning which has much to recommend it was pioneered by the Northern States Power Company of Minneapolis, Minnesota, in 1970. Northern States Power (NSP) had a reputation of being methodical, aggressive, and quick. It planned well and moved decisively in implementing its expansion needs. However, in 1970 it needed to provide for a number of new power generating plants to be built before the year 2000 amid increasing opposition. The opposition was beginning to organize, thus becoming more potent and more vocal.[19] The utility told its stockholders, "Recognizing the public's right to participate in such public matters as the placement of large generating plants, Northern States Power pioneered in creating a Citizens Advisory Task Force on Power Siting. . . ."[20] The task force, in conjunction with a new environmental affairs department, also established by the company, was to participate in deciding where plants should be located, what kind of fuel they should burn, how the sites should be landscaped, and how waste materials should be removed.

The company approached all the major environmental groups and asked them to send representatives to the task force. None refused to participate, though some were hesitant. Said one, "You have to be pretty arrogant to ignore NSP's invitation. You can't raise hell and then refuse to sit down and talk."[21] The governor's environmental cabinet was also invited to participate.

The group began meeting in early 1970 to choose a site for a generating plant that needed to be in service by 1976. In this initial effort the company limited the group to consideration of four sites the company already owned. The task force chose a site in Sherburne County, forty miles northwest of Minneapolis, which was admittedly the least desirable economically from the company's point of view. The company then asked the task force to look at the long-range problems of plant siting and transmission lines. The procedure had worked. The company was able to begin construction on schedule based on the mutually cooperative plan. The Sherburne County plant is now operating.

Numerous states have since enacted provisions for regulating power plant siting. These regulations range from authorization or licensing the choice of the utility to site selection and site designation. In 1972 Minnesota institutionalized a form of open planning by legislating responsibility for plant siting to the Minnesota Environmental Quality Board which was attached to the State Planning Agency. The twelve members on the board come from state agencies and from the public.

The board has the responsibility to investigate and review environmental problems, policies, and regulations in the state; to coordinate state programs; and to "insure agency compliance with state environmental policy." Topics which it may consider are "future population and settlement patterns, air and water resources and quality, solid waste management, transportation and utility corridors, economically productive open space, energy policy and need, growth and development, and land use planning."[22]

In addition, a Citizen's Advisory Committee was established which provides broad-based citizen access to the planning process. It looks to the board for its support and has three of its members on the board. It is composed of one resident from each congressional district and three members at large "as a vehicle for citizen participation in the activities of the board." The committee has the responsibility to hold meetings throughout the state to gather information and a feeling for public opinion concerning environmental quality. It then meets with the board at least four times a year to give advice and counsel based on the information it has gathered.

The board holds an annual environmental quality congress to receive reports and exchange information from state, local, and federal agencies; citizen organizations; industry; and any other enterprise which is active in or has an impact on environmental quality. It can also establish interdepartmental or citizen task forces to study particular problems. No employee or agent of a utility can serve on an advisory committee. The energy producers, in turn, must provide to the board every other year at least a fifteen-year forecast of projected energy demands and available supply.

With respect to power plant siting the board has also been given the authority to

> . . . choose locations that minimize adverse human and environmental impact while insuring continuing electric power system reliability and integrity and insuring that electric energy needs are met and fulfilled in an orderly and timely fashion.[23]

It thus is authorized to select both sites and routes.

Once the utility obtains a "Certificate of Need" from the Minnesota Energy Agency, then it is obligated to select a preferred and alternate site from those which the board has already identified. To date, the board has not been able to choose sites, and new legislation has given it until January 1979 to identify potential power plant sites.

Thus since the 1970 experiment the Northern States Power Company has not been able to select any new sites, but has sought permission to enlarge the Sherburne unit.

The Minnesota state institutionalization of open planning appears to have been no more successful than the utility effort; in fact, the bureaucratization of the process appears to have bogged it down somewhat. The state may have been better served if it had encouraged the company to make open planning a permanent company procedure and required the process to be used by other utilities. In recent years government is often mistrusted as much as industry.

Conclusion

There is no panacea which will provide an input for all relevant values and still allow a democratic process to expeditiously determine policies that will induce societal energy needs to be met. Achieving greater participation from a wide segment of society is costly. It takes time. It may increase conflict. It may alter existing power relationships. It may require changes in organizational structures. It may make decision making more difficult. Furthermore, there is no evidence that "better programs result from administrative participation, nor that democracy is in fact furthered, nor that alienation is reduced."[24]

But circumstances demand that participative efforts be promoted in order to achieve timely decisions and actions in a period of critical energy supply. Open planning worked reasonably well in the Northern States Power experiment of 1970. It allowed all interested parties to participate in the significant decisions of the planning process. Its accomplishments outweighed its hazards; thus those experienced with it became its proponents rather than its detractors. It is probably unfortunate that it was formalized and incorporated into state agencies. As has been observed, officially sponsored citizen participation tends to be co-optation rather than representation;[25] and government action tends to increase the size of bureaucracy dealing with the issue. It is not the only process which has allowed widespread participation, nor did it bring about the most expeditious action; but as a combination providing for both, it compares well with other procedures. The adoption of some additional processes may encourage energy producers to pursue open planning as a private effort.

One potentially useful approach to provide for citizen participation is a bill introduced in 1977 by Senators Kennedy and Mathias entitled "The Public Participation in Federal Agency Proceedings Act" (SB 270, 95th Congress). It provides for a federal fund which is to be disbursed to worthy, qualified citizens groups which have concrete interest in regulatory decisions of federal agencies. In effect, the government would support citizen opposition as a useful method of public participation by paying for reasonable attorneys' fees and other expenses. During the past decade the courts have recognized taxpayers' standing to intervene in proceedings in which a public interest is present. However, the expense of participating has effectively kept many citizens from taking advantage of this new opportunity. As Senator Kennedy has observed,

> While the cost of participation is high, the value of public involvement in agency proceedings is unquestionable. In the last nine years there have been over 25 hearings in Congress focusing upon the need to foster greater public participation in federal proceedings. The extensive record of these hearings leads to one inescapable conculsion: without increased citizen participation, our regulatory systems cannot function properly.[26]

The Kennedy/Mathias proposal has much to commend it, but in energy production planning it would promote delay as it encourages the ponderous route of litigation. However, it would encourage serious utilization of open planning for power site planning and would be useful in many other regulatory areas.

In the early 1970s legislation was introduced in the House of Representatives (HB 5722 and HB 6970, 92d Congress) which would have provided for arbitration on power plant and high-voltage transmission projects. The utility company would have been required to prepare and publicly disclose its long-range plans; but they would also have been given access to the federal power of eminent domain, if necessary, to acquire sites after arbitration. This legislation would have removed control from the energy producers over choosing plant sites, yet not hindered the process of increasing energy production.

The House bill was never reintroduced after dying in committee, and the

Senate proposal was still in committee in the second session of the 95th Congress. The House bill should be resurrected, and both it and the Kennedy/Mathias proposal passed as alternative processes to open planning. The states could legitimize open planning, thus encouraging the energy producers to adopt it as a means to achieve both public and private interests without excessive government involvement or pressure. Where cooperative mechanisms exist, there should be no desire to seek more complex or authoritarian methods to solve problems. However, should the participants in the policy process be unwilling to cooperate, opportunities should be available to achieve solutions which at least satisfy the general needs of the public.

In this democracy there is still room for rational people to disagree and still serve the accepted needs of society. But we should collectively and publicly bear the responsibility for making important policy decisions and neither expect nor encourage the private resolution of basic public problems. However, once the basic decisions have been made, we should encourage a private response to public needs. Therefore let government decide if we need increased energy supply; if so, then let the energy producers provide a cooperative procedure to accommodate the public energy needs and the diverse values of society.

Notes

1. I use *energy producers* to include those which transport or market energy supplies as well.

2. I am indebted to Allen schick for this concept.

3. "Conserving Today's Energy for Tomorrow's Needs," *Exxon USA,* Fourth Quarter, 1977, p. 28.

4. See Norman Wengert, "Citizen Participation: A Practice in Search of a Theory," *Natural Resources Journal,* January 1976.

5. James Riedel, "Citizen Participation: Myths and Realities," *Public Administration Review,* May/June 1972, pp. 212-213.

6. Wengert, "Citizen Participation," pp. 25-27.

7. James D. Carroll, "Participatory Technology," *Science,* February 19, 1971, p. 648.

8. Martha Derthick, "Defeat at Fort Lincoln," *The Public Interest,* Summer 1970, pp. 22-23.

9. See Howard W. Hallman, "Neighborhood Councils: Their Status in 1976," *Neighborhood Decentralization* (Washington: Center for Governmental Studies, May/June 1976), for a description and discussion.

10. Erasmus H. Kloman, "Citizen Participation in the Philadelphia Model Cities Program: Retrospect and Prospect," *Public Administration Review,* September 1972, p. 405; and Edward R. Lowenstein, "Citizen Participation and the

Administrative Agency in Urban Development: Some Problems and Proposals," *Social Service Review,* September 1971, pp. 289–301.

11. Jon Van Til, "Citizen Participation in Social Policy: The End of a Cycle?" *Social Problems,* Winter 1970, pp. 320–322.

12. M. Kent Jennings, "Public Administrators and Community Decision-Making," *Administrative Science Quarterly,* Winter 1963, pp. 42–43.

13. Joseph L. Sax, "Emerging Legal Strategies: Judicial Intervention," *Annals of the American Academy of Political and Social Science,* May 1970, p. 72.

14. Lloyd C. Irland, "Citizen Participation—A Tool for Conflict Management on the Public Lands," *Public Administration Review,* May/June 1975, p. 267; and Lloyd C. Irland and J. Ross Vincent, "Citizen Participation in Decision-Making—A Challenge for Public Land Managers," *Journal of Range Management,* May 1974, p. 182.

15. Spenser W. Havlick, "The Construction of Trust," *Water Spectrum,* Fall/Winter 1969–70, p. 14.

16. Ibid., p. 13.

17. Ibid., p. 19.

18. Environmental Quality Laboratory, *People, Power, and Pollution* (Pasadena: California Institute of Technology, 1971).

19. "Enlightenment Strikes a Utility," *Business Week,* March 28, 1970, p. 142.

20. Northern States Power, "Report to Shareholders," (Minneapolis, Minn.: NSP, 1972), p. 4.

21. "Enlightenment Strikes a Utility."

22. *Minnesota Statutes Annotated,* vol. 9, sec. 116C.04, p. 370.

23. *Minnesota Statutes Annotated,* vol. 9, 1976 Supplement, sec. 116C.53, p. 21.

24. Norman Wengert, "Public Participation in Water Planning: A Critique of Theory, Doctrine, and Practice," *Water Resources Bulletin,* February 1971, p. p. 28.

25. Riedel, "Citizen Participation."

26. Edward M. Kennedy, "Beyond 'Sunshine'," *Trial,* June 1977, p. 43.

Index

Index

About the Contributors

Steven C. Ballard is an assistant professor of political science and a Research Fellow in the Science and Public Policy Program at the University of Oklahoma. His research has been in applied policy analysis, and his publications include articles on knowledge utilization technology assessment, and social indicators.

Hanna J. Cortner is a research associate in the School of Renewable Natural Resources at the University of Arizona. In her principal field of interest, natural resources policy and administration, she has written several articles and monographs focusing on problems of land use, water resources, forest-watershed management, and energy.

Gregory A. Daneke is an assistant professor of policy and management in the School of Natural Resources at the University of Michigan on leave with the U.S. General Accounting Office in Washington. He has published works on the methods of planning and management and in the areas of natural resources and energy policy.

David Howard Davis is a professor of government at Cornell University. Several years ago he was an NASPAA Public Administration Fellow assigned to the U.S. Environmental Protection Agency headquarters in Washington. He is the author of *Energy Politics*.

Terry D. Edgmon is an assistant professor of political science at North Carolina State University. He previously served with the Division of Public Administration, University of New Mexico. His areas of specialization are intergovernmental relations, energy policy, and water resources administration.

Osbin L. Ervin is an assistant professor of public administration in the Department of Political Science and a research associate in the Coal Extraction and Utilization Research Center at Southern Illinois University, Carbondale. His major research interest is municipal budgeting and policy analysis.

Patricia K. Freeman is an assistant professor in the Department of Political Science and in the Bureau of Public Administration at the University of Tennessee.

Kenyon N. Griffin is the director of the Center for Government Research and associate professor of political science at the University of Wyoming. His research includes the politics of taxation and international relations.

Timothy A. Hall, formerly a research associate with the Science and Public Policy Program at the University of Oklahoma, is currently an assistant professor of social sciences at Georgia Institute of Technology. His research has been in the applied energy policy area, and his publications include articles on technology assessment and energy conservation.

Mary Hamilton is the manager of the Energy Policy Department at the BDM Corporation in McLean, Virginia. Her research activities during the past two years have included analyses of the role of government in the development and commercialization of new energy technologies for the Department of Energy and its predecessors.

Michael S. Hamilton is a doctoral student in political science and Colorado Energy Research Institute Fellow at Colorado State University. Since 1976 he has been engaged in research for the Western Interstate Nuclear Board, the Los Alamos Scientific Laboratory, and the National Power Plant Team, U.S. Fish and Wildlife Service, concerning industry and government power plant siting practices.

Helen Ingram is a Fellow at Resources for the Future, on leave from the University of Arizona where she is a professor of political science. She has published extensively in public policy, with particular emphasis on water, energy, and the environment.

Charles O. Jones is a Maurice Falk Professor of Politics at the University of Pittsburgh. His recent publications include *Clean Air: The Policies and Politics of Pollution Control* and *An Introduction to the Study of Public Policy.* He is the editor of the *American Political Science Review.*

Alfred R. Light is an assistant professor of political science at Texas Tech University. He is currently on leave to attend Harvard Law School.

John R. McCain is a research associate with the Institute of Government Research, University of Arizona, and doctoral candidate in political science. His main areas of interest include public policy, natural resources, and American Indians.

David A. Schaller is a staff member of the U.S. Solar Energy Research Institute, Golden, Colorado. Previously he served with the U.S. Environmental Protection Agency.

Robert B. Shelton is the associate executive director of the Assembly of Behavioral and Social Sciences at the National Academy of Sciences in Washington. Previously he was on the staff at the Brookings Institute and at Resources for the Future.

Richard Timm is an assistant professor of engineering at the University of Wisconsin-Extension. Previously he directed the Oregon Department of Energy's planning program where he was responsible for the development and application of the state's energy forecasting model. He has also supervised the Wisconsin Public Service Commission's Bureau of Environmental and Energy Systems.

Norman Wengert is a professor of political science at Colorado State University where he specializes in land-use policy, water policy, and energy policy. During the academic year 1978–79 Professor Wengert is on leave, serving in the Headquarters, U.S. Forest Service, Washington.

Irvin L. White is a professor of political science and assistant director of the Science and Public Policy Program at the University of Oklahoma. He has been the principal investigator or coprincipal investigator of several technology assessments in the energy area.

About the Editor

Robert M. Lawrence is a professor of political science at Colorado State University. He is the author of *Arms Control and Disarmament: Practice and Promise;* with Joel Larus, editor of *Nuclear Proliferation: Phase Two;* and with Norman Wengert, editor of *The Energy Crisis: Reality or Myth.*